THE JOLLY JOSSMAN R.N.

The Jolly Jossman R.N.

FREDERICK DALE

UPFRONT PUBLISHING
LEICESTERSHIRE

The Jolly Jossman R.N.
Copyright © Frederick Dale 2003

ISBN 1-84426-247-2

First published 2003 by
UPFRONT PUBLISHING LTD
Leicestershire

Printed by Lightning Source

This book is dedicated to my parents, the late Frederick and Bertha Dale, whose hard work, deep love and devotion to their family and each other, gave each of their four offspring, first the encouragement, then the rare opportunity during that period, to pursue a career of their own choice. I can but hope that my children, grandchildren and (quite recently) great-grandchild, remember the humour and laughter of my beloved late wife Bette and myself as I remembered that of my own parents. I also hope that they will all enjoy these recollections.

INTRODUCTION

I joined a Naval training ship in the middle of 1942 as an underling trainee, and left the Royal Navy as a Fleet Master-at-Arms late in 1974. The following yarns mostly cover the bits in between those times. I can but hope that you enjoy reading both the yarns and the daffy poems at least half as much as I enjoyed the reflections and subsequent chuckles I had whilst committing them to paper.

It was always my opinion that the position of the master-at-arms, in the Royal Navy had two basic but very necessary requirements. They were:

He needed a very good sense of humour (jolly),

He needed a very strong personality (jossman).

Without humour he would have sunk without trace, and therefore having the strongest personality in the world would not have helped him. I never met a master-at-arms of any consequence who did not have those two very necessary requirements, and in the correct proportions.

It is believed that the word jossman (occasionally he was called jaunty or jonty, which, during my time in the Royal Navy, were looked upon as disparaging nicknames for the ship's master-at-arms) was somehow derived from, or a corruption of, the words 'justice man'. He is, in fact, the ship's 'chief of police', and responsible to the captain, via the ship's executive officer, for the maintenance of discipline and the general behaviour of the ship's company. Readers may recall the film *Billy Bud*, starring Gregory Peck, who played the part of a Royal Naval master-at-arms. However, the film was not very complimentary to masters-at-arms in general, and I feel that it is best forgotten.

CHAPTER ONE

I think I had had the desire to join the Royal Navy, or at least to go to sea, since the day I started to walk. I never remember wanting to do anything else with my life. The consequence of this was that in 1942, at the ripe old age of thirteen, I joined a Naval training ship. Just prior to that event, I had seen the film *Tom Brown's School Days* and had thought that Tom Brown was treated pretty rough and tough with the beatings he received at the boarding school he went to. But, in comparison with that training ship, I now believe that Tom had it reasonably cushy. I had been rather a live wire with my fists in the school I had been educated at, and the confidence of youth, plus some tussles with pretty hard-hitting wartime evacuees, had led me to believe that I would be able to hold my own in any group of my peers. How wrong that proved to be. I was beaten up on several occasions during the first few weeks, as were all the other boys who had joined at the same time as me. It seemed that being beaten up by the senior boys was part of the initiation ceremony.

The hardest beatings seemed to be reserved for a boy named Savanti. He was immediately nicknamed 'the wop' because of his Italian-sounding name, and because the Italians were, at that time, at war with us. If there were any items of bad news regarding the war, poor Savanti caught yet another beating. He was a rather small and skinny lad but he had a toughness that belied his physical appearance and nothing seemed to get him down or overly upset him. He was something of an inspiration to the rest of

1

us 'new entries'. Savanti eventually joined the Merchant Navy, and very many years later I heard that he was the captain of one of the world's largest oil tankers, though I was never able to confirm that information. He is one of the very many fine characters who life has had me rubbing shoulders with, who I would dearly love to meet again, if only to find out if any one of them has enjoyed their lives as much as I have enjoyed mine.

Some twelve or fourteen years after I left that training ship I read William Golding's book *Lord of the Flies* and I realised how close to the workings of boys' minds Golding had actually got. I remember reading that he had once been a teacher and I realised at the time that, with his psychological understanding of a boy's way of thinking, he must have been one hell of a good teacher; I wished that the training ship had had a teacher in that category. Perhaps the beatings from the more senior boys would have thereby been less severe, or would they just have been more cleverly directed?

The bullying practices of the senior boys rather quickly sorted the wheat from the chaff however and several of our group were visited by their parents who 'bought them out' of the training ship, for the then rather exorbitant sum of ten pounds. My father did visit me on one occasion, and my parting words to him were 'I'll stick it, Dad'. To his dying day, he said that that was the most disturbing statement that any of his four children ever made to him. He was the world's greatest dad and I know he would have done anything for me, but deep in my heart I knew that if I had 'chickened out' then, I would never have been able to look any of my friends straight in the eye again.

It was about this time that my father was called up for his induction medical examination for the armed forces (although he was then well into his forties). He had been asked previously if he would like to join the Royal Observer Corps on a full-time basis (aeroplane spotting and plotting), and thereby be excused having to join the fighting services, but he had stubbornly refused, stating that he would not have people saying that he had taken the easy way out or that he was dodging doing his bit for his country (the expression 'doing your bit' was much in vogue during the Second World War). He was always a very proud man. Unfortunately it was found during the medical examination that his physical grading was 3C, which was the lowest medical grade he could have been given, and there was no way any of the armed forces would have accepted him, so he then joined the Royal Observer Corps on a part-time basis, though I don't think that he was ever quite the same man after that medical examination. He had always appeared to be a fit and healthy man, but I am sure that that medical examination robbed him of his confidence. He did, nevertheless, live for a further nineteen years.

The training ship had originally been a ship moored on the River Mersey at Rockferry in Liverpool. It had been bombed and sunk during the German blitz of the city, and in consequence all surviving personnel had been moved to a former holiday camp for deprived children, which was situated in the heart of the mountains in North Wales. It was rather strange joining a place that was referred to as a 'training ship', which was, in fact, a camp perched halfway up a Welsh mountain and many miles away from the sea; a cold and very desolate place to be for sure, and the two winters I spent there were rather horrendous. I would have given my right arm to have had my dog Paddy there lying at the foot of my bunk keeping my feet warm, as he had done at home when I had managed to sneak him past my parents and into my bedroom. He was better than any hot-water bottle or electric blanket.

A point that I remember very well about the training ship was the awful food we were served and the fact that we had very little of it in any case. What food we did get we needed to eat very quickly or one of the more senior boys would soon have it off our plate. To this day I eat very quickly and I know that it is a habit I acquired at the training ship, an obvious aftermath from that time of the survival of the fittest. Whilst I was there, there was something of a mutiny by the boys because of the poor food, and as a result the food improved in both quantity and quality for a week or so but soon slipped back to its original poor state. This shortage of food at a very important point of my physical development had something of an effect on my conscience, and to this day I just hate to see food wasted in any capacity. When I see children throw away a half eaten apple, for instance. I just feel like forcing them to try a little harder to eat more of it.

Prior to joining that training ship, I had enjoyed the luxury of a wonderful childhood in the heart of the Cheshire countryside. My parents had, by their own very dedicated endeavours, built up quite a reasonable business, which could best be described as a general store. After their wedding, which was solely financed by the two of them, they were left with twenty-three pounds, their joint life savings. They then rented premises and opened a shop. My father took on several tasks outside of the business, such as window-cleaning and part-time postman, whilst my mother attended to both the business and us children. They succeeded by hard work, sheer determination, and an abounding faith and love in and for each other.

I had undergone a pretty fine toughening-up period some two years or so prior to joining the training ship, which I am sure helped enormously with my capacity to overcome the beatings I suffered there. The arrival of the evacuee children in our rather sleepy country town in the latter part of 1939 altered all of our lives for ever. They came from a very tough neighbourhood in Liverpool where, I was assured, even the babies spoke with their fists. Within days of the evacuees' arrival, my chum Fred Clark and I were out getting conkers from the horse chestnut trees some half a mile or so outside the town. Fred was one of those natural athletes, and despite the fact that he never removed his clogs to go tree climbing he was a better climber than any ape or monkey I ever saw. He was always the one who climbed the trees and shook the branches whilst I stayed on the ground and collected the conkers as they fell, a method we had happily adopted over the years of our childhood. The season in question had a slight difference, however. There was a greatly increased number of boys collecting conkers due to the evacuees being in our midst, and one of the bigger evacuee boys started to pick conkers from those that had fallen from Fred's efforts of branch shaking. I pointed out to him that we had an unwritten code of conker picking, whereby we only picked up the conkers that our partner had shaken out of the tree, which were later shared between the partners. A pair of hands grabbing my lapels quickly answered my remarks, and I was virtually lifted off the ground. I managed to get one of my hands in front of my face a split second before my assailant delivered the 'Liverpool Nod' (i.e. head butt) and, fortunately for me, my right leg was swinging free; I was therefore able to swing my knee in an upward direction, which caught my assailant neatly in the crotch. As he released his hold of my lapel he seemed to push me with his right hand and this, fortunately, gave greater momentum to my right fist, which was already heading towards his face. In fact it caught him flush in his left eye, and he sank to the ground moaning like an old billy goat. All the other evacuees gathered around with amazed looks on their faces. I heard one whisper to another, 'A 'turnip top' has decked Butch Manning!' Evidently in the language of the evacuees, the local populace had quickly acquired the name 'turnip tops'. Fred Clark and I were wily enough not to hang around for a post-mortem. Fearing some form of retribution and realising that we were sadly outnumbered, we left the scene at the gallop, our conkers being shared out on the run home.

After that first encounter with Butch, which, I have already explained was in front of quite a large audience. I learned to sympathise with the cowboys in the old Wild West who were hounded because of their ability to draw their six-shooters faster than their peers. Rarely a week went by when I was not supporting at least one black eye. The rather silly truth was that I was beginning to enjoy the cut and thrust of being the champion of the turnip tops. I just wish that I had been afforded the luxury of a boxing coach at that period of my life, it would certainly have helped the transition to my later pugilistic ambitions, and would have been a distinct advantage in the experiences I had on joining the training ship.

I should, however, insert a little note about the boy, Butch. He and I eventually became quite good friends and in fact, underwent a few punch-ups standing shoulder to shoulder. He was a large and quite loud-mouthed boy, but he had a pretty good sense of humour and a heart of pure gold to his friends. My one outstanding memory of him, though, was the morning he arrived at our shop rather early, while my father was on his knees scrubbing the shop floor. Butch seized the opportunity to fulfil his ambition to be a cowboy, and jumped on my father's back, shouting 'Ride 'em, cowboy!' My father pivoted and inserted his dirty floor cloth right into Butch's open mouth. He then bucked in the air in the method one sees in the Wild West horse-breaking scenes, and Butch rose some two feet off my father's back to land head first in the bucket of soapy and heavily disinfected water. The soap could have possibly done some good but the strong disinfectant surely hindered his taste buds for many days afterwards.

By this time our shop had become quite a busy business and because of his extra work with the Royal Observer Corps my father had been virtually forced to give up his additional tasks like temporary postman, and as my uncle, who my father used to assist with his window-cleaning business, had by that time joined the army himself, my father was glad to relinquish the window-cleaning job also. There was, however, an incident that happened in our shop about that time that has stuck in my mind as if it happened yesterday. That was when a very smartly dressed lady came into the shop and my mother said, 'Good afternoon, Miss Renee, how nice to see you again.' Whilst she was making this welcoming address I was sure I saw her doing a little curtsy. Miss Renee looked most surprised but she answered my mother by walking around to her side of the counter and giving her a really big sisterly hug. Apparently Miss Renee was the only daughter of the local landowner and my mother had worked at the 'big house' when she went into service below stairs as a young girl of thirteen. It seemed obvious that my mother had been Miss Renee's favourite member of staff out of the dozen or more who had worked in a similar capacity at the 'big house'.

After that first meeting, Miss Renee visited us quite often; she really was a most likeable person and we always enjoyed her visits.

I can still see her in my mind's eye. She was a rather tall, very bubbly lady, who seemed to be almost larger than life itself, and I remember she spoke with a slight lisp. She seemed to be a person that you could rely on to keep any secret and a person you could pledge your soul to. Alas, though not regrettably, the days of the 'big house' were fast coming to an end, and tax problems soon brought down the gentry, as they were then known. The 1940s surely brought about the greatest changes in one single decade in social behaviour that this country has ever known.

Shortly after my first meeting with Miss Renee I had joined the Naval training ship, and soon lost all thought of her. I was, however, quite distressed to hear that she had died in very distressing circumstances some years later. I will always remember her as a very nice friendly lady, who was always most welcome in our home.

After leaving school for the day and completing the delivery chores for my parents' business, which I always did at the gallop, I would scoot off to one of the nearby farms and enjoy the pleasure of riding one of their shire horses back to the paddock. This was a normal event, and country boys had done this chore since time immemorial. To this day, I cannot imagine a more wonderful feeling than to be sat high on the back of a shire horse. Those wonderful and gentle animals were at that time the power tools of agriculture and I for one was greatly saddened when their dominance was superseded by mechanical power. I know that my father, who was a dyed in the wool country boy, passed down his love for those wonderful animals to me. Unfortunately my riding of shire horses came to a rather abrupt end shortly after the outbreak of the war when my cousin Charlie, who was apprenticed to a baker – in fact the baker was his father (my mother's brother) – volunteered (via the Boy Scout movement) and was accepted into the Royal Navy as a signalman. This meant that my uncle was now short-staffed, and because of the shortage of workers, due to so many young men having to join the fighting services, my mother immediately volunteered me to work in the bake house on completion of my school lessons. My homework then went by the board and I was working in the bake house five evenings a week, often until after 10 p.m., and all day on Saturdays from eight until very late, for which I was paid a weekly wage of four shillings (twenty pence). My mother allowed me one of the four shillings (five pence), the rest being put into my wartime savings bonds. It was pretty hard graft too, because automation in the baking industry was almost unheard of in those days.

I think that one of the worst aspects of being a baker's boy was the awful delivery cycle I had to use. It was truly a monstrosity and seemed to have a will and obstinate mind all of its own. Whenever I could, I preferred to put the goods I was to deliver into a basket and do my deliveries at the trot. I was always glad to roll into bed when I got home, and certainly did not need any rocking to sleep. I remember receiving very black looks when I fell asleep during Sunday school one week. I suppose that was par for burning the candle at both ends.

Early in 1944, after almost two years at the training ship, I was accepted into the Royal Navy, having passed the education test, which had been increased in its difficulty (or should that word be severity) several times during the war. This was obviously brought about because of the ever-increasing numbers of boys and young men wanting to join the forces. I often wonder if a future war would find such enthusiasm among the young men and boys wishing to join the fighting services. Anyway, it meant that the Navy could choose the cream of the country's youth. I think that I rather surprised our schoolmaster. I had formed the impression that he had written me off as one of life's eternal thickies, and my success made me feel that I had put one over on him.

Because of the bombing in the war, the Royal Naval training establishment for boys, which was named His Majesty's Ship *Ganges* (that place was also a shore establishment), had been moved over from near Ipswich on the east coast to the Isle of Man, which was about as far to the west as they could move it, and it had taken the new name of His Majesty's Ship *St George*. It was a former holiday camp, and a reasonably nice place to be. In fact the boys, such as I, who had joined from training ships thought that the place was wonderful in comparison to the places we had recently come from. The food was edible and there was more or less enough of it for our ever-empty stomachs. The first couple of nights that we were there, we lay back in our bunks thinking that we really had hit the jackpot. Life seemed to be full of all that was good for us, but nevertheless several times we would hear the boys who had joined straight from home sobbing under their blankets, and I am sure we ex-training ship boys all thought, 'They don't know how lucky they are to be in a place as good as this.' Homesickness for a young person is a hard cross to bear though, and we ex-training ship boys had all experienced it.

We were billeted in what had originally been holiday chalets, each to accommodate two people, but as space was rather limited, each chalet accommodated four boys. We had been billeted in the alphabetical order of our surnames, which fortunately placed me in the next bunk to a friend who had joined from the same training ship as myself. His name was Dawson, and for a reason I never did find out he was always know as 'Doc'. One of the other two inhabitants of our chalet was a huge boy called 'Buster' Elson, and he seemed very spiteful and bitter towards Doc. He used to take every opportunity he could find to rile or belittle him. One day the clash of personalities really came to a head and he grabbed Doc by his collar. I leapt across my bunk and both Doc and I laid into him with all the gusto we could muster. We were both considerably smaller than Buster but the odds of four very determined fists against two soon made him realise that he had bitten off more than he could chew. The punch-up certainly cleared the air, and gradually all four of us became a pretty close-knit quartet. On leaving the induction programme and going to our respective classes, Doc and Buster were put into the same class, but in a different part of the establishment from the one I was put into, and in consequence I saw very little of them from that time. Buster became one of the highlights of the establishment's boxing team, and eventually became the Heavyweight Champion of the establishment.

Intakes, as they called them, were groups of about 200 boys who were all taken into the Navy together and underwent an induction programme of some six weeks' basic training. One very unpleasant chore that all new entry trainees got was that their names had to be sewn into every item of their kit. It was done in red silk thread and had to be sewn in chain stitch. I thanked my lucky stars that I had such a short name and that my parents had been very sensible and given me only one first name. In the next chalet to us was a boy named T (Tom) M de Lacey-Leacey, and poor Tom seemed to be sewing night and day. The new entry trainees were kept completely separate from all the other trainees during that six-week period. They had numerous vaccinations and inoculations. Every orifice of their bodies was looked into. There was a point during this period when I wondered if I was being indoctrinated into some special and secret type of service, but eventually the day of our release came to pass and we were released into the main camp and into a class of 'proper' trainees.

Apart from our set-to with Buster, one thing that I remember very distinctly about the six weeks that I spent in the induction aspect of my Naval service was the sports day that we had. One of our numbers, who looked quite an ordinary type of boy, turned out to be something of an extraordinary athlete. He won the sprints, long jump, high jump and several other events. In fact, he gained more points on his own than any other complete team. He was a very quiet and unassuming chap who the majority of us had paid little or no attention to. After he had graciously accepted almost all the sports day prizes, I juggled myself into a position to be able to speak to him, and the first thing I wanted to know was, what was his name? He said, 'Call me Lucky. My surname is Spears, I am Lucky Spears'. I remember thinking; with a raw talent like you have it is no wonder that you acquired the name Lucky. A few days after our sports day, Lucky Spears was taken into hospital with an appendix problem, and the next day we were told that he had died on the operating table. Many years later a friend of mine named Jack Spears wanted to name his new pet puppy dog Lucky.

I begged him not to do so, and felt greatly relieved when he gave in to my pleas, though I never did explain my reasons to him.

While in the vein of sad nostalgia, one other person that I often think about when reflecting on this period of my life is my very special pal we just called 'Smithy'. We joined the training ship in North Wales on the same day, and we were always the very best of friends. He stayed with me at my parents' home on a couple of occasions and they liked him very much. He was a few months older than I was so he went to the Navy several months prior to me. Shortly after I joined HMS *St. George* as a boy seaman, Smithy left there to join HMS *Dido*. His ship came into Douglas, on the Isle of Man, soon after he joined her and he rather proudly showed myself and a couple of my other chums around her. Shortly after her visit to Douglas, HMS *Dido* took part in what proved to be one of the last European sea battles of the Second World War. I heard many months later that Smithy was amongst several boy seamen who were killed when X gun turret was blown up. That was a few days before his seventeenth birthday. I wish I had recorded his address, I know he had several brothers and sisters and I am sure that they were a very close family. I really wish I had been able to convey my very sincere condolences to them and to explain what a very special friend he was to me. Unfortunately, looking for someone by the name of Smith when you do not know their address would be like looking for a needle in a haystack.

At last we started our seamanship and gunnery courses, and one of the two instructors in charge of our class of trainees was a Chief Petty Officer Gunnery Instructor by the name of Langsdown (known as 'Charlie' Langsdown, but only well behind his back). Such people went under the dreaded title of 'Chief GI'. I think that his bark was just that little bit worse than his bite, but he was nevertheless rather a frightening sight to fifteen-year-old boys. The fact that he was well in excess of six foot tall and almost the same measurement across the chest tended to make him seem even more intimidating. One of the subjects he tutored us in was rifle drill. I had missed the first two lessons because I had some kind of an infection and had to attend the sickbay. When I arrived on the parade ground at the beginning of the third lesson I just did not have the courage to approach such a formidable person as the Chief GI and tell him that this was the first time I had attended, so I just followed what the remainder of the class did. The first order was 'slope arms', and I followed the first two movements easily, but the third and final movement was unfortunately done a little too fast for me and instead of bringing my right arm to my side I brought the left arm down. The class was spread out in single file along almost the whole length of the parade ground. Charlie was standing right in front of me when my ghastly *faux pas* occurred. He first turned smartly to his right and marched the length of the file. He then did a smart wheel and marched down the rear of the file. I could hear him coming to a smart halt directly behind me and he turned even more smartly to his left, then he swung his right boot and on connection with my posterior I, and the rifle I was still holding in the totally incorrect manner, were lifted at least two feet into the air. 'You will not make that bloody mistake again son will you?' He was totally correct. I never did, or ever will, make that mistake again.

There were about two thousand boys under training at any one time, and by general principle we used to spend half of each day under normal instruction (gunnery, seamanship etc.) and the other half of the day was spent at school. Unfortunately the school we used was some three or four miles from the main camp and we had to march each way in a very orderly fashion; each class was considered to be a platoon. Each marching session consisted of about a thousand boys, so the method used to keep the parade in a smart and orderly style was by means of drums. This drum aspect consisted of two side drums and one tenor drum. The tenor drum beat the pace rhythm (in other words kept the step) whilst the two side drums played alternate solos. For some reason I always fancied playing a side drum, and I found that one of the boys in the same cabin as myself had been a drummer in a Scottish pipe band. I acquired a pair of drumsticks and he was quite willing to teach me the rudiments of drumming. After several weeks my cabin-mate considered me capable of drumming a fair selection of side drum solos. In consequence I offered my services as a drummer for the purpose of the march to school.

The day of my inauguration as a drummer (on the school march) was unfortunately a very windy day and, having never previously played the drums whilst on the march, I was not aware of the fact that sometimes a drummer needed a leg strap to hold the drum in the correct place for it to be played. The consequence of this was that each time we passed a side road the crosswind caught hold of my drum and virtually whipped it around my back, thus creating a breakdown in the rhythm and consequently throwing the whole marching column out of step. I think that it would be much easier to say that my drumming caused mayhem and unfortunately I was banned from ever taking the drums again. Actually I suppose that I was rather lucky that I faced no disciplinary action as a consequence of my poor drumming activities. Incidentally, I have never played a drum since that day.

The officers and instructors of HMS *St. George* were really quite a fine group of characters. They were, almost to a man, long past their sell-by date, or retirement age, and were still in the Navy because of the shortages of manpower due to the war. One of the divisional officers was a lieutenant commander by the name of Enright (known to all of us as Danny, but only behind his back, though he was fully aware that we all referred to him as Danny. Incidentally, his brother became an admiral). He must have been well into his sixties. He was very popular with the trainees, but thinking back, I realise that he was as mad as a March hare. He would take the whole of his division sailing or rowing, and when we were well out to sea he would send the signal 'Instructors to the helm'. On receipt of such an order we all knew what the next signal was going to be. 'Stand fast the instructors, remainder abandon the boats.' I suppose that we were rather fortunate to have been in his division during the warmer months of the year, but it was still a long cold swim to the shore, and being fully dressed did not help very much. I should point out that all the boys had to be proficient swimmers to have got to that stage of their training. In fact if a boy could not pass a rather stiff swimming test he was released from the service. I must emphasise that this was a very rare occurrence and I only heard of one boy who was discharged from the service because he was unable to eventually pass the swimming test. One thing that endeared Danny Enright to all of us was the fact that sometimes he would join in the swim, and he took some keeping up with, which goes to prove that mad March hares can be good swimmers.

The second and last summer of my time on the Isle of Man was memorable because of the visit of the King (George VI) and Queen. Because our class had finished our course and were awaiting a draft to sea, we were not fallen in with the main parade. We were, in fact, used as first aid personnel. Because it was such a hot and sultry day the boys on parade were falling over like flies due to the unusual heat. The occasion sticks so firmly in my mind for the following reason. A friend and I were stretcher-bearers, and were kept very busy picking up the prostrate bodies of the trainees. We had to run and pick up one boy who had collapsed virtually a few feet in front of the King and having loaded him onto the stretcher I looked up to find the best direction for us to make our most surreptitious retreat. My face was but inches away from that of the King and my jaw must have dropped several inches as I looked into his face. I was so shocked at seeing his heavily made up face that I almost dropped the stretcher. It was some time later that I realised that the King was not in good health at that time, and because of the many cameras that were always around him he had to look his best. I remember many years later making my face up for the part of the Fairy Queen in a pantomime and wondering what the King would have thought of my make-up.

Why

The word *why* is the key to man's being,
His ambition, his aim and his goal.
Why controls most of his actions.
It pervades his whole body and soul.

Why creates powers of invention,
The incentive to overcome fear.
Why can give reason for laughter,
But is often the cause of a tear.

Why was man's need to split atoms.
It carries him deep into space.
Why is the word that controls him,
That gives him direction and pace.

But if man really knew all the answers,
And no longer deemed to ask *why*,
The whole human race would lose purpose.
Then man would just wither and die.

The Jolly Jossman's Ball

'Roll up and buy a ticket,' was the happy sailor's call,
'Come and buy a ticket for the Jolly Jossman's Ball.'
I said, 'I would love to dance upon the ballroom floor,
But I've just been in an accident and my feet are rather sore.'
The sailor raised his curly head and gave me the strangest glance
And then he said, 'You've got it wrong, it's a raffle, not a dance.'

Sea Sick

I was lying in the gutter, having been tossed out of a bar.
I needed a taxi back to the ship; I could never walk that far.
Oh, I really must remember not to use my caustic charm,
Landing on one's head like that could do a sailor harm.

I must try to keep my mouth shut when I go out on the spree,
I foolishly told the barmaid that she reminded me of the sea.
'Ah,' she said, 'It's my deep blue eyes I bet have done the trick.'
I said, 'No dear, it's because you're rough and make all the sailors
    sick.'

Farmer Giles

Old farmer Giles thought life hardly worthwhile,
When told by the vet that his bull was infertile.
'Don't worry,' the vet said, 'we can cure all such ills,'
And presented old Giles with a bottle of pills.

The pills were accepted with gracious glee,
And Giles was quite happy to pay a large fee.
The vet said, 'To administer pills of this type,
Blow 'em down the bull's throat by means of a pipe.'

All set and ready Giles waited the 'off'
Just as the bull decided to cough.
Giles' face went red and then it turned blue,
And he swallowed the pills without even one chew.

He went to the pub, washed the pills down with beer,
Woke the next morning saying, 'Gosh I feel queer.'
His wife brought his breakfast up to his bed,
And proceeded to pour it all on his head.

'Why have you done this?' he asked of his wife,
Then just managed to duck as she threw him a knife,
She said, 'You dirty old man, I'd be silly to stay,
You've put two barmaids and me in the family way.'

'Oh dear,' said old Giles, 'I'm sorry my pet,'
And hurried to town to visit the vet.
'Good grief,' he said, 'I've behaved like a goat.
I hope that those pills have an antidote.'

'They have not,' the vet said, 'but worry no more,'
And he pulled some medicine out of a draw.
'Will this stop the sex urge?' Giles asked in a bleat.
'No, but it should stop you *crapping* all over the street.'

A Courting

My grandson said, 'Could you lend me your torch? I'm going
out on a date.
The girl I've got is a beauty and I don't want to make her
wait.'
I said, 'If I'd carried a torch when courting, my girl would
have thought me a clot.'
'That doesn't surprise me a bit,' said the boy, ''cause just
look at the one that *you* got.'

Young Football Spectator

The poor boy was crying profusely, he was lost in the football
crowd.
By the time a policeman got to him, his crying had become
very loud.
'Why the tears?' the constable asked him. 'I've lost my dad,'
the little boy sighed.
'What's he like?' asked the friendly old copper. 'Beer and
women,' the young lad replied.

CHAPTER TWO

After a pretty enjoyable year on the Isle of Man, it was time for my first ship, and she was to be HMS *Devonshire*, an eight-inch gun cruiser and a really beautiful lady. She was commissioned the year I was born. Some ninety or more boys were to join the ship in Guzz (Devonport, Plymouth) for the purpose of taking passage in her to Sydney in Australia. The war in Europe had come to an end and the war in the Far East was in its dying throes. As the European aspect of the war had drawn to a close, almost all of our fleet had been sent out to the Far East, but once the Germans surrendered, the government decided that they should immediately start to demobilise the personnel who had joined for the 'hostilities only' period. This meant that the ships in the Far East quickly ran out of sailors to man them, hence our hasty departure for the Orient. Japan finally surrendered as we were on our way out there. I have always maintained that Tojo surrendered because he heard that I was on my way out there to finish him off, but it would be very hard to prove this fact so long after the event.

There was one very noteworthy incident that happened to the ship whilst we were on passage through the Mediterranean. A ship had caught fire in the southern part of the Med, a hundred miles or so above Port Said and the Suez Canal. We made all the speed we could on hearing the mayday signal of distress. Then the details came through that she was a ship that had been carrying displaced persons, which meant that her passenger manifest was certain to be mostly women and children. When we got to the position given, the ship had already sunk and the sea seemed to be a mass of floating bodies. We lowered all our available boats, and for some twenty-four hours we were picking up mostly dead women and children and laying the bodies out in rows along the decks. There were a few survivors but they were suffering from the effects of the fire that had eventually sunk the ship. Every available man (and boy) manned the boats' falls (those are the ropes that are used to hoist and lower the boats). I don't think there was a single person on the ship who did not have badly blistered hands by the time we were finished. There were no such things on HM ships as electric winches for hoisting boats in those days.

Although I had seen dead bodies before, that was the first time in my life that I had been completely surrounded by death and human destruction, and I now realise that the fact that we were all kept so busy during that period and given very little time to dwell on the subject obviously made our initiation to such a gruesome happening a little less distressing than it could have been, had we been merely spectators. Some time after the event we learned that the fire and the subsequent sinking had most likely been brought about by sabotage. How anyone could seek to sink a ship, which was mostly full of women and children is well beyond the comprehension of the brain of a mere mortal like me. What plea could such people make if they ever come face to face with their maker?

The many bodies on our decks were very quickly cleared on our arrival in Port Said the following morning and we were soon heading south down through the canal. We had to stop for a short period in the smaller of the two bitter lakes that form part of the canal and 'Hands to bathe' was piped. Many of us were able to enjoy a swim in the lovely, clear blue water. How times have changed since then. The last time I traversed the canal (which was quite recently) I would not even have wanted to put my foot into it because of the pollution.

We quickly fuelled in Aden, but no shore leave was given. It was only on our return from the Far East when we stopped at Aden that I realised how little we missed not stopping on the way out. The place still remains a place of dread to me and I, like almost everyone else I know, was most pleased when we gave it back to the local populace.

Our stay at Colombo in Ceylon was quite short but we were allowed an afternoon leave and several of us went on a trip to a place called Mt. Lavinia, which was a fair bus ride away. Whilst we were there we were able to get the young local boys to climb the palm trees and collect fruit for us. They also brought us pineapples, which we ate until our mouths started bleeding due to their acidity. None of us had seen such fruits since before the war. I returned to the place fifty-five years later and still remembered it. I closed my eyes for a minute or so and could picture it as it had been. My mind's eye saw all those fit young sailors swimming in the sea like fishes, as if it had been but yesterday.

From Colombo we had a heavy pound through the Indian Ocean and landed at Fremantle in Western Australia, which is pretty close to Perth. Apart from the really wonderful weather there, it was almost like being back home. The strange thing is that I have never lost that feeling about Australia. I was there relatively recently and I still had that same feeling. The slight difference in the two visits was that when I was there the first time, most of the people we spoke to referred to the UK as the old country, or 'back home'. During the most recent visit I felt that people seemed to keep us just that little bit more at arm's length, but were still very friendly. The one thing that I remember most distinctly was the surprise we all had at seeing all the children walking around without shoes. It was obviously not because of poverty. It was just because the weather was so good that I suppose the kids thought that boots and shoes were unnecessary.

We were soon off through the Great Australian Bight and heading for Sydney. That was one of the several times I have been through the Bight, and the only time I can remember doing it in totally calm weather.

What a sight to behold when the ship eventually entered Sydney! It was virtually days after the end of the Second World War and I don't think that one harbour has ever held as many

21

British warships as were on display there. There were five, possibly six battleships, at least a dozen aircraft carriers and even more cruisers. There were destroyers and frigates by the dozen, and they were all lined up at least five abreast on the jetties. We were trooped off the ship almost as soon as she berthed and immediately transported to the Naval base ashore to await our draft to one of the ships of the British Pacific Fleet. The shore establishment was HMS *Golden Hind,* which consisted of a series of Nissen huts. Each of the huts had iron bars running across them, and these bars were about seven feet above the deck of the hut and about nine feet apart. There were no chairs or other furniture in the huts so we were apparently going to have to sling our hammocks between these bars and then swing in a Tarzan-like manner and hopefully land in our hammocks. Whoever designed these structures had obviously never seen, and was even less likely to have slung or slept in, a seaman's hammock.

One really amusing aspect of *Golden Hind* was that we were the first boy seamen that had joined the place, and the Catering Officer informed his staff that boy seamen were entitled to eat as much food as they wanted. We certainly took advantage of his order. We had not seen food like it since the beginning of the Second World War. We were served such things as banana trifle, and we had not seen bananas for years. The consequence was that we all ate until we were sick. Then back to our Nissen huts and the pantomime of trying to get into our hammocks. It was a good job that we did not have enough money to be able to afford booze. I shudder to think what the consequence would have been then. Perhaps it would have meant a severely bruised night on a very cold concrete deck.

After only a few days at *Golden Hind* we were all whisked off to join our various ships. I was lucky enough to be in the group who were to join the battleship HMS *Duke of York.* She really was a fine ship and I think I loved her from the first time I set eyes on her. Like all battleships, she seemed to lie low in the water but had that appearance of space that is certainly not present in smaller ships like destroyers, frigates or even cruisers. We were mustered on the quarterdeck, our names called and boarding cards were issued to us, which gave us all the necessary information we needed, like the number of our mess, action station etc, then the Master-at-Arms appeared. He was about six feet four inches tall and dressed in tropical rig, which consisted of white shorts, shirt, shoes and stockings. He had dagger handles tattooed on the outside of his thighs, which gave the impression that he had two daggers stuck into his stocking tops. He was one of the most impressive looking characters I had ever seen and I soon learned that he ran the ship's discipline with a rod of iron. He seemed to be everywhere. At one period I started to think that there must be about six masters-at-arms, who all looked identical. I often wonder if I first acquired my ambition to become a master-at-arms during that first briefing on the quarterdeck of the old *Duke of York*.

There was one incident that I remember well during our stay alongside in Sydney, and that was during one quiet weekend when most of the sailors were ashore on their usual sailor-type adventures. Unfortunately boy seamen had an aversion to going ashore very often, due mostly to their lack of funds, which was, in turn, brought about by their very low income. In other words, they were mostly poverty-stricken.

Volunteers had been asked for, to assist in helping former prisoners of war to disembark from a troop ship and to board their waiting transport, which consisted mostly of a series of ambulances and buses that had been lined up on one of the jetties. As I have already mentioned in a previous chapter, most of us had seen and been virtually surrounded by death during our passage through the Mediterranean. Unfortunately most of those bodies were past any help that we could have possibly given them. They were, in fact, mostly dead or dying. It had been virtually impossible to render any noteworthy humanitarian assistance. This opportunity to give help to the needy seemed to be more in line with our capabilities, so almost all of the boy seamen on the ship volunteered to lend a hand.

We all found that the job we had volunteered to do was just as distressing as our experiences in the Mediterranean. Some of these ex-prisoners of war were so emaciated they were in fact, just skin and bone; they had been so grossly ill-treated that just getting them onto a stretcher was obviously agonising for them. None of them complained verbally, but the expressions on their faces told a silent story of their agony. Some of them even smiled at our fumbling efforts to lift them, but their clenched jaws showed a totally different aspect of their true feelings. Most of them were devoid of teeth, which had fallen out due to the several years of starvation and malnutrition they had suffered. Many of them were obviously in excruciating agony. I often wondered just how many of those poor men died before getting back home, though the much more prevalent thought in my mind was, how could the Japanese have behaved so inhumanly as to treat fellow human beings in such a way as those poor men had obviously been treated? On our return to the ship, I was pretty well bushed as the Aussies say, but I found an out of the way toilet cubical and was able to shed a few tears in private, and then to pray that the people we had so ham-fistedly helped, would all return to the people they loved.

I have been to Japan numerous times since that incident, the last time being fifty-five years after the event I have just described. In truth, I never feel comfortable in that country, nor do I feel comfortable in the company of Japanese people. I regret to say that I am going to take that aversion to my grave.

To go to sea on a 'battle-wagon' (as battleships were usually referred to) for the first time was quite a thrill for us boys, and our first port of call was to be Hobart in Tasmania, where we were to rehearse our landing parties in preparation for taking control of Hong Kong after the recent surrender of the Japanese. I fell head over heels in love for the first time in my life whilst the ship was in Hobart and like a hundred billion young men before me I was sure that my love for the pretty young lady would last for ever. Shortly after we left Hobart to return to Sydney however, I was scrubbing the upper deck one morning and no doubt wearing the vacant expression of a love-struck goat. The chap alongside me in the line of deck scrubbers had a similar appearance and soon he was telling me about the smashing girl he had been dating in Hobart. Then he started to describe her and I sensed some feeling of familiarity. I asked him if he had a photo of her and sure enough, we had been dating the same girl. I was sure that I was going to die of a broken heart. I have tried to remember the girl's name but for the life of me I cannot remember the name of my first (and rather untrue) love, a sure sign that my dotage is upon me.

I do remember that other love-struck young man, in fact we became rather good friends. His first name was Jimmy, and I suppose that his surname was rather immaterial. I do remember that he was quite good and rather jovial company, in fact we eventually worked together in the ship's telephone exchange. Unfortunately he was struck down with tuberculosis, which was a most dreaded disease at that time because there was no known cure. I later learned that almost his entire family had been wiped out by it and the last I heard was that he was in a sanatorium. It was not uncommon for entire families to be completely obliterated from existence by such diseases in those days.

After a fine time in Hobart (except for the broken heart) it was back to Sydney, and there it was discovered that all our food storage compartments were virtually alive with cockroaches. In fact the whole ship was alive with cockroaches. All the storage compartments were treated with DDT (Dichlorodiphenyltrichloroethane), which was supposedly a very strong insecticide. Soon after the job was done it was discovered that DDT was considered to be unsafe to use in food storage compartments – in fact in the quantity it had been used it was virtually poisonous – so all the compartments had to be cleared out again and steamed out to clear the poison.

We boys were rather disappointed with the delay that such an operation created. We were all keyed up to sail off to pastures new and to swan off around the Orient, but a consolation was presented to us in the form of seven days' leave to each watch of the sailors on board. The Australian people were most wonderful to the thousands of sailors that were in that area during and shortly after the Second World War. They had built a large temporary building in the centre of Hyde Park, which is in the middle of

Sydney. This building would accommodate many hundreds of sailors who wished to stay ashore overnight, and the building also contained a large office where sailors who were due for leave could find addresses where they could spend that leave. I went to this office with a friend of mine and we were given an address of some people in the far north of New South Wales, and we were issued a travelling warrant to get there by train.

What a wonderful place our holiday address turned out to be; we had a most superb seven days' leave there. I always had a great respect and liking for the Australian people and that feeling was further enhanced by my experiences during that leave. What a wonderful time we were given. It was a large farm that we stayed at and nothing was spared to ensure that we enjoyed every minute of our stay. We tracked emus, hunted dingos, chased kangaroos and just had a ball of a time, though our bottoms soon became sore due to the horse riding. I had done very little horse riding since riding the big shire horses on the paddocks when I was a young boy. The owner of the farm was a man well into his eighties; he had virtually retired from working on the farm and the younger members of his family actually ran it. He was really a grand old man and I spent hours talking to him. What an interesting character he was. In his youth, which must have been in the late 1880s, he had toured the United Kingdom on a cycle. The only place in the country that he could remember distinctly was Chester, because he could remember that it was possible to shop on two levels. As the nearest large town to my address in the UK was then Chester, he and I felt we had something in common.

It was very hard saying goodbye to the family. How could we ever have thanked people like that sufficiently? They said, we owe it to the old country. How could we ever repay our debts to them? They had sent the cream of their youth to fight in our European wars on two occasions and they had suffered such a tragic consequence. There are just no words that I could muster that would express the thanks that I feel towards the wonderful people of the antipodes, and for their acceptance of the large amount of

Naval personnel that our country found it necessary to park in that beautiful harbour of Sydney.

At last we sailed for Hong Kong. We performed several exercises on the two-week passage, and one of them was firing our small anti-aircraft armour at air targets. Unfortunately the depression stop on one of the Pom Pom guns failed to work and in consequence several of the other gun crews on the deck below it were injured, one of them fatally. He was a chap named Mick Furniss, a really first-class man. We buried him at sea the next day, and in consequence the sharks followed us for many days afterwards. I believe they were still there as we entered Singapore harbour over a week later. I remember talking to the sail-maker who had sewn Mick into the canvas shroud in which he was to be released over the ship's side. I asked him if it were true that the last stitch was made through the nose of the deceased, and he assured me that he had sewn up many bodies, especially during the early part of the war, and he always put the last stitch through the nose. The reason was that if the person who had been sewn into the shroud had any life left in him, the stitch through the nose would certainly make him give at least a reasonable twitch. He also said how he appreciated the extra tot of rum he received prior to doing the job. By the looks of his large, shiny red boozer's nose, I think that the extra tot of rum was the biggest attraction of the rather macabre task. If *he* were ever buried at sea the sail-maker who sewed *him* into his shroud would have little trouble finding *his* nose for that last stitch.

A call into Singapore, where our Admiral (Bruce Frazer), Commander-in-Chief, British Pacific Fleet, had a conference with Admiral Mountbatten. On completion it was on to Hong Kong but unfortunately, on the way we unexpectedly ran into the worst weather that any of us boys had seen. We were told later that the wind registered typhoon force on the wind scale. The seamen of the cable party were rushed onto the foc'sle (forward part of the ship) to secure the anchor cable properly. The First Lieutenant, being the officer responsible for that part of the ship, was the first to arrive at his post. Unfortunately his arrival coincided with the arrival of one of the largest waves to hit the ship and he was washed clear over the side. Several others were hurt, a few of them quite seriously. There were several acts of bravery performed by members of the ship's company in recovering the injured. In the circumstances we were rather lucky that there was only the loss of one life. I have often thought about what must have gone through the mind of Lieutenant Commander May, the First Lieutenant, as he watched one of the most powerful ships in the world drawing away and leaving him to drown. We had a large cruiser in company with us at the time, but neither of the ships could even turn in such foul weather. Had we found him there would have been little chance of recovering him alive. He had been possibly the most popular officer on the ship. He always had a quip or a pleasant remark when he met you, and his face seemed to wear a permanent smile. He had a great zest for life and it was obvious that he truly enjoyed the work he did. His was a very sad loss to the Navy but very much more so to our ship.

Hong Kong was, and to my knowledge still is, one of the most exciting places on earth. I have been back there several times since that first visit. In fact I was there just one year prior to writing this. I have always enjoyed my time there. It is often said that if it cannot be found in Hong Kong, it cannot be found anywhere. During that first visit, though, things were a little different. The Japanese had proved to be very hard taskmasters and the population had suffered a miserable existence while under their control.

Our ship landed almost a thousand men who were going to have the job of policing the whole colony. Looking at the situation now and taking into account the vast population of the place, it seems almost farcical to have attempted such an undertaking with such limited manpower. However the job was done with some reasonable degree of efficiency, which says a lot for the organisation involved and the adaptability of the sailors taking part.

There was a rather lengthy border between what was then known as The Hong Kong New Territory and the mainland of China, and Royal Marine Commandos policed that border. A group of us boys from the ship went on a trip up to that border and we found the Commandos to be tough and rugged characters. The local Chinese had a tradition of burying their dead for a period of many months, and then digging them up and putting what was left of their remains into large earthenware pitchers, which were lined up, in family rows along the hillsides. The Commandos used to take the lids off these pitchers during their night patrols and extract the gold teeth, which many of the Chinese wore. Some of the Commandos had pockets full of gold. I often wondered if the teeth were of much value and how the Marines managed to convince the jewellers in this country that they acquired the gold legally. We considered that the macabre practice rather smacked of the English grave robbing period, which I believe was some time during the middle ages.

Over the three months that our Hong Kong sojourn lasted, we noted many changes in the behaviour and attitude of the local populace, and it was mostly for the better. There were, however, a couple of rather nasty incidents involving our ship's company, who were taking part in the police duties. Several of the locals were caught in the act of looting and were shot on the spot. This was totally legal, because martial law was in force at the time. This naturally involved a lot of reports being submitted to the various authorities and many of the sailors involved could be guaranteed to be sitting at a desk doing paperwork for several days, often having to forego their time off. Remember that this was happening long before the advent of photocopiers. In consequence of this dislike of paperwork and the loss of their leisure time, it is believed that several of the looters were shot and their bodies were quietly pushed into the monsoon ditches. Nothing was heard or known about such incidents until spring arrived and the temperature rose. This was naturally accompanied by a most unpleasant smell. When the bodies were eventually recovered there was a hurried investigation, and a few of the sailors who had carried out patrols in the area where the bodies had been found were questioned but no charges were made. Little was said and even less was done about it. I think that the blame was eventually placed on the

Japanese, but just about everyone on the ship believed that the bodies were those of locals who were trying to loot or rob and were shot by our own sailors, who subsequently kept quiet to avoid the paperwork and loss of their own free time. The .303 ammunition was readily available to anyone at that time, so there could not be any successful questioning from that angle. I still find it hard to believe that life could have been deemed to be so cheap and expendable though.

The number of boys in the boys' mess fluctuated considerably; decreasing as the more senior ones were rated up to the exalted rank of ordinary seaman and increasing as more boys were sent out from the UK to relieve the 'hostilities only' ratings who were being sent back to the UK in ever-increasing numbers for demobilisation. We boys were a pretty fit and enthusiastic crowd. Tug o' war was a little out of our reach because of our lack of size. The Royal Marines who seemed to be able to dig up a team of giants when such events were arranged invariably won that event. We usually gave a pretty good account of ourselves in sports such as deck hockey and rowing. I think that we would have been best described as full of the joys of youth. Money was the one commodity that we had very little of, our pay was thirty shillings (£1.50) a month. Even taking into account the huge inflationary effects of the many years that have passed since the days to which I am referring, our pay was rather paltry, and hardly kept us in toilet equipment. Then one day a veritable windfall occurred to me. I received a postal order from the auxiliary fire service in my hometown for the sum of five pounds. They had apparently been running dances, and the money raised had been spread around all the local servicemen who had lived in the town, and each one of us had been sent five pounds. A lucky drop in the ocean for some of them, but for me it was a plutocratic fortune.

My close chums were 'Dinger Bell', Tom King and 'Little Joe', and having had a meeting of this 'brotherhood of reprobates' we decided that we would indulge our newly gained fortune in a 'rip roaring run-ashore' in Wanchai, which was the red light district of Hong Kong at that time. The services of a local prostitute cost the princely sum of five Hong Kong dollars (thirty-two pence in the present sterling currency).

The ship was moored in the middle of the harbour, so we caught the first Liberty Boat early one Saturday afternoon, and were duly landed at the jetty by the Fleet Club in Wanchai. We went into the club, and for the first and only time during our sojourn in Hong Kong we were able to afford a meal there. It was great to be able to eat whilst ashore, and in fact I think we almost licked the plates having enjoyed the meal so much. After the meal we strolled around the corner into the main street of Wanchai and viewed the women, of whom there was quite a good selection. The main snag in our situation was that our own sailors policed the place and it was their job to keep us out of the brothels. We were told that the main reason for such strictness was to prevent the spread of venereal disease, but in our youthful and rather 'bolshie' opinions of that time, we considered that the reasons were just a fascist doctrine. I suppose that those ideas were a reasonable reflection of both our political and moral immaturity.

I vaguely remember that Dinger was the first one to notice Lotus. She really was a charmer and was doing an excellent job of displaying her bewitching charms at the entrance to the brothel in which she worked. The four of us soon followed her up the stairway to the first floor, where we sat down on the wooden benches just inside the door of the flat. The flat was really just a long corridor that was divided off into rooms by means of very flimsy and fragile screens. Each of these divisions, or rooms, was allotted to one of the girls, of whom there were, I figured, about six attached to this particular brothel. However, with the possible exception of Little Joe, the woman that we all fancied going to bed with and had followed up the stairs was the one known as Lotus, and because Dinger had been the first one to notice her he was deemed to have the first choice. I suppose that such behaviour merely emphasises the inbred discipline in us young sailors, even in such frustrating circumstances as are being described.

The Hong Kong prostitutes were quite strict about their protection from venereal disease and were rather meticulous from the point of view of hygiene, particularly considering their limited facilities. Everyone going to bed with them had to be wearing a condom and they would give the condom a really thorough examination. If they thought that there was anything wrong they would shout for the house madam, whose long whorish experiences were considered to be the ultimate yardstick necessary to give them the confidence that everything would be okay.

Dinger was quickly relieved of his sexual frustrations and as I did not fancy any of the other women I also chose Lotus after Dinger had left her. Tom King who, like me, had not fancied any of the other women followed me. By the time that Tom had achieved satisfaction, Lotus had earned almost one pound. We then realised that Little Joe had been sitting down very quietly during all these frustrating proceedings and despite the fact that several of the women had paraded in front of him in several states of undress and displaying very provocative states of sexual encouragement, with the obvious intent of relieving him of his five dollars, he had remained totally unmoved. It was then that madam brought on her *piece de resistance*. This was in the form of a young teenage girl; I doubt she had reached the age of sixteen but she was very pretty in an Oriental, blushing, shy and retiring sort of way. I suppose the main attraction for Little Joe was the fact that this girl was the only one that was smaller than he was. Little Joe was immediately smitten with the girl and she had little trouble in arousing his passions and getting him into one of the cubicles.

As Little Joe and the girl withdrew to the cubicle, the three of us, who had already had our worldly way and satisfied our sexual frustrations, then carried our chairs quietly to the outside of the cubicle that Little Joe and the young girl had entered. We then stood on the chairs and looked over the top of the flimsy screen to what was going on inside the cubicle. Our surveillance was being carried out in a very quiet and surreptitious manner, but unfortunately the girl, being the only one of the couple to be in an upward-looking position, caught a glimpse of one of our heads, and she let out the most horrific scream.

The scream frightened the living daylights out of the three of us, and what had really started out as a skylark almost turned into a major tragedy. The screen collapsed and the three of us fell into the cubicle in a heap of wooden slats and cardboard (from the screen) and arms and legs (from the three of us, plus Little Joe and the girl). It was soon obvious that Little Joe was bleeding rather profusely from the area of his genitals. Having three rather weighty young sailors fall across your back whilst you are in the middle of deep sexual penetration, which obviously had promoted high blood pressure – I am sure that one hardly needs to stretch ones imagination to realise what a predicament we were all in. However, the problems of three of us were relatively minor in comparison with those of Little Joe.

Our major problem was the fact that the girl could not be stopped from screaming, and the four of us were fully aware that there were several patrols outside in the street trying to stop sailors from using the brothels in Wanchai and arresting anyone caught in them. The patrols had something of a bonus system. If they caught someone in the brothels, their next duty could then be spent in the police station composing a patrol report, and in inclement weather this could prove a great asset.

It was rather fortunate that we were the only customers in that particular brothel at the time, so on hearing the sound of heavy boots on the stairway leading up from the street, the four of us were able to make a dash for the fire escape at the rear of the building. We were virtually carrying Little Joe, who was still busy pulling up his trousers and trying to mop away blood at the same time.

The fire escape was something after the style of the ones seen in the old films of New York, with the possible exception that this particular fire escape had obviously never been maintained since its installation very many years earlier. It really was very rickety and almost in a state of collapse, and its bottom flight had long since disappeared or been stolen. Despite the need for urgency in our flight we descended the ladder just one step at a time, realising that too much weight would surely lead to an accident. The first three of us made the final jump with little other than a few scratches and bruises. Unfortunately Little Joe, who had had his fair share of trouble for one day, having climbed down the part of the fire escape that was still intact, then froze above the missing last flight. Little Joe really was very short, and the distance to earth from where he was then standing must have looked to be one hell of a drop. Then one of us had the flash of an idea. Almost without words being spoken, the three of us who had already made the descent gathered up all the cardboard and paper rubbish we could see lying around, and piled it in a heap below the fire escape. Little Joe then made his daring leap and luckily landed right in the middle of the heap we had constructed.

I have felt very dubious about using the word 'lucky' at the end of the previous paragraph because we had, in fact, created a further problem whilst trying to solve the one described in that paragraph. Our enthusiasm for enlarging the pile of rubbish to afford Little Joe a reasonable landing had obviously masked our sense of smell, and one of us had inadvertently thrown a box of rotten fish onto the top of the pile of rubbish. On landing, Little Joe found himself to be up to his chest in the most foul smelling fish any of our nostrils had ever encountered. We could see the maggots on Little Joe's clothes as he fought his way out of the heap. The smell was just nauseating. I had the job of giving him a push up and over the wall that surrounded the yard we had landed in, and I was almost sick whilst doing so. By that time we could hear the boots of the Naval patrol in the flat we had just left, and I certainly did not have time to hang around and indulge in the luxury of a good puke.

Once over the wall, the four of us must have run something in the region of half a mile before stopping. Fortunately for us, Little Joe had rather short legs and stayed well to the rear during this escape flight. When we stopped and took deep breaths of air and allowed Little Joe to catch up with us, we realised that we were going to have a problem getting back to the ship. As already stated, the ship was moored in the middle of the harbour, and the only way of getting back to her was by boat. There was not a boat coxswain in the whole of the Far East who would have let Little Joe onto his boat in the stinking state he was then in.

Our flight from the rear of the brothel had taken us in a virtual circle and we found ourselves back at the Fleet Club. We attempted to enter the main door of the club in the order we had taken in our flight from the brothel. In other words, Little Joe was walking several paces behind the other three of us, and as he got within two yards of the doorman, the said doorman let out an ear-piercing yell, whereupon the manager's office door burst open and the manager came out in a rush. He took one sniff of the air and stated that if Little Joe attempted to enter the club in the state he was then in, he (the Manager) would immediately call the shore patrol. We pleaded that the reason for our entering the club was for the purpose of getting Little Joe cleaned up enough to make him acceptable to the coxswain of a boat for our return to our ship. The manager would have none of our pleadings, and in hindsight I am very much inclined to agree (and in fact sympathise) with his point. Little Joe was given a very firm 'Thou shalt not enter' hint when the doorman reappeared with a very long handled broom and proceeded to push him in the direction of the outer door.

In true musketeer fashion we all left the club with Little Joe, and were walking rather forlornly along the harbour front when one of us espied the fish market, where we knew there was a tap and a hosepipe. One of us produced a few cents and bribed the attendant to let us use the hose, Dinger took the hose nozzle and trained it on Little Joe whilst I turned the lever that was suppose to act as a tap. At least I thought it would act as a tap, whereas the lever just fell to the ground and the water came out of the hose with such force that Little Joe was almost cut in half by it. We all had a try at wrestling with the tap-cum-lever, and were all well and truly soaked to the skin whilst doing so. The attendant rushed off somewhere, we assumed to shut the water off at the main tap, but our suspicions were such that the four of us, fearing the worst, rapidly legged it for the third time that day.

We headed back to the jetty where our ship's boats landed and picked up our liberty men, and were lucky enough to see one of our ship's boats coming alongside. The boat was one of our ship's picket boats, which was normally used only by officers and senior ratings, but there was a small compartment in the after part of the boat that often carried lowly sailors like us. We were about to sneak into this compartment when the coxswain of the boat, who was unfortunately downwind of Little Joe, caught a whiff of his fishy BO. 'You smelly little bastards are not going back to the ship on my boat,' he said. 'What is more, you are all soaking and I have just had all the seat covers changed, so piss off and wait for another boat.' Boy seamen would never dare to argue with a boat coxswain even if their lives depended on it, so we rather dejectedly turned to leave the boat.

Fortunately our forced and dejected exit from the boat had coincided with the arrival of the boys' Divisional Officer. 'Hell,' he said, 'what in the world happened to you? You look like four drowned rats.' Tom (the more imaginative member of our quartet) came up with an answer as quick as a flash. 'We missed the last liberty boat by the skin of our teeth, Sir, and decided to hitch a lift back to the ship on a Sampan (a small Chinese boat), but unfortunately it got caught in the wash of a junk (a small Chinese ship) and was capsized. Boy Seaman Crocket here (he then pointed to Little Joe), did several plunges under the capsized Sampan to rescue the woman who had been sculling it and he managed to get her to the surface after finding her jammed in the bilges of the Sampan. She was virtually encased in a box of rotten fish, Sir.' The other three of us just looked on in awe and wonderment at the imagination and the gall of Tom. We had often referred to him as 'the baron of bull-shit hall'. But to have brought a story like that one right off the top of his head, well, we all later agreed, it was a masterpiece. Our Divisional Officer was most impressed, but then he came up with a very harrowing question. He asked if we could point out where the Sampan was now. Tom then gave some further long spiel, which culminated in the words 'towed away rapidly, Sir.' In answer to this the Divisional Officer gave a pleasant smile (which I later realised was what my parents used to call a 'knowing smile'). He then turned to the coxswain of the boat and said, 'Let the boys into the after compartment and take the boat back to the ship, coxswain.'

Our soggy return to the mess was greeted with a whole tirade of jokes, laughter and mickey-taking and it took the four of us several days to live it down. In truth, I was once reminded of the incident some fifty years after the event. Some sailors have memories like elephants. I must admit that I often wonder if the dedicated people who worked their bums off organising and running dances in order to provide the local servicemen of the town with an extra few pounds could ever possibly have imagined what some of those ''orrible' young servicemen did with that money. God forbid that they should ever find out.

Several of our mess members were sat quietly playing cards one evening when a seaman named Ginger Shaunessy from one of the other messes, came down to visit one of his friends on our mess, and after a while the conversation got around to venereal disease. One of our mess members said, 'I heard that you have recently had a mess change to Rose Cottage, having caught the boat up, Ginger'. ('Catching the boat up' was the Naval expression of the time for having caught a venereal disease and 'Rose Cottage' was the nickname of the mess that was laid aside for all the people who had a contagious disease. This was governed by a law that was in force at the time: 'the Contagious Diseases Act). 'Yes,' said Ginger, 'I've had a shanker, which started as a small lump in my groin'. He then dropped his pants and showed us all where his shanker had first manifested itself in the form of a small soft lump. He went on to say how lucky it was that such a thing could now be cured relatively easily by means of penicillin, which, at that time, was rather a new drug and the first of all the antibiotics that were to follow. Shortly after watching the card game, I decided to have a shower prior to jumping into my hammock for a night's sleep.

I think that a nice shower in the quiet of the evening is one of the most pleasurable events of a sailor's day, and on the evening in question I was really enjoying my shower. I had soaped down and washed it all off well and was then part way through the towelling down process. Then, when I got to the area of the groin, I felt the lump. A small soft lump, and in the precise spot that Ginger Shaunessy had described where he had found his. It was one of the most frightening moments of my life. My entire life's picture flashed before my eyes. Most of it was not too good to look at. I was sure that, despite penicillin or any other antibiotic, my time on this earth was as good as over. Years later I was to travel around the West of England and South Wales, taking on all comers in the boxing booths of the fairgrounds there. Sometimes fighting people almost twice my own weight. None of them ever frightened me as much as that little lump in my groin did. I wondered if I would receive a mess change to Rose Cottage. I had not heard of any boy seamen ever being mess changed to Rose Cottage and I wondered if I would create a precedent. I am sure that my teeth must have chattered with fright.

As a result of my find during the shower, I had one of the most awful and sleepless nights of my life. I had never before had trouble sleeping but that night I was totally devoid of even the remotest sign of sleep, every roll of the ship and every creak of my hammock clews seemed like a loud and frightening signal of trepidation. The morning seemed a very long time arriving. I neither drank nor ate anything at breakfast and was one of the first in the queue at the Sickbay Fresh Cases Muster that morning.

The ship had three doctors, the senior of whom was a Surgeon Commander by the name of O'Brien. He was a wise old Irishman, with that Celtic twinkle in his light blue eyes, and his face seemed to wear a permanent smile. I doubt very much if there was anything in the whole wide world that could have upset him or even taken him out of his normal stride. My luck was in, Surgeon Commander O'Brien was taking fresh cases that morning. I was greeted with the usual smile, followed by the question, 'What seems to be the trouble with you this morning son?' I answered by dropping my pants and pointing to the lump in my groin. 'Jees,' he said. 'You have been talking to that bloody fool Shaunessy. I'll ring that bastard's scrawny Irish neck the next time I see him. You must be the tenth one to come up here to see me, having listened to that bloody Shaunessy. There is nothing wrong with you boy, so pull up your drawers, piss off and get on with your work, and for God's sake keep away from those pox-ridden women. If you see Shaunessy, tell him that I will be using his guts for garters if he has the cheek to come back to my bloody surgery.' I am sure I heard a very distinct chuckle as the door closed behind me.

On arrival back at my place of duty, I confided in my chums as to the problems I thought that I had and of the comments made by the Medical Officer, particularly in respect of Shaunessy. It passed off with a laugh and a joke and was soon forgotten.

A couple of weeks after the above event, a number of us members of the boy's mess were enjoying an after lunch break in the sun on the fo'c'sle deck prior to going back to work for the afternoon. We were sitting quite near to a type of skylight window of the sickbay. Suddenly we heard a most horrific scream. We were all confident that it was surely the last outcry of a man before he was overcome by a most sickening and horrible death. I would think that all our faces must have lost colour and our agitation must have been obvious to anyone. We all looked at each other in awe and hardly any words were spoken. Then some able seaman passed by and said, 'Did you hear that poor bastard scream? It was Dutchy Holland getting the umbrella. They found out that the poor bastard is allergic to penicillin and he has a tear' (meaning that he had gonorrhoea, a venereal disease). Apparently the so-called 'umbrella' was some sort of a surgical instrument that was pushed down the urethra tube (which is the tube that connects the bladder to the outside world via the penis); it was then opened out like an umbrella and pulled out, taking all the mucus and scabs that had been created by the gonorrhoea off the lining of the urethra tube. This operation was usually done without anaesthetic and, in truth, the very thought of such an operation would make every man I know squirm. That scream of poor Dutchy Holland sure enough scared the living daylights out of all of us boys and it sure enough dampened any further desire to visit Wanchai again.

Many years after the above event it was discovered that I am very strongly allergic to penicillin, though I am glad to say that this discovery was not made due to a venereal infection. I thought long and hard about poor Dutchy Holland when my allergy was discovered. However, the thought of that umbrella and the memory of Dutchy's scream still make me shudder.

I do wonder from time to time if Tom King ever wrote of his adventures, because with the imagination that he had he could surely have been in the best-sellers lists. I have never heard of him since leaving that ship. I met Dinger several times over the years. He left the Navy after serving more than fourteen years, and he joined the civil police force somewhere in the south of England. After his retirement from the police he had several problems with cancer and I am sad to say that he died quite recently. I have met Little Joe only once since the time of the above happenings and that was some ten or twelve years afterwards. I was by that time a regulating petty officer, and I was in charge of security on the main gate of the Royal Naval Barracks in Devonport (Plymouth). A Naval lorry that was proceeding out of the barracks was stopped and checked by my staff and me. When I looked inside it, there was Little Joe. He had attained the exalted rank of able seaman, and had obviously decided he was quite happy to remain as such. He was still wearing his usual big broad smile, and I doubt if he had grown an inch since I had last seen him. My greeting to him was, 'Shit, it's my favourite Cornish pixie! Where the hell are you off to?'

'I am away to join a frigate that is about to sail for the Far East,' he replied. I was unable to hold the lorry up any longer so I bade a quick 'bon voyage' to him and my parting words were, 'If you get to Hong Kong, don't forget that some woman in Wanchai still owes you thirty-two pence or a roll in the bloody hay, Little Joe.' By the time I had finished that parting statement, the lorry was well on its way so I doubt if he heard it. I am sorry to say that I have seen or heard nothing of Little Joe since that day. He will, nevertheless, for ever remain my favourite Cornish pixie, even though the memory of him is still tainted by the smell of rotten fish.

The ship had remained in Hong Kong for about three months, apart from a visit to Amoy, which is some distance along the

Chinese coast in a north-easterly direction and in what was then known as the Straits of Formosa. The visit was well received by the then nationalist Chinese people, and several gifts were bestowed on Admiral Frazer. One of the gifts was a very large hamper of Chinese tangerines, which the Admiral sent down to the boys' mess, and we all ate tangerines until we were well and truly sick. We also found that the tangerines gave us the runs, which meant that when you got to the heads (toilet) you were not sure which end was going to shed its excrement first.

Eventually the ship handed over her policing duties and after the sailors who had so successfully carried out those duties, laid on a wonderful and very professional and entertaining tattoo, the ship left Hong Kong for what I think could best be described as a grand tour of the Orient. The first place we called at in Japan was Kagoshima, on the southern tip of the country. There was a volcano very nearby and the ship was covered in volcanic ash; it was like a very fine powder and it seemed to get into everything. We left there after a couple of days and fortunately ran into some heavy weather, which washed off most of the ash. I did hear that the volcano erupted shortly after we had left and there were many people killed in the explosion, but news was very flimsy and uncertain at that time and that report was never confirmed to us. Then on to Nagasaki, where the second atom bomb was dropped. The Americans laid on several trucks to transport us around the site of the damage, and it really was astounding to think that such damage could have been caused by one bomb. I remember one of our party picking up a small glass bottle that had been flattened by the heat of the explosion. It was still in the shape of a bottle but completely flat, a very good indicator of the intense heat that the atomic explosion created. There was also the charred outline of a man on a rocky outcrop. He had obviously been blown against the rock with the force of the explosion, and when his remains were eventually removed from the rock (which I should imagine was done by a high pressure hosepipe) it left a virtual silhouette of him. It was really quite macabre, and to this day when anyone mentions atomic bombs, my mind conjures up that strange silhouette. I think it is going to be with me for the rest of my days. I sincerely hope that the silhouette has long faded from view, though I have no particular desire to return to confirm it.

Then on to Kure, where we were able to catch a train to visit Hiroshima, where the first atomic bomb had been dropped. That was the most devastating sight I have ever seen, for the reason that it was a very flat area and the devastation could all be seen in one panoramic view. As far as the eye could see, everything was flat. It was only a few months since the bombs had been dropped and I distinctly remember wondering if anything would ever be built on the site and if anything, would ever grow on it. I had just turned seventeen years of age and I distinctly remember thinking, *will man ever grow out of the need for such barbarism?* I hope I never live to see such a sight of devastation again.

The allies could hardly be chastised for dropping such devastating bombs when one considers the totally underhand way that the Japanese had entered the war by their raid on Pearl Harbour. There is a possibility that my own life was saved by the act of dropping those bombs, as I was on my way out to the Far East to take part in the war when they were dropped. Everyone was convinced that the Japanese would fight to the last man, as had already been borne out by the defences they had put up at the islands that the Americans had taken up to that time.

One nevertheless, has to consider deeply what the consequences of such an action as dropping nuclear bombs would be. Mankind entered a totally new zone of conflict with the introduction of the nuclear aspect of war.

I have thought long and hard about the consequences of the atomic age and realise what a problem the world still has to face. I sincerely hope that we can come to some agreement whereby all the countries of the world agree to forgo the use of nuclear weapons.

The United States of America have nothing to be embarrassed about in the way they fought and, mostly due to their efforts, won the Second World War.

But the formation of the United States often brought about a contravention of those very principles that we have since fought wars over.

There is one chapter in American history that was recently brought to my attention. I think that it is a part of their history that the people of the United States ought to have imprinted on their souls. They are the words of Chief Seattle, when he surrendered Indian (native American) land in the territory of Washington to the United States Government in 1854. I quote:

> The shining water that moves in the streets and rivers is not just water, but the blood of our ancestors. If we sell you our land, you must remember that it is sacred and you must teach your children that it is sacred.

> The rivers are our brothers, they quench our thirst... The air is precious to the red man, for all things share the same breath – the beast, the tree, the man, they all share the same breath...

> This we know. The earth does not belong to man: man belongs to the earth. This we know. All things are connected like the blood which unites one family. All things are connected.

> Whatever befalls the earth befalls the sons of the earth. Man did not weave the web of life; he is merely a strand in it. Whatever he does to the web, he does to himself...

> The white man too shall pass; perhaps sooner than all other tribes. Continue to contaminate your beds, and you will one night suffocate in your own waste.

That wonderful and most profound statement was uttered almost a whole century before those two atomic bombs were dropped. But the point that should not be lost is the fact that that speech was made by a person who most of the known world, at that time, referred to as an ignorant savage. Who are the savages now?

The next stop was Yokohama, from where we were able to visit Tokyo, and again the devastation was sickening to behold. I am aware that Japan started the war with both the Americans, and us but the cost in innocent lives that was brought about by the stupid and bigoted beliefs of the Japanese leadership was truly nonsensical. God forbid that such people should ever rise to power in any part of the world again: I nevertheless fear that such a possibility is still feasible.

After a long and truly wonderful journey through the Pacific islands we returned to Sydney once again, but this time it was to make our last farewells, and the actual goodbyes were quite something. There were so many paper streamers thrown between the ship and the jetty that I had the idea that the ship's engines would have quite a struggle to raise enough steam to break them all. There were several sailors who jumped over the side of the ship because they could not bear the thought of leaving their sweethearts and I have no idea how many actual deserters the ship left behind, but it must have eventually been quite a large number.

Sydney was left behind us, and the ship would never again return there, except in the possible guise of razor blades after she was broken up and sold off as scrap in the late 1950s. First it was back to Hong Kong to pick up Admiral Frazer, and from there it was quite a good run home. I was told that we broke the record in the Suez Canal, we ran aground only six times, and the other three ships of our class all ran aground more than us. All of us were topped up with food for the UK donated free by the kindly Australian people, so it is pretty certain that all the ships of the class were drawing at least a foot more than their normal draught. I heard that the *King George V* was aground nineteen times. Fortunately the canal bottom was sandy and as battleships had a double bottom there was obviously no damage done to any of them.

Our next stop was Malta. This was my first visit to Malta, where I seem to have since spent a large part of my life. The island was slowly recovering after some hectic bombing raids during the war. The place was nevertheless back in full swing as a sailor's attraction, and our ship's company certainly put the place to the test. I remember that two of our Marines were arguing who was going to hit them and who was going to stack them when they got into a punch-up with some other ships' companies. There really were some hard characters on board that ship.

Gibraltar was our last port of call prior to arriving in dear old Guzz (Devonport, Plymouth). We were able to top up with such things as bananas, which we knew were still not available in the UK. The war had only been over for a few months and prior to the lend-lease by the dear old Americans, our country was virtually stony broke and could hardly afford to buy enough food to feed the population. It must be hard for today's generation to realise that our country was so short of food that all HM ships returning from the various Commonwealth countries were virtual obligated to bring home all the food that was offered to them and which they were able to carry. Food was very strictly rationed in the country, an example being that a week's ration of butter was two ounces per person per week, and one was only allowed three eggs per month.

We arrived in Guzz (Devonport, Plymouth) on 11 July 1946. It was a bright sunny day and the ship was soon overrun with family visitors. Shortly after our arrival the first leave party were on their way home and I was amongst them. On the way from Australia, the only land of any consequence that we had seen for any reasonable period of time had been when we were traversing the Suez Canal, and that had been mostly rather bleak desert, so it really was lovely to see and appreciate those lovely, rolling green fields whilst travelling up to my home in the North West of England.

Oh, the green, green grass of home.

The Lifeguard

'I don't attract the women,' said the lifeguard on the beach.
'All the pretty girls I see are way out of my reach.'
'I'm sure I know what you need,' said I, 'and I'll soon put it right.
Drop these large spuds in your bathing trunks and tie the cord up
  tight.'
He paraded up and down the beach but not a girl came near.
'The idea doesn't work,' said he, 'and that is pretty clear.'
'Don't raise your wrath at me, mate,' I stated very blunt,
when you put spuds in your bathing trunks you should put 'em
  down the front.'

Hunger Pangs

The hunger pangs were biting when I entered the kitchen door.
My wife was in her rocking chair, the dog lay on the floor,
A pan of soup boiled on the stove that would not go to waste.
I filled a ladle brimming full and had a darned good taste.
Then I looked at the wife and spluttered, 'It needs salt, I declare.'
'Put as much salt in as you like,' said she, 'I'm boiling my knickers
  in there.'

Shipwrecked

Poor Jack, the shipwrecked sailor, in the cannibals stew pot sat.
To think that life could end like this made him feel a proper prat.
He was glad he had kept the laxatives that were issued by the Navy,
At least he would get some sweet revenge by ruining their gravy.

A Medical Opinion

I went to the doctor's surgery, I was not feeling very well.
My nose had started running and my feet had begun to smell.
'I think I know what your trouble is,' the doc said with a frown,
'But you don't need pills or medicine, you're just standing upside-
    down.'

The Rocket Man

The young sailor stood in his space suit, looking up to the sky.
Soon he would be in the rocket, and heavenward he would fly.
'Where will your journey take you?' shouted someone in the
    crowd.
'I'm going to the sun,' said he, and they all laughed out loud.
'You will shrivel like a cinder, a blackened, awful sight.'
'Not me,' replied the Jolly Tar, 'I'm going up at night.'

The Bank Robber

He entered the bank with a mask on, his intention was to rob.
'Put your hands in the air,' he said to the staff, 'this is a stick up job.'
But they all fell about with laughter; they thought it hilarious fun,
This stupid twit with the mask on had forgotten to bring his gun.

To My Darling

'You are my only darling,' said she whilst removing her dress,
'The only man I will ever want, I really must confess.'
And as she spoke, her silky slip tumbled to the floor,
Followed by her brassiere and several items more.
As naked as the day she was born she got into the bed,
She was going to sleep there all alone after telephoning Fred.

The Dustman

The dustcart was well decorated, a truly magnificent sight,
I think that the driver was sober but the rest of the crew were tight.
They were due for a grand celebration, it was Tony the dustman's
   day,
'Twas his shotgun wedding to Two Ton Cath, she was in the
   family way.
The church was full to the rafters, even the atheists came,
They had all played cards for the hand of Cath and Tony had lost
   the game.
So he was to be the bridegroom, with the full approval of Cath,
But when he carried her over the threshold, he spilt some of her
   on the path.

48

The Gangster

The gangster boss was in a bad mood and looking for someone to
   blame,
One of his aids, just to make small talk, said, 'I saw you last night
   with a dame.'
The boss-man said, 'Unfortunately, she died last night of VD.'
'I didn't think that was terminal, boss'. 'Yes, it is when they give it
   to me.'

Acrobatics

'That's a nasty gash on your forehead.'
'Yes, I bit myself up there.'
'You can't bite yourself on the forehead.'
'Yes you can, if you stand on a chair.'

CHAPTER THREE

My family were quite pleased and rather excited to see me after my first spell abroad, and the first thing I presented to my mother was a large bunch of bananas, the like of which had not been seen in the country for something like seven years. She took them into our shop and presented one to every young child who entered the shop, and as the news spread the bananas went as fast as a forest fire and none were left for our own family. Some people are born givers and some are takers. My dear old mum was one of the world's truly born givers.

It was an enjoyable leave, and by that time my cousin Charlie had been demobilised from the Navy and was back in the bakehouse, so I spent the whole of my leave without hearing a cry of help from my uncle, the baker. My leave was soon over and it was eventually back to Devonport and the dear old *Duke of York*.

I really ought to insert a rider here about my cousin Charlie. He had had quite a war. He had spent his whole war just sailing back and forth across the Atlantic, mostly in very slow convoys. How the hell he had managed to survive is really something of a miracle in itself. A year or so after his demobilisation from the Navy he got married. It was a great match and they were both very happy. He was a man who truly deserved a happy life. Regrettably, shortly after his wedding, he died of cancer. Luck is a very strange animal.

One incident that I recall during that very enjoyable home leave was that my brother Peter, who had become one of the junior bell ringers in the parish church, asked me if I would go down to help with a problem they had with the bell ropes in the church tower. They could not get new hemp rope because of the import restrictions at that time and they were told the only way that the ropes could be repaired was by splicing the old ropes together. Some local man had tried that method but found that the ropes were then too thick to traverse the large pulley wheel. I therefore spliced the ropes with what is known as a 'long splice', which increased the width of the rope considerably less than the ropes spliced during the original attempts. The ropes were then able to pass successfully over the pulley wheel and in consequence it was then possible to ring a full peel of bells. The one snag that this rather egotistical exhibition of my seamanship prowess brought about was that every time I was home on leave thereafter, I was asked to splice bell ropes. That is, at least, until the time that hemp ropes were again available, and the parish were able to renew them all.

There was one memory of HMS *Duke of York,* however, that I should relate, and that was that ships, like most villages, have their idiots. The *Duke of York* was no exception to this rule. Our supposed idiot was named Campbell, and in deference to the late Sir Malcolm Campbell, who held both the land and water speed records, he was often referred to by the nickname of 'Flash' Campbell, so anyone in the Navy whose surname was Campbell automatically acquired the nickname Flash. It would have been impossible to find a nickname less appropriate to its owner than the one our Flash Campbell therefore acquired.

Our Flash Campbell seemed to have been for ever under punishment, due mostly to his almost total inability to get to where he should have been by the time that he should have been there. Poor Flash seemed to have been in a permanent daze, and although the ship had carried three doctors, none of them could find anything physically or mentally wrong with him. In consequence of his tardy timekeeping, which we all believed was due to his laziness, his life was truly miserable. One specific incident does stick glue-like in my mind, and that was the time that Flash was seconded to the Bridge

Staff for lookout duties. He was given a post on the starboard side of the bridge and had to cover an arc of some 45°. He was issued with the standard binoculars and, as an able seaman, he was expected to be conversant with the duties and responsibilities of a lookout. After Flash had been on watch for about fifteen minutes, he seemed to be holding his binoculars fast on one specific spot, as if concentrating on a particular object on that bearing. The Officer of the Watch noticed the apparent concentration of the lookout and he brought his own binoculars to bear on where he thought the object to be, but he could find nothing there. He then walked over to Flash and tapped him on the shoulder, whereupon Flash fell to the deck. He had obviously been fast asleep.

Flash was immediately relieved of his duties and marched down to the cells, and incarcerated there whilst a full investigation into the incident was carried out. Again no medical evidence was forthcoming to prevent poor Flash receiving yet more punishment.

On our return to Devonport, Flash was sent up to the local Naval hospital at Stonehouse (Plymouth) and eventually it was diagnosed that he had a brain abnormality. I suppose that goes a little way to proving that not all ships' idiots are really genuine idiots. Poor Flash, had that happened during the present time he would surely have received a lot of money in compensation.

After my return from leave I settled into a routine that my itchy feet and deep desire to travel had not prepared me for. The ship remained in Devonport and was no longer of the seagoing variety, a situation which suited me not one little bit, though in one respect it pushed me in a different direction. I took up running and became very interested in general physical fitness. I had always had the urge to take up boxing seriously and this static period seemed to be the ideal opportunity for me to make a start in that direction. I became quite a dedicated athlete and I used to run at least five or six miles every evening as well as doing a pretty strenuous workout.

We did have a very slight change in our scenery about this time. HMS *King George V* came into Devonport, and all the personnel just changed ships. In other words the Duke of York was taken out of reserve and replaced by the 'KGV'. Several of us had hoped that we would go back to sea on the old *Duke* but unfortunately there was not the slightest chance of such a happening. One small consolation was that we knew our way around our new ship because she was identical to the old *Duke of York*.

Soon after the changeover, the *KGV* went into dry dock, and in fact she spent many months there, which was not the most pleasant situation for either the comfort or convenience of the ship's company, and just using the heads (toilets) necessitated a very long walk. One incident that happened during that period raised a good laugh amongst us, and it happened to the Leading Seaman in charge of the mess I was in. He was an Irishman by the name of Murphy, he was far from the most popular man on the ship and quite lazy regarding his own ablutions and toilet affairs. One day he urinated into an old tin can because he was too lazy to walk across the brow to the heads. He then emptied the tin can out of the open porthole. Unbeknown to him, there was a dockyard worker who was working just below that porthole and he was soaked with the urine. The dockyard worker was a huge man and he was soon on the ship and searching out the mess where the responsible person was ensconced. Murphy was flabbergasted when he saw the big 'docky' approaching, and the only way he could think of placating him was by offering him his tot of rum which had just been dished out. The docky took the tot and sank the lot in one gulp. Murphy had intended the docky just to have one good sip of it and then hand it back to him. To my knowledge that was the only time that Murphy ever gave away any of his rum, and although we bore sympathy for the urine-soaked docky we all enjoyed the fact that Murphy got his comeuppance, and certainly enjoyed the fact that he had lost his tot. I was too young to draw my rum ration at the time, but the more senior members of the mess all banded together in their denials, and in consequence I am delighted to say that Murphy got no rum that day.

There was one other rather unpleasant character in the mess other than Murphy, and that was an able seaman by the name of Simmons. He was one of the world's great moaners and I don't think that anything ever happened on that ship that Simmons could not find something to moan about. One day he came back from a trip ashore with an even bigger moan than was usual, even for him. He had been to retrieve a pair of shoes that he had had repaired and he considered the price of the repair was extortionate. Another AB (Able Seaman), by the name of Jones, who had recently arrived on the ship, took a look at the shoes and stated that the shoe repair was a very poor job, as well as being overpriced. Jones then said that he had served some time as a shoe repairer prior to joining the Navy. I could see Simmon's expression change, and imaginary pound signs flashed up in his eyes like the figures on a shopkeeper's till. 'Do you think you could teach me to repair shoes?' asked Simmons.

'It would cost you quite a bit of money to get the thing off the ground,' said Jones, 'and although I would be quite happy to show you how to do the job, I have no intention of coming in with you in a cobbling firm, or even investing in one.'

Simmons must have dug very deep into his savings to purchase all the tools, the leather and rubber etc. that were evidently required. He also had to get permission from the Executive Officer, via the Master-at-Arms, to start what was called a 'ship's firm'. A notice, containing a price list, as per regulations, was displayed on the Daily Orders and boots and shoes in quantity came into the firm's collection point. Simmons then received his first lesson from Jones. That lesson was, how to strip the old sole and heel off the boots and shoes. The following day Jones was sent ashore for some medical tests, and before going he suggested to Simmons that he carried on stripping the boots and shoes and when he (Jones) returned he would execute lesson number two, how to sole and heel. Simmons consequently spent all his off-duty hours stripping the soles and heels off the large quantities of footwear that came into his caboose (a little compartment set aside, normally for storage purposes, on a ship) in preparation for the return of Jones and lesson number two.

Alas, tragedy struck. Jones was retained in the hospital he had been sent to, and it was discovered that the poor fellow had tuberculosis (TB). In those days the letters TB were a virtual kiss of death as there was no known cure. We were all quite dumbstruck, because he had looked so fit and healthy. The next we heard of his situation was that he had been sent to a sanatorium in the north of England, near to where his family lived. None of us ever saw him again, and in fact that was the last we heard of him. The one person who the tragedy struck rather hard was Simmons. He was left with umpteen pairs of footwear, minus their soles and heels, and not the remotest idea of how to repair them. The general consensus of opinion was that of pity for poor Jones and his family, but none of us seemed to feel any sympathy for Simmons. I left the ship shortly after the departure of Jones, so I do not have any idea of what happened about Simmons' footwear tragedy. All I can say is that it could not have happened to a more deserving character. I bet it cost him a pretty penny to sort out the problem and I wish I had kept in touch with someone on the ship and found out the outcome, if only to have enjoyed a good laugh at Simmons' comeuppance.

By early 1947 I had attained a pretty good standard of fitness, and despite the fact that I had not had the opportunity to get in much sparring practice, I entered the Devonport Command Novices Boxing Championship. Boxing was one of the country's major sports at that time and most boxing competitions were very well subscribed. The Command Novices Boxing Championships were no exception to this, and I think that I had about seven or eight bouts before I eventually got to the finals, which I won solely because of my outstanding fitness rather than my boxing ability. I do feel that had I had proper coaching at that period of my boxing career I could have advanced much better and faster than I did. I had the dedication and the will to train hard. The Command Trainer eventually dragged me into the Command Boxing Team, but I still felt that what talent I had was not being properly nurtured. I did have several contests shortly after the Command Novices Championships, losing only one of them and that one was to a rather awkward 'southpaw'. I did have a very good result in beating the RAF representative in two rounds, but for the life of me I cannot remember his name, though I do remember the look of complete surprise on his face when I landed the final right cross flush on the button.

I volunteered for the 1948 Devonport field gun crew during the latter part of 1947, and because of my very good standard of physical fitness I was readily accepted. Shortly after I had joined the gun crew, the Command Boxing Championships took place, and in the finals of that competition I was boxing the Imperial Services Light Heavyweight Champion. He had sweated himself down to middleweight because he had been told that he had a strong chance of being selected to represent the country in the 1948 Olympic Games, providing he could reduce his weight whilst retaining his fitness, then to enter the competition as a middleweight. I lost the fight on a very close points decision, and I have no complaints about that decision. It was several days later, however, that a friend of mine made a critical comment about my tactics in the fight. He said that I should have concentrated more on my body punching, because shortly before the fight with me, the man I was boxing had boxed Randolph Turpin (who later became the World Professional Middleweight Boxing Champion) and Turpin had quite severely damaged his ribs. If only I had known that before my fight with him, it is possible that the whole course of my boxing career could have been changed. As it happened, the man who beat me in those finals had to withdraw because of the damage to his ribs. The boxer who eventually won the Navy Middleweight title that year also won the Amateur Boxing Association title and then represented the country at the Olympics in 1948, and in fact he won a silver medal, the highest achievement of any of our Olympic competitors during those Olympic games.

I would like to say that I was very pleased and truly proud of the fantastic support I had from the Devonport field gun crew members, who attended the Command Boxing Finals almost to a man. They all shouted themselves hoarse on my behalf and made me very proud to be a member of such a wonderful organisation, and to be one of such a fine group of men. I am pleased to say that I have never lost that pride in my brotherhood of field gunners. Such a statement certainly demands a further explanation and I hope that the following paragraphs give that satisfactory explanation, and in a comprehensive manner.

The largest military tattoo in the world, The Royal Tournament, had its last showing in 1999, and it had been going in its various forms since 1883. As I have already stated, I took part in it as a member of the Devonport field gun team in 1948, but 1999 will remain in my memory as possibly the most nostalgic. To have joined several hundred ex-field gunners marching before Her Majesty the Queen, some having travelled from the far corners of the earth, well, it was close to overpowering. (The oldest ex-field gunner on parade was Bill Bedford, 99 years of age. He had run in 1926, two years before I was born.) I still find it hard to believe that it has all come to an end, despite my normally hardbitten common sense having told me for many years that, in this modern world of high technology, its time was surely fast drawing to a close.

The first year that the Field Gun Competition was introduced into the Royal Tournament was 1907. It was a competition consisting of an 'obstacle race' in which men carried and pulled a field gun, weighing more than a ton, over and through obstacles like walls and chasms. The gun had to be taken apart and reassembled several times. Two supposed actions took place during the competition, where three rounds had to be fired from the gun. Each gun crew (or team) consisted of eighteen participants.

Its origin is a throwback from the Boer (South African) War when, in 1899, men of Her Majesty's Ships *Powerful* and *Terrible* landed several guns and towed them to Ladysmith, where they were deployed for its defence and thereby eventually, after a period of 119 days, were instrumental in breaking the siege there. To get from the ship to Ladysmith, the guns were towed many miles over rough terrain. On several occasions the guns had to be taken apart and carried over or through obstacles, then reassembled, which took great endeavour and proved the courage and tenacity of the crews involved. On their return from the war all the guns crews were paraded before Her Majesty Queen Victoria who gave them lunch at Windsor Castle and thanked them for their valiant and heroic efforts. Rudyard Kipling wrote glowingly of the gunners' exploits. The Prince of Wales took the rare step of conveying his gratitude by shaking the hand of a humble gunner during an inspection on Horse Guard's Parade. I would imagine that the kernel of an idea for the Field Gun Competition was sown at about that time.

Over the years, the Field Gun Competition was proved to be one of the hardest and most competitive sports in the world and certainly the hardest team sport that I have ever seen or taken part in. I always advised any young sailor wishing to volunteer for selection to one of the three crews which took part in the Royal Tournament, to make sure that he was superbly fit, or he would have no chance of selection.

Some time in the mid-1990s a group of 'work-study' students were shown all the pieces of equipment and asked to devise a method of shifting them as fast as possible from one end of the course to the other, using eighteen men. Eventually they presented a plan that would have kept the crew busy for something like nine hours. The Devonport crew hold the record for the course, which stands at two minutes and forty seconds. Over the years the times have obviously got faster and faster. When I ran in 1948, no crew got below four minutes.

I was very lucky to be selected for the Devonport Crew of 1948, and for more than half a century my mind has carried the question, how in the world did they get it out? The explanation for my quandary is this: our gun's crew was several weeks into the training programme when we were hit by a spate of injuries. It got so bad that the trainer decided to call a halt to any further drill. A bus was ordered for the following day, and the whole crew and the staff were wheeled away for a break. Eventually we stopped at an old coaching house inn far out in the country. We all piled into the rather friendly bar, and were soon enjoying genial banter with the locals. That is, all except one farmer, who had a very caustic tongue and a distinct lack of humour. Fortunately none of our crew took offence, and the enjoyable afternoon seemed to have passed all too quickly.

Well before the afternoon 'stop tap' was called, all the crew were outside and ready to board the bus. One of our crew then mentioned that the car of the caustic-tongued farmer was parked in the small courtyard of the inn. Without, it seemed, a single word being spoken, the car was lifted, turned end on, and in that mode placed between the two walls of the entrance, with each of the bumpers of the car some two inches from the walls; the car was totally undamaged. We quickly left the area and I have no idea where that old coaching house inn was, but I have had many a chuckle imagining those locals trying to move that car.

There was only one other member of the 1948 Devonport crew at the 1999 parade before the Queen, and we both really enjoyed a few chuckles over the happenings of our year's field gun escapades. However, I am sad to say I recently heard that he had passed on (crossed the bar), so it seems that I am the only one left to carry the 1948 banner. All us field gunners obviously have wonderful, though hard-earned memories of our field-gunning days. I was reminded of the time that my partner and I fell into the supposed chasm, each of us carrying a 120 lb wheel on our shoulder. It was the occasion when the King (George VI) and Queen were the royal spectators. We were told later that it was the first time a pair of wheel carriers had fallen into the chasm without at least one of them breaking a bone, a record that both my wheel carrying partner and myself were happy to have achieved – though both of us suffered from other physical problems as a result of the fall. The drop was about six or more feet. We were both in the gun run the following day though.

In 1948, out of many hundreds who volunteered for the Devonport crew, there were fifty chosen, out of whom, eighteen would eventually be chosen to represent Devonport as the first team (the 'A' team) and a further eighteen would act as a sort of reserve (the 'B' team). Our 'A' team 'angel' was an able seaman named Danny Boon and although, perhaps like most other years, we had many great characters, I think that Danny was one of the most memorable. I had better explain at this stage that the 'angel' is the last man to be pulled across the chasm on the run back from the supposedly enemy territory. He comes over at great speed carrying a ten-foot spa. The spa is dropped to his right whilst he bails off the traveller to the left. It is because of this rather dramatic high flying and spectacular looking activity that his job acquired the name 'flying angel', which was soon shortened to 'angel'.

I think that the following part of my story started with a bet. I say this because I knew that Danny liked a little 'flutter' on the horses. We were having a great run back from the supposed enemy territory on one particular day and the time seemed to be much better than on our previous runs. Danny came across the chasm in the usual way. The ten-foot spa went wheeling off to the right and Danny peeled off to his left in the traditional manner, but then he seemed to slightly correct his balance and he ran through the fourteen-foot cross spas as they were falling. The spas seemed to miss him by inches. There were a few spectators there at the time and Danny got quite a cheer. He nevertheless got a pretty good rollicking from the number one trainer, but Danny's ego had been inflated and a seed had been sown. From that time on, whenever he felt the time was right, Danny would run through the falling spas.

Anyone who has ever watched field gun runs must know what this paragraph will contain. Danny tried his luck just once too often, and four hundred pounds of spas fell across his back. We all gasped in horror (the more tight-fisted members of the crew possibly cursed the high price of flowers we were surely going to have to buy). We all looked on in dread as Danny was spreadeagled in the cinders. There seemed to be a lifetime of total silence, then we all rushed to the scene, we lifted the spas, and up jumped Danny like a jack-in-a-box. I don't think that a word was spoken for several seconds. We were obviously all so relieved and surprised by the fact that he had not sustained serious injury. Then we all spoke as one man, as if we had rehearsed what we were going to say for many days beforehand. 'Danny, if ever you do that again we will all kick the living excrement out of you.' Danny had just about enough brain never to try it again.

At the time in question, the field gun accommodation was right beside the field gun pitch and within spitting distance of the church. We worked a six-day week in those days, and the bells rang out to call us to church on the morning of the seventh day. Danny hated the sound of the bells and promised for weeks that he would find a way of silencing them.

One Sunday morning we all awoke to an unusual silence. We breakfasted to silence. We lunched to silence; in fact the silence was rather eerie. We all looked at Danny but apart from his usual vacant smile, he was virtually expressionless. It was possibly 2 p.m. when the Padre entered the mess. He was red faced and full of bluster. His day had obviously been totally destroyed by the absence of the lilting tones of his church bells. I am glad that I had not heard his sermon that morning; it must have been full of fire and brimstone. I can imagine that his sermon was in the category of John the Baptist at his best. 'Someone has sabotaged my bells,' he said, 'and I am sure it was one of you field gunners.'

Sunday was the only day that the field gunners could enjoy their tot of 'Nelson's blood' (rum), and several of the crew were silently glowing as the flush of the raw spirit crimsoned the pallor of their facial appearance and caused their cheeks to glow. (I was, at that time, under the age of twenty, so was not one of the crimson-cheeked members of the gun's crew; I was, alas, too young to draw my tot.) At this very point in time, the light from the doorway of the mess was almost totally obliterated as the huge frame of Scouse Rawlings appeared in it. Scouse Rawlings was our number eighteen and he could hold up the barrel of the field gun with one hand. He was the type of man who could have made King Kong beg for mercy. His deep bass voice boomed out the question, 'What seems to be the problem, Padre?' The Padre strained his neck to look up at the six foot six inch figure of Scouse. 'Someone has silenced the church bells,' he said. 'I have heard about it, Padre,' said Scouse, 'and I am sure that, short of hiring a helicopter, the silencing act could only have been brought about by the actions of an angel.' Every member of the mess unsmilingly nodded in unison. As the Padre turned and left the mess, a toast was proposed to the angel.

A powerful telescope later revealed that a seizing (a method of lashing ropes together) had secured the three bell ropes firmly together. It had been done with sail-maker's twine and on hemp bell ropes it was almost impossible to detect from the ground. Whoever had tied that seizing had performed one fantastic climbing feat, and it had obviously been done in the dead of night. We were all quite sure that it could only have been done by someone who was mad enough to run under 400 lbs of falling spas. Danny never admitted or denied any involvement in the incident; in fact he was never really questioned about it. I ask you, who would ever have the audacity to pose such a question to an angel?

There was one incident that occurred during our sojourn at the Royal Tournament in London, the memory of which has often brought a smile to my face. Each member of the field gun crew was allotted two complimentary entrance tickets to hand to our family or friends, but like many of us, Scouse Rawlings had no relatives living anywhere near London, though we certainly found out in a very amusing way what happened to his two complimentary entrance tickets. The two competing field gun teams form up outside the two large gates which form the entrance to the actual arena, and I can assure you that the short period of waiting to enter that arena is very much akin to the nerve-racking period suffered by a prizefighter when he is waiting to enter the boxing ring. One day, whilst the two competing crews were undergoing this nerve-racking and perspiring wait in the usual tense silence, it was then that two very effeminate voices rang out in unison, 'Hello Scouse.' Every eye turned to look where the sound had come from, and there, just a few paces from us, were two obviously very gay men. Their faces were beautifully made up and they were waving rather limp-wristedly and blowing kisses at Scouse. When you are six foot six inches tall it is rather difficult to hide, and Scouse's face turned a rather dark crimson colour. We all burst out laughing and at that very moment the arena doors opened, the band played, and we marched into the arena all wearing the broadest of smiles. The great consolation of the incident was that it had taken the tension out of the crew and that day we performed at our very best and we did the fastest run we had done in the whole tournament. Scouse Rawlings was never allowed to live down his part in the improvement of our performance though.

On completion of the Royal Tournament in London, our return to Guzz (Devonport, Plymouth) was a rather sad affair, as we were completely devoid of cups or medals. If anyone tells you that it is not the winning but the taking part that matters, tell them from me they could not possibly be a former field gunner. Despite such failure, I have remained a staunch supporter of the Field Gun Competition and the Devonport crew in particular. I carry my association membership card with as much, nay, more pride, than I would an Oxbridge Blue.

Alas, as already stated, 1999 was the last year of the Field Gun Competition. All that fire and enthusiasm which has lasted for a whole century will be no more. It seems so dreadful to the likes of me, who, having joined the Navy as young boys, were virtually fed field gun in our cradles. Such enthusiastic men were the lifeblood of the Navy, as we carried our newly gained passion for team work, total dedication and supreme effort back to the fleet on completion of our stint at the Royal Tournament. I knew throughout my Naval career, particularly as a seagoing master-at-arms, that field gunners were special. Field gun did not just promote enthusiasm, it made it infectious. I feel that the loss of such dedication and ebullience will have a far greater effect on the Navy than the mere loss of a competition. Dartmouth may have produced the top admirals but field gun built the best sailors.

Such a sad passing filled me with a deep despair.

My Queen

She had long blonde hair and deep blue eyes, the nicest ever seen,
I walked across the gilded room and begged her to be my Queen.
'I could live in those lovely eyes,' I said, 'so beautiful and bright.'
'You would really feel at home,' said she, 'there's a sty in the one
    on the right.'

Worries

Joys and worries, like boots and shoes,
Invariably arrive in twos.
Will we be healthy or will we become ill,
If we are going to be healthy then our worries are nil,
If we are going to get sick we'll look up to the sky,
And ask our maker will we live or die.
If we are going to get better then our worries are few,
but if death be the outcome then we're back to the two.
If it's heaven, no worries, everything will be well,
But the devil usually wants us old salts down in hell.
So we're going to be busy at hell's fiery gates,
Shaking the hands of our old shipmates.

The Fiery Shed

Our Chief Stoker was a giant of a man, he was known as Two Ton
   Ted.
One night he caught a burglar nicking some gear from his shed.
The burglar's testes he locked in the vice and the key was hidden
   from sight.
He said to the burglar, 'I'll tell you mate, you're in for quite a
   night.'
Then Ted put a rusty knife by the vice, the burglar turned to say,
'Oh, don't use that knife on me mate, don't cut my testes away.'
'You are the one with that problem,' retorted Two Ton Ted,
'What you do with the knife is up to you, I'm just going to burn
   down the shed.'

Church Parade

They sat in the church just waiting for the service to begin,
The organist struck up a chord to introduce a hymn.
'Twas then a thunderous flash occurred and filled the aisle with
   light,
The congregation were terrified; it gave them an awful fright.
Then the devil appeared in a blinding flash and everybody ran,
The stampede quickly emptied the church except for a sailor man.
The sailor man just sat there, his demeanour very cool,
The devil approached and said to him, 'You must be the local fool.'
As the devil neared the sailor, his hot breath raised a blister,
But the sailor said, 'You can't scare me, I'm married to your bloody
   sister!'

The Grumpy Bishop

We all attended the funeral, after the Bishop passed away.
One thing we thanked the Almighty for was a dry and sunny day.
It was sad to see him lowered to the bottom of the grave,
His family showed great fortitude and acted very brave.

'Twas the early hours of the morning when the Bishop arrived at
    heaven.
And when he rang the doorbell a voice said, 'Wait until seven.'
The wait seemed to last for ever, his patience was wearing thin,
When at last an angel came to the gate he said, 'You can't come in.'

By this time the bishop was furious; he'd never been stood up
    before.
Wherever he'd arrived, whilst down on earth, someone opened the
    door.
'What do you want?' said the angel, 'we're expecting no one today.'
'I've been sent up here,' said the Bishop, 'and here I intend to stay.'

'Well, you'll have to wait for Gabriel, no matter how much you
    insist,
'Cause there's no way I can let you in, when you're not even on
    my list.'
It was afternoon when old Gabriel arrived, looking quite calm and
    serene,
By then the Bishop was explosive and ready to create a scene.

Gabriel said, 'Take it easy old man, we don't lose our tempers up
    here,
Come in and watch our grand parade and enjoy a nice cold beer.'
So at last the Bishop stepped inside but he couldn't find a seat,
And he was getting a bit disgruntled as the crowd trod on his feet.

66

Then he saw a flashy Rolls Royce car gliding over the cloud,
The cheers were almost deafening from the large and happy
crowd.
Why the Rolls Royce and cheering crowd, the Bishop had no
conception,
And what's this man in the Roller done, to deserve such a great
reception?

The Bishop was most despondent and said, 'I've been treated very
bad.
Yet on seeing this bloke in the Roller the angels sound so glad.'
Gabriel replied, 'The reason is, we get a bishop almost every year,
But this is the very first master-at-arms we've ever had up here.'

CHAPTER FOUR

Of the millions of people we meet along life's highway, the vast majority we completely forget, though a few stay in our memories just about for ever. To me, Henry Lang was one of those memorable characters. I had met Henry whilst we were both with the field gun. As I have already said, in the 1940s and early 1950s, field gunners were picked mostly from known athletes, and Henry was chosen because he was one of the best known boxers in the Navy. Henry had twice been a British Schools Boxing Champion as a young boy and he was, having been born in Birkenhead, a wonderful example of the classical style for which the Merseyside area was at that time, quite famous. In my boyhood I looked upon the Merseyside boxers as virtual Gods within the boxing fraternity. Such wonderful British champions as Nel Tarleton and Ernie Roderick (both Merseysiders) were, in my opinion, the epitome of style and courage. Their defensive skills and ability to slip and evade punches and then counter-punch effectively proved them to be true masters of their craft and their chosen profession.

I have felt for a long time that boxing lost something in the 1950s. It was then, it seemed, that total physical fitness, brought about by bodybuilding and muscle enhancement became the password to boxing success. It seemed that the in thing was to train and body build to the ultimate physical perfection and then with a vocabulary of only the basic punches, coupled with an ability to plough ever relentlessly (and often flat-footedly) forward, due mostly to this enhanced muscle barricade, to overcome one's opponent in a tank-like battle. I think that Mike Tyson is (or was) the embodiment of this theory and in my opinion it was the death knell of true boxing. As far as I was concerned it was also the end of my love of the sport that had been my great passion from early childhood until that time.

Henry Lang was due to leave the Navy in 1950, after having served the twelve years for which he had signed up, but his release from the service was held up due to the Korean War; in fact at that time all service personnel were retained for a further eighteen months over the time they had contracted to serve, so you can surely imagine the moans that were (and I think quite rightly) heard from such people. I went out to the Far East in 1950 and a number of the people on the ship were retained in that way; in consequence they were not the most pleasant company to be with. The situation had little effect on Henry's rapier-like Mersey wit and humour however. I am sure I was never in Henry's company when he was stuck for a topical reply, which was usually also a comical one. He seemed to have a boundless wit and it was always great to meet him and to be in his company. I remember the very last time I saw him, he was back to being a stoker, having been reduced from the rank of leading stoker for the fourth time in his Naval career. I said, 'Tell me what the hell happened this time, Henry?'

He said, 'This time I was drunk and disorderly and refused to fight the Officer of the Watch.

There used to be an annual boxing tournament held at Belle Vue in Manchester; it was between the Royal Navy and the Royal Marines. Belle Vue was one of the largest sporting venues in the country at that time, so it was a fair indicator of the esteem that the tournament was held and it was invariably a sell-out ticket-wise. Henry had been chosen to box Marine Johnny Rice who was, at that time, the ISBA (Inter-Services) Light Heavyweight Champion. Henry's great weaknesses had always been his reluctance to train for a fight and his liking for drink. On this occasion however, he had trained very hard for the contest and had been kept almost totally off the booze by his teammates. In consequence he was highly favoured to beat Rice, in fact it was said that quite a lot of money was riding on Henry as Rice, being the ISBA champion, would have been the bookies' choice.

Unfortunately Henry was allowed home to Birkenhead on the evening prior to the contest and he went out for a quiet drink with his brothers. When the locals saw Henry drinking half pints of shandy they were aghast, and people came from other parts of the pub to see this most unusual spectacle; in fact it was said that people even came in from other pubs to see it. Someone said that they were even considering bussing spectators in from other parts of the county but let us not get too carried away with over enthusiastic exaggerations. The appearance of spectators supposedly embarrassed Henry, though I must state now that I had never imagined any situation that could have embarrassed him. Anyway, he soon converted to his usual pints of stout and the consequence was that, carrying a king-sized hangover, he lost the fight the following evening by quite a large margin of points, after which he said to Rice, 'You were lucky in that last round, Johnny.' Rice replied in a very indignant fashion that he could not agree with Henry's comment because he had, quite rightly, considered that he had won the fight clearly, to which Henry replied, 'No John, what I mean is, when you hit me in the belly in the last round I almost spewed all over you, so in that respect you were certainly very lucky.' I don't think that there ever could have been a situation in which Henry Lang could not have seen, or created, something to laugh about.

The Naval Field Gun Competition was, in fact, a rough, tough and very demanding type of sporting competition, and during the training period prior to the actual competition taking place at the Royal Tournament in London, there were often periods of almost total depression when everything seemed to go wrong. It was during such periods that a person like Henry Lang was truly worth his weight in gold. Nothing seemed to get Henry down. Nothing, it seemed, could wipe that smile (or was it a smirk) off his face or prevent that resounding but always friendly repartee that met every little mistake in our drill. I suppose there were times when we must have turned with vicious intention to do physical harm to him, only to be met with a friendly pat on the head from Henry. If Henry ever had a temper, I never saw him lose it.

After leaving the Navy, Henry evidently helped in the running of a boxing club and I heard that he went up to Blackpool with a team of boxers from that club. At the last minute he decided to take part in the tournament himself because one of his club members had failed to turn up. He evidently collapsed during the contest and died shortly afterwards due to a blood clot on the brain. I did try to gain more information about the incident but I only heard the story long after it had actually occurred, and not having knowledge of his address it would, by that time, have been almost impossible to confirm.

I have often thought about Henry and tried to guess what retort he would make in certain circumstances that occur in my life, but my addled brain could never match his quick fire wit and repartee. Either St. Peter or the devil must be enjoying some merriment. If he has landed with the devil, I hope that he (the devil) has the good sense not to promote Henry to a leading stoker again, because he will never be able to hang onto the rate, and five is not a very lucky number anyway. Though, on reflection, Henry could surely not have been committed to the devil's fiery depths. If anyone was able to make as many friends as Henry made along life's path, there must certainly have been one hell of a heap of good in him.

On completion of the field gun escapade I was given a temporary job whilst awaiting a more permanent draft and the temporary job was one known as 'travelling escort'. It involved travelling all over the country as a threesome – a leading hand and two sailors. Our job was to pick up all the Naval deserters, mostly from the Second World War, who had been arrested by, or had surrendered to, the civil police. I think that I was doing the job for about a month and I was not sorry to eventually leave it. The job did however do me one great favour, in as much as it was through doing it that I met the girl who was eventually to become my wife, to whom I was happily married for forty-seven years, until her untimely death in 1997 due to cancer. I met her in Swansea, South

Wales and the meeting came about because of the fact that we went there to pick up a man who had served at HMS *St. George* at the same time as me. He had deserted from his ship whilst it was in New Zealand and on hearing that his father was ill, he, being a trained seaman, had managed to work a passage back to the UK on a merchant ship. One day, a friend of his, who happened to be a policeman, went to see him and told him that it had been reported to them that he was now back in the country and living at home, so it would be much better if he reported to the police station and surrendered to the police because they were due to come and arrest him the following day. He took this very sensible advice, and in consequence his punishment for desertion was reduced to a suspended sentence of detention, wholly because of the fact that he had surrendered himself as a deserter.

Eventually I received a 'draft chit' (that is, the little *Billet-doux* telling me I was about to move), and written on it was 'Harrier for Dale'. I thought it must be some kind of a mistake because it stated my name on the top and then said Harrier for Dale at the bottom. I went along to the drafting office and asked about this supposed mistake. When I poked my head into the hatchway of the office and stated that my name was Dale, I could both hear and see that several people in the office were laughing. Someone said that there was a closed down Royal Naval airfield called Dale and it was controlled by the RN Radar Training School at a place called Kete, which was nearby and, which went under the full title of HMS *Harrier*. I then realised why the people in the office were all laughing. They had obviously put my name on the draft as some sort of a joke to confuse people. I was quite disappointed because I had both wanted and expected a seagoing ship. It had, by then, been two years since I had last felt the movement of water under a ship's keel, and I had joined the Navy to travel. Within a couple of days I was on a train chugging its way as far to the west of Wales as trains can get.

The job at RNAS (Royal Naval Air Station) Dale was about as easy a job as one could ever possibly hope to find, and I spent most of my time keeping fit by running around the airfield. I was also able to get to Swansea quite often, which was where my fiancée was living. I spent almost two years at both RNAS Dale and HMS *Harrier* and I must say that it really was two wasted years, because I really should have been doing something much more with my career at that time. Being so near to Swansea and my girl was obviously the incentive that held me back from requesting to go back to sea or some other course that would have put me in line for promotion. There was another incentive in the latter part of my stay in West Wales, and that was that I met Ron Taylor, who ran the boxing booth in the fair that travelled that area. I boxed for him on several occasions and we became quite good friends. I had, however, boxed under an assumed name to ensure that my amateur status was untarnished.

Shifting the subject back just a little though, an incident that happened whilst I was at RNAS Dale has often got me wondering about the supernatural, but I have to admit that despite the incident I am about to describe, and the one about the elephants in the jungles of Kenya (which you will read about in later chapters), I still do not believe that there is such a thing as the supernatural. Nevertheless, here is the story of the incident, which is truly how it occurred, and I leave it to your own judgment and imagination as to whether you want to believe it or not.

At the time in question I very rarely drank alcohol, primarily because of the fitness requirements of my boxing. In truth, at that time I had lost all desire and taste for drink, in fact I used to feel rather contemptuous of people who took drink, and particularly those who drank to excess. The consequence of this was that I was often the only person out of the twelve or fourteen of us on the air station of Dale who was sober during the fortnightly pay weekends. Taff Foster, the Petty Officer, who did the job of bar manager, often just used to sink slowly into a chair, which was a signal for me to throw him over my shoulder and carry him over to his cabin. After I had carried out that first part of the regular pay weekend chore (or was it a ceremony?), I just used to run the bar myself for the remainder of the drinkers who were sober enough to order further drinks. The strange thing was that I felt no objection to this chore, which I had virtually allotted to myself. I felt that I was serving with some very good people, despite the fact that the majority of them seemed to be 'pay weekend drunks'.

On one of the payday weekend evenings, I was running the bar, having carried Taff Foster to bed in the usual manner. I was standing alone behind the bar whilst all the other members were sitting around the well banked fire, which was some five or seven yards in front of the bar. Everything was very quiet and there was no wind or turbulent weather to mask any external noises. In fact, it could be virtually described as a night of relative deadness, when even the smallest of sounds would have seemed to be magnified to great proportions. This created something of a creepy atmosphere amongst the people in the bar, which was reflected in the fact that the few who spoke, did so in whispers.

It was three minutes to midnight when we all distinctly heard the outer door open, followed by the sound of a lady's high-heeled shoes walking across the cement floor from the outer door and across the ten or twelve paces of cloakroom to the door of the bar. Ten or eleven pairs of eyes were focussed on the door of the bar; waiting for it to open and display the female who we were all sure must have been about to enter. Then, a deathly silence, followed by an even more deathly pause by all the occupants of the bar. It seemed an eternity before the eight or nine occupants jumped up from their seats and ran towards the door, which was thrown open, to reveal – nothing. I jumped over the bar and quickly joined in the search of the building and the surrounding area but there was not the slightest indication of another person being in the area.

I was the duty security person that night and I had the job of walking around the whole air station to check on boilers and the general security. The moon was quite bright and I must admit to seeing shadows jumping around in places where I had never seen shadows jumping before but I am pleased to say there were no further happenings of a ghostly nature.

The following morning we rang everyone we could think of who might have been able to account for the presence of a woman on the air station at midnight the previous night, but we were unable to get an answer to our question.

Being the only one there during the above incident who was totally sober, I have often wondered if we had all had something of a rush of mud to the brain, but on reflection I am sure that it all happened exactly as I have described it and there were too many people there for it to have been just imagination.

If, as I am told, there is a life after this one, I hope that some one up there (or should that be down there) is able to offer me some explanation as to how the incident described in the last few paragraphs occurred: if for no other reason than to relieve me of the query that has bothered me for more that half a century.

The latter part of my stay in Pembrokeshire was spent wholly at HMS *Harrier*, which was one of the RN radar training bases. By that time I had got myself into a very good physical condition and I took it upon myself to organise, and eventually captain, their cross-country running team. We entered the team into the Devonport Command Cross Country (Xcountry) Championships, but the day after our entry was accepted, I received a draft back to Devonport to join a ship that was due to sail for the Korean War in the not too distant future. The Sports Officer at Harrier made some frantic phone calls and then informed me that I would be able to represent Harrier because I was on their books when the application to enter the Xcountry race was made.

I left Harrier about a week before the Xcountry team were due to travel to Devonport (Plymouth) for the race, and on my arrival in Devonport I realised that the Command Boxing Championships were just about to start and I was in the nick of time for my entry to be accepted. Then one little snag raised its head above the parapet, and that was the fact that the boxing finals would be on the evening of the Xcountry race. Superb physical fitness often carries with it a virtual contempt for lesser mortals, and I was confident that I was in the type of physical condition whereby I could have jumped over the moon. During the two evenings prior to the Xcountry race I managed to eliminate the three boxers who were blocking my way to the finals and I did so in a total of five rounds, one slight snag being that I damaged my right hand during the last of those three contests. However, having seen and made an assessment of the other finalist (who was a pretty hefty Royal Marine Commando, but rather cumbersome), I was confident that I had the beating of him, even with my damaged right hand.

I had taken part in several prominent middle distance races and I had run in several Xcountry races before, but until that time I had never taken part in a Command Xcountry race. There were some six hundred and fifty entries and it was to be run over a very demanding six and a half mile course. I was told that most of the entries had walked the course the previous day but the Command Boxing had precluded me from that opportunity. I therefore did not realise the necessity of a good start, and I allowed myself to become trapped amongst a group of sloggers when I should have started with a sprint and got amongst the *crème de la crème*. I had a hell of a fight to get within sight of the leading group and I think that I must have run the whole of the last mile at a virtual sprint. I finished in a creditable sixth position. I know that I could have done much better had I given myself a better start but that is now water under the bridge. Because of my high finishing position in the race, I was asked to represent the Command in the Navy Xcountry finals, but that was to take place long after I was to have sailed for Korean waters, and wars don't wait for Xcountry races.

It was about this time that I was called up to see the Personnel Selection Officer, because I did not have what was then known as a 'non-substantive rate'. In other words, I was an able seaman with no other branch job like gunnery or radar, and the PSO was supposed to be the man who would select the branch to which I would be most suited. I was rather surprised at his friendly attitude and at the warmth of the greeting he gave me. Then when he started to talk I realised that he was a boxing fan, and had watched me eliminate the three other contenders for the Command Middleweight title. He then said, 'I have the ideal job for you and that job is as a leading patrolman.' In other words he saw me in the role of Naval policeman. I had never really thought much about taking on that type of job before, and I immediately realised that I would be rather suited to the job. I told him that I had already been detailed to join a ship that was due to sail soon for the Korean War, and he said that if I was willing he would make a move to stop that draft. I was already on the verge of arranging the wedding to my fiancée prior to the ship sailing, and the news that I might not have to sail with the ship was most welcome.

I returned to my mess in a rather elated mood and was soon chatting to other mess members. One mess member who I had become quite friendly with was a man by the name of John Corrin. He was a big Cornishman who was quite well known in the rugby circle. He played for both Devonport Services and his county of Cornwall. He had also been detailed to join a ship that was soon bound for the Far East and like me he was just on the verge of getting married. I told John what was happening to me as regards to my possible change of branches, and he said he would go and see the PSO the following morning. When I saw John the following day he told me that his draft had already been stopped and he was due to go to Portsmouth within a few days to start the course for leading patrolman. He thanked me for the advice I had given him, and though I heard quite a lot about him over the following few years that was the last time I actually saw him.

The Command Boxing Finals were a disaster from my point of view, and I was knocked out for the first, and really the only time in my life. Looking back on the situation, I really was due for a fall. To have imagined that I could have run in the Command Xcountry race and then boxed in the finals of the Command Boxing Championships (and with a damaged right hand) some four hours later was the height of egocentric stupidity. I hoped that the rest of my life would reflect the lessons that that period of my being should have taught me; though I regret to say that that was certainly not the case, as the rest of this biography will surely, and rather regretfully, confirm.

The Devonport Command Physical Training Officer then asked me if I would box as a light heavyweight in the Naval Championships in

Portsmouth. I said that I would do so if I could be assured that Peter Messervy was not boxing. I knew that there was not a middleweight in the country, possibly in the world, who could have given a stone in weight to a man like Peter Messervy. I was assured that he would not be boxing that year, so I consequently offered my services as the Devonport representative at light heavyweight. However (I bet you have all second guessed me here), the first person I was drawn against was Peter Messervy. Peter won the Amateur Boxing Association Light Heavyweight title that year (in other words he became the British Amateur Light Heavyweight Champion) and I was, more or less, his first stepping stone. I threw a fight for the first and only time in my life. Peter was sixteen pounds heavier than I was and I could feel every ounce of it in his punching, so I bailed out at the end of the first round. Peter really was a nice chap and certainly deserved that title. He was one of the really hard men of amateur boxing but always a gentleman. I felt some sad pangs of nostalgia recently when I read about his memorial service in the Navy News. I really would have liked to have attended that service and to have said a fond farewell to a fine character.

I was so incensed by the way I had been deceived by the Devonport Command Physical Training Officer that I swore I would never again box as a representative for the Navy, and I never did. The Devonport Command boxing training staff all said that I had done the right thing in throwing the fight but my conscience troubled me for years afterwards, and in fact, it still does. It belittled my basic honesty and made me feel like a cheat. To me, a cheat is a person who does not give his all when his conscience tells him he should do so. So, to some extent, the sourness remains.

Shortly after the debacle over the Navy Boxing Championships, I was introduced to a man named Mick Kielly, who ran the boxing booth that operated in the west of England. I liked Mick; he was like Ron Taylor, whose boxing booth travelled the Welsh circuit of fairgrounds. Their word was their bond, and I never remember either of them ever breaking it. I boxed many times in the booth that Mick Kielly ran (which was called Whitelegs Boxing Booth). The way I met Mick was quite strange, however. I have always enjoyed looking around second-hand bookshops, and one Saturday, late afternoon, I was looking around a shop in Plymouth and found a most wonderful set of eight books containing the entire works of Shakespeare. It was gold-bound and had been edited by Henry Irving, the famous actor (later Sir Henry) and published by Blackie & Son in 1895. The price was three pounds ten shillings, but unfortunately my weekly pay was much less than two pounds so I reluctantly conceded that the price of the set of books was out of my reach, and I dejectedly went to leave the shop. In the doorway I virtually bumped into an old boxing friend of mine. He said to me, 'Hell, I wish I had met you yesterday.' I asked why, and he told me that the boxing booth was in Plymouth's Home Park, and the boss of it was desperate for a couple of reasonable class boxers to challenge his resident performers, and that he had to cancel one of the shows the previous evening because of the lack of challengers.

I am not sure if my immediate following action was due to the confidence of youth or just my desperate desire to acquire the set of books or, perhaps just a sudden rush of mud to the brain which made me want to take a big gamble. I went back into the bookshop and asked if the set of books could be held for me if I placed a reasonable deposit on them. The proprietor accepted my last ten shillings (fifty pence) to reserve the set for a week. I was soon on my way to the fairground, and I was introduced to Mick Kielly for the very first time. On the Monday I was able to pay off the full amount for my set of Shakespeare books and I can see them sitting on one of my bookshelves as I type. They are looking a trifle more battered than when I acquired them more that half a century ago, due partly to the thousands of miles they have travelled. They are, of course, now well over 100-years-old.

The time for me to join my ship was fast approaching and I had heard nothing from the PSO or the drafting office as regards my course for leading patrolman, so I went to the Office of the PSO to find out what the latest news was. He informed me that he had stopped the draft of another able seaman who was due to sail for the Far East, and had received a rollicking for doing so. It was therefore obvious that I would be joining my ship as nominated. It was also most obvious to me that the able seaman who had gone to join the regulating branch was John Corrin, and I was the one who had talked him into doing so, (I think that was akin to cutting my own throat).

Alas, the Korean War was raging and the frigate I was to join was needed out there quite urgently. She had recently undergone a major refit but due to the fact that a major fault had been found in the gunnery circuitry the refit was extended for a couple of weeks. I asked my fiancé to marry me and we were married a few days before the ship was due to sail for Korea. Our honeymoon lasted a full twenty-four hours. I was soon to sail and would be away for two and a half years. What a wedding present for a young bride and groom! It would be interesting to read what the newspapers would have to say if young married servicemen and their wives were to get that kind of a wedding present today.

The ship I joined was a frigate of some notoriety, with a penchant for getting stuck up rivers. The following disclosures will clarify the reason for me not revealing its name. The Captain was surely the worst ship handler in the Navy (possibly the worst ship handler in the whole world). We sunk barges and mooring buoys. We also rammed jetties and chopped the ends off several piers. This was before we had even left our home port of Devonport. I remember a year or so ago seeing a TV programme about an elderly lady from Cardiff who was learning to drive a car. She made numerous mistakes and was something of a disaster from her driving aspect, but I swear that she could not possibly have been any worse at handling a car than our captain was at handling the ship. In fact, I bet it would have been a more interesting commission had she been running the show, and possibly less harrowing from the ship's company's point of view.

Our first port of call after leaving dear old Guzz (Devonport, Plymouth) was Gibraltar. I cannot remember what damage we did there but I am sure it was quite substantial. It was in Gib where Petty Officer Electrician Longholm went to the sickbay with a 'tear' (that is sailor language for gonorrhoea, a venereal disease). There is a strong likelihood that some woman in Guzz gave it to him as a farewell present. He was a tall handsome man of very striking appearance, who obviously had a very strong sexual drive, but, he was virtually devoid of an ability to choose the right woman to take to bed.

On to Malta, always a happy stamping ground of mine. We had been allotted a berth in Grand Harbour, and we were to secure to a buoy there. Our motor boat landed the two 'buoy jumpers' onto the buoy, which is the normal procedure. Then the Captain brought the ship up to be secured to the said buoy. The big snag was that the ship was doing at least twice the speed it should have been doing, and we hit the buoy a real clout. Both the buoy jumpers were knocked into the water and we had quite a performance recovering them, unfortunately; and because we were a ship of some notoriety there was quite a crowd of spectators there at the time, in consequence we all felt quite embarrassed by the Captain's poor ship handling. Worse was to come though.

I seem to have spent a large part of my Naval career in and around Malta. It was there that we had to work the ship up to its full wartime potential, and that meant stacks of gunnery practice; we also had to exercise landing and boarding parties. I was not on the published list of those who were to take part as a member of the landing and boarding party but the Yeoman of Signals, who was in charge of the platoon, had recognised me as one of the Guzz (Plymouth) Command Boxers and I was consequently roped into his platoon. I never did figure out why my ability to box should have made me more acceptable to carry a rifle than anyone else, but in the eyes of the Yeoman it obviously did. I think that I should insert a rider at this stage and state that the Yeoman, (Fred Burnet) was a really hard, tough and likeable character, who I was proud to serve with and whose friendship I felt very privileged to enjoy.

The mention of the name Fred Burnet brings to mind several of the characters who were on that frigate. I used to think that they were mostly bonkers. I suppose that anybody who spends a large part of their lives dodging around the oceans of the world in a big metal box (ship) just has to be bonkers or have something missing from their brain box. One day whilst the ship was in Malta, Fred Burnet and several of his cronies had been on a run ashore and were returning to the ship by means of one of the *dhiasos* (Maltese water taxis propelled by oars). The ship was lying in Sliema Creek at the time, and as the *dhiaso* pulled alongside the ship's gangway, one of the group hung onto the lower platform of the gangway. Unfortunately for him, though, the *dhiaso* drifted off a little so he was virtually at full stretch, with his hands holding onto the lower platform of the gangway and his feet still in the *dhiaso*. The remainder of his cronies just walked across him as if he was some type of bridge. Several of them made it without mishap but the last one of them, plus the one who had been forming the bridge, just collapsed into the water.

Several of the men used to swim back to the ship after they had had a few drinks, until someone drowned (fortunately he was not from our ship). I assumed it was because of the large amount of booze he had consumed. The consequence was that an instruction was circulated that sailors were not allowed to swim back to their ships. I am afraid that such orders had very little effect (Come to think about it, it was like telling a flock of ducks that they were not supposed to swim), except for the fact that those who did swim back to the ship were put on a charge for disobeying instructions – unless they managed to sneak on board without anyone noticing, and a lot of them actually did, which I suppose did not reflect too well on the ship's security.

There was a camp in Malta in those days, where ship's landing and boarding parties were trained. The place was run by the Royal Marines, and if there is one thing that Royal Marines like, it is to get a platoon of what they referred to as 'sloppy fish-heads' (meaning sailors) under their control, and I can assure you they gave us hell. Soon after our arrival in their grasp, our platoon was divided into three sections with a Marine NCO in charge of each section. The Corporal in charge of the section I was in, realised that he had received a very special present from our ship, and that present was in the form of our 'ship's idiot'. The man's name was

Watson, and if there were two ways of doing anything he could always be relied upon to find the wrong way.

The patience of the Corporal was well tested by Watson, but that patience eventually snapped on the third or fourth day of our training. We were doing what was known as the 'Sten walk' and for this, the trainee had to walk along a boulder-ridden cliff face while someone pulled levers and up would pop spring-loaded wooden or cardboard cut-out figures of the supposed enemy. Each time that one of the figures rose up, the trainee had to fire a quick burst from his Sten gun. After the first one or two figures had appeared, everyone doing the walk realised that the rise of the supposed enemy figure was preceded by a distinct click. Everyone, that was, except Watson. He was more that halfway through the walk before he cottoned on about the clicks. So, having fired at a target to his right he heard another click from a figure rising on the other side of the walk, which, in fact, was now right behind him. Unfortunately, Watson took what he considered to be the quickest way round to put a burst of fire into the new target, and in doing so he passed the muzzle of the almost fully loaded and cocked Sten gun across the chest of the Royal Marine corporal who was walking close behind him.

The Corporal was not a very big man, but was in the age-old tradition of someone who had just been frightened enough to have soiled his trousers, and who had also obviously gained enhanced strength from both fear and anger. He grabbed Watson by the collar and shook him like a dog shakes a rat, and he kept shaking him until he let go of the Sten gun. Then he carried him, dangling like a puppet, and dropped him at the end of the Sten walk. He said, 'Get him out of my bloody sight, and if I see that bastard again I'll shoot him before he kills somebody.'

During the following year, the boarding and landing party was called upon to perform some rather arduous and tricky tasks in the Korean conflict, and I feel sure that we were all grateful to that Royal Marine corporal for sorting out the wheat from the chaff. There is a strong likelihood that his sensible action saved at least one of our lives.

We had a long hot march back to the ship on completion of the agony of our landing and boarding course with the Royal Marines, and we were all longing to get back aboard to enjoy a shower. The ship had been berthed in dry dock whilst we had been away playing soldiers (as the rest of the ship's company put it), and as we crossed the brow (gangway onto the ship) we found that most of the mess decks were closed off and were being fumigated, because it had been found that the ship was virtually alive with 'crabs' (*Pthirus Pubis*) perhaps better know as pubic lice. The temperature had been well over 100°F for a couple of weeks, and at the rate that that type of lice breed, it is not surprising that the ship was soon overrun with the darned things. We found that all the members of our mess had had a dose of the crabs. It was later realised that our mess seat cushions, being stuffed with horsehair, had been virtually a reservoir for the crabs because of the high temperature. Poor Andy, the quartermaster, being of a very fair skin and complexion, had even suffered from crabs in his eyelashes, despite the fact that he was possibly the best groomed and cleanest man on the ship. Fortunately all the horsehair-stuffed mess cushions were taken ashore and burned, but I will never be sure that the substitute foam plastic stuffed cushions were any better.

We spent several weeks 'working-up' in and around Malta, and one incident comes to mind that bore out our conviction of our Captain's incompetence at ship handling. It was during some exercise off Malta that necessitated our ship having to fuel at sea from an oil tanker. I was on the wheel at the time that 'special sea duty men' were called to their stations. That meant that the Captain would get up onto the ship's bridge and the Chief Coxswain would come to the wheelhouse to take over the ship's steering wheel from me. The Navigating Officer was the officer of the watch at the time, and he gave an order to put the wheel twenty degrees to starboard to acquire the course that would bring the ship near to the tanker. I put the twenty degrees of wheel on and then that order was soon followed by the order 'midships', which meant that the wheel had to be returned to its original position. I did a quick spin of the wheel to the position of midships just as the Captain was passing up through the wheelhouse to get to the bridge. I was almost deafened by the Captain shouting in my ear. 'It is people like you that are ruining our tele-motors,' he shouted (they are the motors that power the movement of the rudder, as directed by the movement of the ship's steering wheel). At the same time he snatched the wheel from my hands and said. 'I will show you how a ship's wheel ought to be handled.' I stepped aside and stood alongside the Coxswain, who had followed a few paces behind the Captain. The ship was now nearing the stern of the tanker, and the Navigating Officer gave the Captain (who was now the helmsman) a compass bearing to steer by.

As one ship nears another there is invariably a time during the manoeuvre that the ship taking up the oiling position is drawn into the tanker she is coming alongside. Everyone who has steered a ship for any length of time knows this, but apparently our Captain did not realise it. He started to put on wheel much too late, and as our ship came alongside the tanker we got so close to her that we pushed all her wind-scoops into her portholes. Fortunately little damage (other than bent wind-scoops) was done, but as it was happening, the Captain turned to the Coxswain and said, 'Have I got the wheel the right way, Coxswain?' The Coxswain replied, 'Yes Sir, but you were just a little slow in putting the correct wheel on.' The Captain just turned the wheel over to the Coxswain, though the turnover was done in a totally incorrect manner. He then walked up the ladder to the bridge with a very red face. The news of the incident spread through the ship like a forest fire.

I was one of the main participants in that incident, which had brought discredit on the Captain in the eyes of the ship's company, but I felt no relish in it. I was mature enough to know what a lonely and sometimes thankless task that a ship's captain has. I heard later that he had been a prisoner of war of the Japanese. Knowing what deprivations such prisoners had undergone I just felt like some kind of a snake for having felt any satisfaction in his embarrassment. I do, nevertheless, feel that some selection board along the way had made a very dubious decision in giving a man of his limited ability the command of a ship. I have served under something like thirty or forty Naval captains over more than thirty years of my Naval career, and I am glad to be able to say that he was the only one with whom I served who I could say was really not up to the job for which he had been selected. If you are willing to accept my judgement on the abilities of ship's captains, it is fair to say that the average of the competence of the various selection boards is therefore pretty good.

At last the ship was considered competent to go to war, so Malta was left behind and we ventured out into the Mediterranean and headed south-west for Egypt and the canal. Our departure from Malta was noteworthy for the fact that it was then that PO Electrician Longholm got the second star on his belt for gonorrhoea. He had thereby received his second farewell present, this time from a Maltese lady. It was lucky for him that we were carrying our own doctor, plus a large supply of antibiotics.

I had been in the Med before and had heard of, though never seen, the heavy seas that sometimes occur in the wide part of its southern area, and by gosh, we caught a real corker. It must have been force nine, going on eleven, and we were in it for at least five days. There are usually two on watch in the wheelhouse, sometime more, when a ship is at sea. The number one is the quartermaster and number two is the bosun's mate, and it is the normal procedure for them to take half hour spells on the wheel (these spells are called tricks of the watch). I was the bosun's mate, and my chum Andy was the quartermaster. Unfortunately Andy was so prone to seasickness that he was virtually useless when the weather was even partially rough. We both came up for the middle watch (midnight to 4 a.m.), and Andy just collapsed on the deck of the wheelhouse; he was, in those circumstances, worse than useless. This was my third four-hour watch on the wheel during this patch of bad weather, and I had been on the wheel for the whole time of the watch. During each of the previous watches we had been running on a course of something like $110°$ and when the watch was turned over to me I was still very sleepy and had obviously not comprehended that we had had a change in course of something like fifteen degrees, the course having been upped to 125°. I had been steering the old course of 110° for almost the entire four-hour watch. The Officer of the Watch on the bridge above me had obviously been as sleepy as I was, but luckily, I was waking up towards the end of my watch and realised what a stupid mistake I had made. Because the weather was so bad the ship's head had been swinging some six or seven degrees each side of the course we were trying to hold, and I was therefore able to gradually set the ship's head back onto the new course without anyone on the bridge noticing the difference. When I turned over to the morning watch the ship was firmly established on the new course, so I was able to make my turnover report 'ship steering 125° Sir.'

Andy had been *non compos mentis* during all the former proceedings and I never mentioned a thing about the above proceedings to him, despite the fact that he should have been the one who was in charge of what went on in the wheelhouse. However, the Navigator's Yeoman (an able seaman) was also a member of our mess, and twenty-four hours after the watch I was describing, he popped into the mess for a cup of tea and mentioned that we were several miles off our course. I looked at him very straight faced and said that the Navigating Officer ought to be ashamed of himself for being so far off course, considering the facilities he had at his disposal. It was several months later when I admitted the real truth to the Navigator's Yeoman, knowing that by that time it was much too late for any action to be taken.

Our passage through the Suez Canal was fairly uneventful. The Red Sea was as hot as usual. Aden was just a short break and it lived up to its reputation as being the last place that anyone wants to spend any time in. The one scary thing that I remember about it was that we had to land one of our officers into the hospital there and he was almost immediately flown home to the UK. He had caught polio, which at that time was a really dreaded disease, since there was no inoculation or vaccination for it at that time. The whole ship's company were rather biting their nails for several weeks afterwards and hoping that he was going to be a one-off case, which, I am pleased to say it later proved to be.

Colombo was but a short respite in our journey to the war we had been dispatched to pursue. Singapore, well, it was just Singapore. I have been in love with Singapore ever since I first called there in 1945. I have been there several times since and the place just gets better. I have yet to sit down and try to analyse why I like Singapore so much, and I think that if ever I do, it could well fill a book on its own. There was one little present that one member of our ship's company received whilst we were there, however. The fact was that PO Electrician Longholm qualified for his 'Lonsdale belt' (I hope the boxing fraternity do not find the analogy too offensive). On leaving Singapore, it was discovered that he had caught gonorrhoea for the third time since leaving the UK. One would have thought that after catching that dreaded lurgy twice, he would have had enough intelligence to keep his trousers well zipped up. Some people never seem to learn from their mistakes. I did hear tell that the doctor suggested that he get the zip of his trousers welded together before the ship ran out of penicillin.

Hong Kong. I have always reserved my deepest love for Hong Kong. I have spent a large part of my life travelling around the world and have been to what are termed the exotic and fantastic places to be, but Hong Kong is the place that I hold dearest to my heart. Perhaps the reason is that a very important part of my youth was spent there. It is possibly where a large part of my maturity occurred, which has already been reflected on in an earlier chapter.

By the time we reached Hong Kong, the northern hemisphere (which, surprisingly to most people, also includes Hong Kong) was deep into the throes of winter and the weather was pretty awful. I had endured a previous winter in Hong Kong and was not as surprised as some of my shipmates were to see ice and a little snow around the place. The young sailors almost ran amok when they found out that they could purchase the sexual services of a woman for five Hong Kong dollars (thirty-two pence). They were no less surprised when they found the prices of clothes were less than half the price that they had been paying at home in the UK.

We had Christmas in Hong Kong, and it really is a smashing place to spend Christmas. Unfortunately we were moored out in the middle of the harbour, so all our trips ashore had to be by means of our boats. The Captain had his wife out there for Christmas, and on Christmas Day she accompanied him on the traditional Captain's rounds of the ship. Unfortunately our mess had only two Christmas garlands, which were strung diagonally across the mess. These garlands were made up entirely of girls' pants (ladies' knickers to the more old-fashioned readers), which the members of the mess had confiscated from the prostitutes after completing their sexual indulgences with them. It had become quite a competition as to who could acquire the most colourful pants. This obviously made the decoration of our mess one of the most colourful, but unfortunately, as far as the Captain's wife was concerned, one of the most embarrassing.

This period of tension between what was then called the Free World and the then Communist World, which had in fact led to the confrontation that had created the Korean War, was really at its most severe at the time that I am writing about. There was very high tension in Hong Kong because the Chinese had entered the Korean War on the part of the North Koreans. Every HM ship passing through, or even just operating within the Hong Kong theatre, had to join in operations to exercise the defence forces of Hong Kong, and our ship had several such chores whilst we were in that area. It was on one of these operations that our landing platoon acquired the opinion that the one past member of our landing party (Watson) was not the only one of his type in the British armed forces.

On one of these exercises our landing platoon's allotted target was to be one of the radar installations guarded by an army unit which, we knew, consisted mostly of national servicemen who, we suspected, were about as keen to be in Hong Kong as a troop of Eskimos would have been. Our Platoon Commander was a sub lieutenant who was the son of an admiral. The Sub Lieutenant was a man of tremendous enthusiasm but unfortunately he was a little short on the necessary ability that was needed to accompany it. Charts had been studied, and in the very early hours of the morning we were taken to a small secluded beach in one of our own ship's boats.

The boat's coxswain was a wily old Leading Seaman who we all knew to be a first-class man at any task he undertook, particularly when he was the coxswain of a boat. He was heading for shore in a very cautious manner, and keeping well over to the left side of the beach as he had been instructed to do by the ship's navigation officer. The Sub Lieutenant then countermanded this previous order by ordering the Coxswain to take the boat over to the right side of the beach, which would be nearer to the radar installation. The wily old Leading Seaman gave quite a grin as he slowly inched the boat well over to starboard, and it soon had its bow embedded in the sand of the beach, or so we thought. I distinctly remember looking at the Coxswain's face at that time and I swear that the grin had become considerably wider. The Sub Lieutenant jumped over the bow of the boat and whilst doing so he bade the remainder of us to follow him. He waded some three paces forward then vanished completely. The Coxswain's grin turned to a side-splitting laugh, and the only words he uttered that I could make any sense of were 'sandbank' and 'chart'. We managed to get the very soggy Sub Lieutenant back into the boat, and the Coxswain then took the boat astern and proceeded over to the other side of the beach, where we all managed to make a relatively dry, or slightly less than waist deep, landing. The boat was then taken back to the ship and I can imagine that the Coxswain could hardly wait to tell the rest of the ship's company what had happened to the Sub Lieutenant.

We were now on our own with the sea at our backs and no possible way of escape. We slowly and cautiously crawled up the rather steep hill to the radar installation. I was quite close to the Sub Lieutenant and I remember smiling at the squelching sound he made, though in fairness to him his enthusiasm was not noticeably dimmed. We neared the installation, and could see only one sentry on guard there. I was unfortunately the nearest one to the Sub Lieutenant at this point, so I got the job of taking out the sentry. The Sub Lieutenant whispered to me that he wanted no rough stuff and that violence in any form was not to be used.

The sentry seemed to be in a world of his own. He was possibly dreaming of his girl back home, or perhaps the pretty Chinese girl in Wanchai that he had slept with the night before. It was a very easy job to get close to him, and I am sure that the first time he realised my presence was when I clamped my hand around his mouth in case he gave a shout. It was then that I realised that I might have created something of a problem for myself. The man collapsed in my arms like the proverbial sack of crap. I was about to tell him that I was a British sailor and that I was taking part in an exercise, and that I did not want him to say anything at that moment and all would be fully explained to him later. The Sub Lieutenant was soon alongside my shoulder and threatening me with 'hell', 'damnation' and a 'court martial'. I said, 'I only put my hand round his mouth and he collapsed on me like a sack of crap, Sir.'

Four of us were detailed to pick up the sentry and, having ascertained that he still had a pulse and was breathing, we carried him into the nearby army barracks and surrendered ourselves, having successfully made our chalk marks on the radar installation, to the effect that it had been supposedly blown up. We were then ushered into their main kitchen and given a supper-cum-breakfast, accompanied by a superb cup of strong tea. I then tried to ascertain what had happened to the sentry who had collapsed. My request for such information was met by resounding laughter and they soon made it obvious that the sentry I had encountered had been the 'unit idiot', who had been furnished with the information that there was a possibility that a Ghurkha unit would be engaged in the exercise, and that if they caught a sentry off his guard the Ghurkhas would slit his throat, because it was against Ghurkha beliefs to return their *kukri* (knife) to its scabbard until they had drawn blood.

The news of the possible impending invasion by the Ghurkhas, which had promoted the sudden collapse of the sentry in my arms, had got me off the hook with the Sub Lieutenant. Fortunately, as he was still picking baby crayfish out of his underpants on the passage back to the ship his interest in me had waned considerably, and he could hardly wait to get a hot shower and a change of clothing. By the time of our return to the ship, there was not a living soul on board who had not heard about the Sub Lieutenant's unfortunate swimming session and I am sure that it was a very long time before he was able to live it down.

Hong Kong used to be virtually the world capital of tattooists, and the collection of tattoos that one could acquire there were boundless. One of the real favourites was the fox disappearing in the anus followed by a pack of hounds, and some of the braver members of our ship's company even went back to have a couple of horses and riders in full hunting red appended on each cheek of their posterior. A couple of the sailors who tried having tattoos on the cheap and went to the real back street artists regretfully found that they soon suffered infections; one was particularly bad and had to go into hospital to have his infection sorted out. I bet he was reluctant to get further tattoos after that.

One of the members of the mess I was in had been at HMS *St. George* in the Isle of Man at the same time as me, and we had remained good friends. His nickname was Hoppy and he, like me, had married shortly prior to sailing, so neither of us had a desire to go ashore waving our five dollar bills and looking for girls in Wanchai. In fact both of us saved all the money we could with the intention of buying very good presents for all the members of our families prior to eventually going home, which at that time seemed a long way away. Most of the members of our mess were aware that we spent very little money, so we were constantly asked to lend money to them. Then on one occasion, one of the people who owed me money left the ship suddenly without the means to pay back the money he owed me. I had a firm promise that the money would be sent to me, but I am still waiting for it to arrive more than half a century later. I discussed this loan problem with

Hoppy but we both agreed that there was no way we could get collateral from the people we lent money to so the risk of lending money without any profit was rather stupid, and that we ought to think about charging interest. We were paid fortnightly and in consequence the second week, which was obviously known as 'blank week', was when all the big spenders were looking around to borrow money off someone.

I am sure that I could never have been accused of throwing my weight around, though everyone on the ship knew that I had boxed for both the Command and the Navy. The most pleasant consequence of that was that I rarely had people threatening to punch my head if I upset them in any way, which I always tried my best to avoid doing in any case. Hoppy and I therefore decided that he was the best one to keep the books for our loan company, and I was the obvious choice to be the collector of the debts. Our firm worked like a charm and I don't remember us ever having a bad debt. Lending money at a profit is obviously an offence against the Naval Discipline Act, and there was some whispering from a couple of the Leading Hands of the various messes on the ship about our firm, but we were never cautioned by anyone in higher authority. I must admit, though, that when I think about the interest we used to charge, I can quite understand why there was a little chuntering in the background.

This was how the company rules worked. If a man wanted to borrow ten dollars in the blank week, he had to pay us eleven dollars on payday. You don't need to be a genius to realise that our profit was near the 500 per cent mark if you take it on a per annum basis. Had we been running our loan company at the present time I think that we would have been referred to as 'loan sharks'. Come to think about it, if the firm had still been running we would have both been millionaires by now.

A Pushing Problem

Work had been hard for a long time,
The job was just getting me down.
My face, which had always been happy,
Now wore a most miserable frown.

The weather was wet, cold and gloomy,
I was glad to get home for the night.
I was happy to climb up to our bedroom,
The bed was a most welcome sight.

It seemed hours before any sleep came,
My senses were just stripped to the core.
But it must have been well after midnight,
When we heard a loud knock on our door.

'Who could be knocking at this hour?'
I sleepily asked my poor wife.
She said that 'It sounds very urgent,
There must be some form of strife.'

I opened the front door with some caution.
A drunken man stood under our bush.
I asked, 'What in the world do you want?'
He said, 'Could you give me a good push?'

I slammed the door shut in my anger,
My wife asked me what was the snag.
I said, 'A drunken bum asked me to push him,
And that's what has made me so mad.'

She said, 'Remember when we had a problem,
Our car broke down one very dark night.
Someone was willing to help us,
Despite that we were both rather tight.'

I said, 'If you're going to nag me,
I'll go down to see him once more.'
So I trundled again down the stairway,
And reluctantly opened the door.

I couldn't see anyone out there,
It seemed such a very strange thing.
I shouted, 'Eh there, do you still need a push?'
He replied, ' Yes, I'm on your garden swing.'

Evils of Drink

The teacher was very religious and despised anyone who took
   drink,
He would rant on about it for ages, until both of his cheeks turned
   pink.
He said, 'Alcohol is quite toxic and I'll show you just what I mean,
I'll put two drinking glasses before you, but first please note they
   are clean.'
One glass he then filled up with water, the other he topped up
   with gin,
A tadpole he put in the water, which was soon enjoying a swim.
A worm was then placed in the gin glass, within seconds the poor
   worm was dead.
'That's proof of my point,' said the tutor, and the whole class just
   nodded their head.
'My point is proved,' he boasted, 'there is nothing more evil than
   drink,
So before you indulge in the practice, I am begging you all to just
   think.
What does this prove?' said the teacher, wearing a self-righteous
   grin.
'I've got it,' said one of the pupils, 'If you suffer from worms,
   drink gin.'

CHAPTER FIVE

Shortly after Christmas we sailed for Japan. January in Japan is cold but worse was yet to come. If you have a yearning to spend your night watches chipping ice off your ship's rigging in order to ensure that the ship does not become unstable, then northern Korea in winter is the ideal place for you to be. When I see the clothing that modern adventurers and climbers wear and then think of the stupid clothing that was issued to us at that time, I just feel like laughing. The ship had no heating system whatsoever, so in consequence nobody undressed for weeks at a time. I feel sure that it was about that time that I lost my sense of smell. My wife blames the loss on my professional boxing career, but I feel confident that it dates back even further, to my Korean experiences. When a human body is uncovered after many weeks, it omits the most obnoxious of odours, and I feel that the sampling of such odours on several occasions brutalised my sense of smell to such an extent that it has never been able to work effectively since.

One further snag to the job that the Yeoman had volunteered me for, i.e. the landing and boarding party, was that the boarding party was very often called upon to board the many junks that were sailing in our area. We had to search the junks to ensure that there were no illegal cargos like ammunition or armaments. These junks were all infested with all kinds of 'crawlies', and as it was not possible to get a bath due to the low temperature, the whole ship's company was obviously soon infested with crawlies. The ship's company at first shied away from us boarding party members in an attempt to avoid the dreaded beasts, but it was soon realised that we were all going to get the infestations. So their attempted evasions of us poor 'boarding party souls' was rather pointless.

It was about this point in the ship's commission that I became the caterer of the mess. In those days, on all the smaller ships like frigates, the caterers were responsible for buying all the food for their messes and for organising the preparation. This was called 'canteen messing'. The prepared food was then taken to the ship's galley, where the cook merely had to put it into the oven for the appropriate cooking time. A caterer's duty was a task not considered above his normal duties, and certainly did not excuse him from the everyday workings of the ship. I got the job by complaining that my predecessor was not up to the task, and I remember very distinctly that he was happy to present me with the books. Such change of mess caterers was a normal event after the caterer had received a firm enough complaint, and most caterers were only too glad to get shot of the job. I can still remember the sighs of relief that my predecessor exuded when I took over the job. I was, nevertheless, determined to do it to the best of my ability. Somewhere along the line I can still laughingly hear the words of the song 'How green is my valley'. My major point was that you had to organise the job properly, and get to know the abilities and inabilities of your mess members. In the days to which I am referring, a ship's company were together for two and a half years. The caterer therefore had to get to know if any of his mess members had a particular talent in a specific area of the culinary art of cooking. One particular mess member, I recall, was a signalman by the name of Bartlet. He had a great talent for making jam roly-poly. Whenever he was off-watch and able to prepare it, I used to put jam roly-poly, on the menu. Several other mess members had a go at various dishes; some were a virtual disaster and some were quite reasonable. Canteen messing was always something of a hit and miss affair. An adventurous caterer (though I doubt that the Navy could boast many of those), and a little cooking talent from the mess members, were a must to ensure a reasonable and varied diet.

After lunch on Sundays, the cook would leave his galley, which was a signal for any of the messes who wished to do a little baking to get in there and use the ovens. One particular Sunday, a mess member and I decided to bake some meat pasties (known throughout the Navy as 'oggies') as a treat for our messmates. We had mixed the meat, potatoes and other vegetables together and were both busy on the pastry when a young radio operator appeared in the mess and with exuberant enthusiasm begged us to let him assist. His enthusiasm masked the fact that he had two left hands; both, unfortunately, were on his right foot. Thinking that even he could do little damage in the simple task of seasoning the oggy contents, I, like a fool, gave him that task.

Pepper was purchased in one pound tins, which had push top lids. Usually a few holes were punched into the lid by means of a sharp nail, so making it into a rather large pepper pot. Our young helper must have had his back turned towards us when the dastardly accident occurred. Unbeknown to me the lid of the tin came off into the oggy mixture, followed naturally by the pound of black pepper. The oggies were then finished and taken to the galley for baking.

As I have previously stated, the ship was under wartime conditions, and because the ship was moored to a buoy in Sasebo harbour (that is in Japan, where we had been taking on supplies prior to returning to the Korean Coast). I had the 'last dog watch' (6 p.m. to 8 p.m.) as the fo'c'sle sentry. The weather was bitterly cold that evening, in fact it had been snowing for most of the day. When someone passed me up a mug of hot strong tea and an oggy, I was most appreciative; I also remember asking if the oggy was hot. The reply was that the oggy was certainly hot. For a few seconds I cradled the hot mug in my hands, enjoying its warmth. Then I took a big bite from the oggy. I estimate that I rose three feet above the deck. The worst part of the incident though was when I took a large gulp from the mug of tea in a desperate effort to quench the burning sensation created by the effect of the pepper. I then scalded both mouth and gullet.

Fortunately my messmates had the good sense to relieve me of my Sten gun before I caught up with that young radio operator.

Again, back up the Korean coast, and this time our searches of the lice ridden junks were interspersed with gunnery bombardments. In other words, we would blow the coastal roads up during the day and the Chinese and Koreans would quickly fill in the shell holes and use the roads during the night. The whole war was just a stupid chess game. Just occasionally there would be an aircraft scare and we would put up an anti-aircraft gunnery barrage. That just meant we had to get as many shells up in the air as we could, and the only people who had any liking for these barrages were us loading numbers on the 4-inch guns, because attempting to get thirty rounds a minute from a 4-inch twin mounting got the loading numbers of the gun crews really warm, the downside being that the body lice got quite excited about this excess heat and became considerably more active. I suppose that it just went to prove that life is all give and take.

After a few of these rather dismal Korean patrols, our Sports Officer had a flash of inspiration as we were on our way down to Sasebo, which was our replenishment base in Japan. He decided to throw a challenge to some other ship for a game of rugby. It had snowed all the time we had been on our Korean patrol, and it snowed all the way down to Japan. We all agreed that the Sports Officer had had a masochistic rush of mud to his head though we soon all decided that a stupid idea like playing rugby in the midst of a snowstorm was a fair indication of his total absence of a brain.

In that one fell swoop our Sports Officer managed to inflict more damage on the allied fleet than the combined efforts of both the Chinese and the North Koreans. At least six of us either limped off or were carried off the rugby field on stretchers. I did hear that someone was lost in a snowdrift but I rather fancy that that was a sailors tot-time exaggeration. By the time that our Medical Officer was sober enough to see any patients, after his escapades ashore in Japan, the ship was well out to sea. It was then decided that my knee needed surgery. My transfer to the hospital ship was done by what is known as 'jackstay transfer'. This is done by rigging lines between two ships as they run along abeam of each other (side by side). It is worked very much on the same lines as a 'breeches buoy'. It is a hair-raising experience in a calm sea. At the time in question there was a force seven or eight gale running. The experience could best be described as trouser-filling. Our Captain's inability to keep the ship on its correct station whilst executing this manoeuvre meant that I was up to my knickers in very cold salt water almost all the way across.

The gale had risen to force ten by the time that the surgeons operated on my leg, and I still have two large and rather nasty scars, which gives me to believe that they went in there with a shovel. I suppose that I should at least be thankful that they at least chose the injured leg and not the good one, or that they were not as alcohol-soaked as our own ship's doctor usually was.

One thing that I well remember about the ward I was in on the hospital ship was the young Chinese laundry boy who was in the next bed to me. He was recovering from a leg injury he had received during bad weather whilst he was working in the laundry on a British destroyer. Each day the medical staff came around and asked all the patients if they had had their bowels moved. After I had been in the ward for about a week, I noticed that the Chinese boy was nodding every time the question was posed to him. I had also noticed that although he was unable to get out of bed, he had not asked for a bed pan during the whole week I was there. No doubt the fact that the poor fellow could not speak or understand English was the main factor that led to this situation. I mentioned to the ward staff one day that the boy must be feeling awful because of his obvious discomfort, so an enema trolley was called for. The poor chap was rolled onto his stomach and as the enema was inserted a fountain of excrement jetted into the air, covering the two operatives and a good portion of the ward. The two operatives looked as if they had had a mud bath but their obscene expletives were drowned by the loud sigh of relief from the Chinese boy. The smell was indescribable, and it was still hanging around the ward when we were all transferred to the British army hospital ashore in Japan a few days later. I would think that that Chinese boy must have lost half a stone in weight in a few seconds.

The army hospital housed many hundred of casualties from the Korean War. Each of the wards was run by a nursing sister from the Australian Army and boy, were they strict and tough. Just about all the doctors were scared to death of them. If one of the doctors came to see you and you wanted to get rid of him, all you had to say was, 'I think the Sister is coming,' and, sure enough, they would be away like a flash. The day we arrived from the hospital ship, the ward sister asked me what the Chinese laundry boy, who had been once again put in the next bed to me, wanted for his meal. I told her that I could not answer her question, as I did not speak Chinese. She replied, 'He arrived on this ward with you so you had better find out what the hell he wants to eat, or you might find that you will not be eating anything yourself.' I formulated a picture in my mind that seemed to be the conjunction of a Chinese dragon and an Australian nursing sister named Ned Kelly, and by far the most acceptable part of the picture was the Chinese half. I nevertheless took the sister at her word. After my whole gambit of hand signals and my two word Chinese vocabulary had been totally exhausted, I managed to get the required answer, though I think that it would have been much better described as a guestimate.

Shortly after my arrival at the hospital it was diagnosed that I was suffering from a post surgical infection and I was prescribed penicillin, which was the only antibiotic available at that time. Within an hour of the first injection, my body swelled up like a balloon, eventually reaching almost twice its normal size. My eyes closed tight and my throat became totally restricted. Within minutes, tubes were passed into just about every orifice in my body. In fact I think that some tubes were passed into orifices I did not even know I had. Two nurses sat by my bed dabbing me from head to toe with calamine lotion. (I thanked my lucky stars that the job was not being done by the Ward Sister, as I feel sure she would have been tempted to use very rough sandpaper.) Each time I recollect this incident, the mental picture of myself makes me shudder. Even my mother used to admit that I am ugly, but on the occasion in question I must have looked like an ugly pink whale caught in a web of transparent tubes. The only plus to this condition was that I was no longer bullied by the Ward Sister into interpreting for the Chinese laundry boy. My great hope is that he did not starve to death.

It was at this very point that the door of the ward virtually burst open and in walked the Commander-in-Chief, with all his entourage (I was told later that he was also accompanied by some high ranking politicians and several famous film stars, but in my rather delirious and sightless state they counted for very little on my list of worries). The doctors were disclosing all the salient facts of each bed case as they came to them, e.g. 'This man's tank was blown up. This man was blown up on Hill Number 92. This man trod on a landmine,' and so on. Then they got to me and I heard later that the C-in-C looked totally astounded, and he said, 'God! What the hell happened to him?' One of the doctors said, 'He did it playing rugby, Sir.' I, of course, had no sense of vision or hearing at the time, but I was told later that the C-in-C and all his entourage, and the other visitors, were gazing at my swollen, pink torso with incredulity. Then the C-in-C said, 'After all that, I hope to hell his bloody team won.' Luckily the restrictions on my senses of sight, hearing and speech totally restricted my ability to inform him that we had been hammered by more than forty points.

I was lucky enough to be sent back to the UK to do a regulating course (Naval Police Branch) within weeks of the above incident. You surely do not need very much imagination to realise the list of uncouth adjectives that were used by the ship's company to describe my luck at being on my way home after only just over a year of what should have been a two and a half year commission. Particularly as I was on my way back to the UK to become a copper. There were no complaints from me however. I also hope that the last wave of my hand really conveyed the sentiment of the total *Adios* that I wished to convey, despite the fact that the wave was made by only forty per cent of the digits of one hand. My sentiments to all the ship's company, but particularly to the Captain were, may I nare come back again; and I am truly delighted to say I never did.

That ship was the only ship I served on that I totally disliked. As I have already said, the Captain was very poor at his job. The Executive Officer (Second-in-Command) was also very weak. The Coxswain was rather pathetically useless and was completely lacking in the necessary personality to hold the ship's discipline together. In those days, smaller ships like frigates had a Coxswain who did the regulating duties, as well as taking the wheel during 'special sea duties'. The Coxswain's branch was amalgamated into the regulating branch in the early 1970s. From then on, all HM ships carried a Master-at-Arms, except for some of the very small ones which possibly carried only an RPO (regulating petty officer). These comments are not intended to belittle coxswains as a whole. In truth, I met some very good coxswains during my time in the Navy, but it so happened that the frigate in question had one who was not really up to the job. Thinking back, I suppose that the experience on that ship, from the point of view of the behaviour of the Coxswain, did me something of a favour. I certainly learned what not to do when I later became the master-at-arms of a ship.

The journey home was by troop ship, and was certainly not the most pleasant sea journey I have ever made. There were only a few Naval personnel on the ship, and we were accommodated in quite a small mess within one of the larger troop decks that accommodated army personnel, and when the sea got a little rough the smell on the troop deck was ghastly. We Naval people all tried to hold our breath as we passed through the troop deck and almost burst our lungs in doing so. Unfortunately when the sea settled a little, another problem arose, and that was in the form of a bug that created dysentery. I think that everyone on board the ship had it at the same time, so the odour on board passed from that of oral excretion (vomit) to one of anal excretion (faeces), and we all stood in a long queue for the limited amount of heads (toilets) available. Whilst the excrement ran slowly down our legs, we all sang very obscene verses of the song, 'Why are we waiting?'

It was great to get home.

The Talking Frog

The old jossman was quite fond of fishing,
He spent hours with his rod and his line.
He would sit all day on the edge of the sea,
And completely forget about time.

Then one day he thought he heard voices,
'Pick me up,' he heard a voice say.
'I need a man to kiss my lips,
Or in this form I'll have to stay.'

He looked around, but nothing,
Sweet nothing could he see,
Except for a frog that was hopping nearby,
So he asked, 'Were you talking to me?'

The frog said, 'I'm glad that you've noticed,
Now listen to what I will say.
I am really a beautiful princess,
But a witch's spell turned me this way.'

The frog said, 'I'll give you great pleasure,
My lovemaking will stand any test.
Forget about the Karma Sutra,
You'll find that I am the best.'

'All you need do is to kiss me,
Then a princess I'll once more become,
And you will be my Prince Charming.
A great victory we will have won.'

The old jossman said, 'I am sorry, my dear,
And I'm sure that you've had a hard slog,
But my libido has left me completely,
So I'll just keep the talking frog.'

The Cursing Parrot

A sailor brought a parrot back as a present for his spouse,
But when he got the parrot home loud swearing filled the house.
'We cannot have this language,' the sailor told the bird,
'The words that you are using are the worst I've ever heard.'

'I am sorry,' said the parrot, 'but when I was on the ship,
They said they wouldn't feed me if I couldn't curse a bit,
So I practised very diligently and now I'm quiet obscene.
In fact, I'm the foulest bloody parrot that you have ever seen.'

The sailor said, 'I've a good idea and I'm sure it'll do the trick,
I'll put you in the freezer and leave you there a bit,
And when at last I get you out, you won't be rude or bold,
You won't do any swearing because you'll be too cold.'

But the parrot couldn't stop himself and let out another curse,
He was dumped headlong in the freezer before his words got
    worse.
After half an hour he was brought back out, he was shivering and
    blue.
He said, 'If I got half an hour in there for swearing, what the hell
    did that chicken do?'

The Cowboy

A cowboy rode in from the prairie,
He'd worked in the snow and the rain.
He needed a good shot of red-eye
To bring him to life once again.

For weeks he'd been out herding cattle,
He had ridden for mile after mile.
Now he'd got back to civilisation,
And intended to stay for a while.

He fed and he watered his bronco,
The reins he then hitched to the rail.
He walked to the back of his trusty old steed,
And then he just lifted its tail.

He kissed his horse right on its anus.
The sheriff said, 'That's a strange trick,
What the hell did you want to do that for?'
He said, ''Cause I've got a chapped lip.'

The sheriff said, 'Hell, will that cure it?'
The cowboy said, 'No, not a bit.
But there's one thing I'm certain of, Sheriff,
That'll stop me from giving it a lick.'

CHAPTER SIX

My wife had managed to rent two rooms of a house near to where her parents lived so we were able to enjoy married life for the first time despite the fact that we had been married for more than a year by that time. My leave passed all too quickly, and I was off to Portsmouth to do my course to become a copper. I enjoyed the course very much, though the judo played havoc with my damaged knee. Nevertheless I had to grin and bear it in case I was removed from the course. I have already explained that all coppers in the Navy are called Regulators, and I found that, with very few exceptions, I liked the type of people who I was working with. During the following twenty-four years I met very few regulators whose company I did not enjoy, so joining the branch proved to be one of my all-time good decisions.

The Regulating School was in Portsmouth, at a place that is known as Whale Island (HMS *Excellent*). The reason it acquired that name was because it actually was an island and could only be approached by means of a bridge, and the island was shaped like a whale. At that time the place was mostly used as the RN Gunnery School, the Regulating School being tucked away in some discrete corner as if the main occupants of the establishment (the gunnery people) did not want to know anything about the regulators. The gunnery branch considered themselves the kingpins in those days, and they considered that their branch ruled the roost. Ironically, the gunnery branch in the Navy is now all but finished and guided missiles are kingpin. As the regulating branch is still in full flow I suppose that we had the last laugh in some ironic way.

There was one incident that occurred during the time I was there which I think about each time I see anything to do with hypnotism. It happened one evening just after we had got back into our mess and were preparing to enjoy an evening of leisure, or more likely to do more swatting. Somehow the subject of hypnotism came into the conversation and one of our classes, a man by the name of Roger, said in a very casual manner that he was a hypnotist. Tom Wilkinson, one of the men in the conversation, said he thought hypnotism was a load of 'bulsh' and that he did not believe him. So Roger took a pack of photos out of his locker and sure enough, from the evidence of those photos he had obviously performed on the stage as a hypnotist.

Tom said that he did not believe that Roger could hypnotise him, and Roger said that he would not even try because it would take too long, due to the fact that Tom would obviously set his will against it. Then one of the other members of the mess, a chap by the name of Scotty, who also happened to be by far the oldest man there, volunteered to be hypnotised. Roger had him under hypnosis within a few seconds. Roger had Scotty performing all sorts of strange things like sitting on a chair in a reversed fashion, and making believe that he was riding a cycle. First he would have him riding his cycle uphill and poor old Scotty would be sweating profusely, then he would reverse the action and have him riding his cycle downhill, at which time he would be relaxed and whistling. After a short performance that proved beyond any doubt that Roger had the power of hypnosis, Scotty was brought back to his own senses with a snap of Roger's fingers. We enjoyed quite a laugh telling Scotty what he had been doing whilst under hypnosis. In fact we told him quite a few white lies, so that in the end he had not a clue as to what the hell he had been up to. He, nevertheless, took it all in good part.

From that time onwards Tom Wilkinson would not look Roger in the eye. Obviously he was scared that Roger might hypnotise him. It became quite a standing joke between all of us and we used to say to Tom, 'Hide your eyes Tom, Roger's coming.' I have often wondered what happened to Roger. He used to perform under the stage name of Roger Dee, but that was not his proper name.

Ten per cent of each class of men qualifying for leading patrolmen were given extra tuition in driving vehicles, and I was one of the lucky ones who were sorted out for that extra tuition. I was lucky enough to obtain my vehicle driving licence, which obviously saved me money in having to pay for private driving lessons at a later stage.

On qualifying as a leading patrolman, and being of the Devonport Division, I was drafted to the appropriate Patrol Headquarters, which was in fact in the city of Plymouth. It was an old and rather dilapidated building, which for most of its life had been a civilian police station. I think that the Navy must have won the place in a raffle. It really was a dump of an address. The basement consisted of what I can only describe as very dank and miserable cells and beyond this row of cells was an even older part of the building, which consisted of a darker and danker single cell. At the time in question this cell was used as a boiler room, and it contained a rather ancient coke-fired domestic hot-water boiler. Rumour had it that this particular cell had been used in days of yore as the condemned cell, and that many people had been hanged in the small courtyard just outside it. That was when capital punishment was rife and rather localised, and when many towns and all the main cities had their own hangman. In consequence, you can surely imagine that ghost stories abounded.

We were all rather exuberant and relatively fit young men and practical jokes were very prevalent, several of which got rather out of hand. One particular prank does stick very firmly in my mind, however. Froggy French, one of our more exuberant colleagues, had caught several of us out with one of his pranks, but his particular success was at catching out one of our more senior members, a patrolman named Jan Davey. Jan was a pretty hefty Plymouthian; he had a very good sense of humour and had taken the jibing quite well, but I had pounded the beat many times with Jan and had got to know him quite well. He and I had built up quite a strong rapport and I knew that something was brewing. Jan had been wearing a 'my turn is coming' smirk on his face for a couple of days.

Beat patrols usually ended at about 2 a.m., though there were always two or more patrolmen actually awake and on duty at the Patrol Headquarters. One particularly cold and foggy morning such a duty befell Froggy French and myself. There was an open fire in the main office and as fuel was rather low, Froggy went down to the boiler room to get a bucket of coke. The door of the boiler room was pretty stiff to open, and the light switch was rather difficult to reach. As Froggy's hand eventually stretched out and reached the switch, a cold wet hand held it and squeezed it in a vice-like grip. The first I knew of the incident was a blood-curdling scream. Despite explicit verbal and printed instructions that the main office was never to be left unattended, I was immediately in full flight and heading for the boiler room. I switched on the light and the first thing I saw was Froggy. His face had turned an ashen colour and his eyes looked like those of a rabbit surrounded by stoats. Jan Davey was lying on the heap of coke, holding his stomach and fighting for breath amidst guffaws of laughter. He was wearing an old leather glove that had obviously been soaked in some kind of liquid, most probably a bodily fluid.

Several days after the above event I was again on the beat with Jan Davey. This time our beat was outside the Naval dockyard at Devonport. This beat used to end with a good and a bad point. The good was the fact that before starting the long hike back to the headquarters, we would get a free bag of fish and chips from Ma Merrin's Chip Shop, and they were about the best in town. The bad point was that we had to walk a complete circuit of Devonport Park, which, on a night like the one I am recalling, was pretty grim. It was drizzling with rain, it was foggy and there was not the slightest breath of a breeze.

We had completed our circuit of the park and also eaten the last mouthful of our fish and chips when we heard a very loud cry of 'Help, help, help'. It was a deep bass voice and it came from the direction of the water reservoir. Both of us must have stared at each other with wide-open mouths. Not a living soul had hove into our sight since leaving Ma Merrin's shop. Then, without a word passing between us, both of us ran to the reservoir and soon found a gap in the high outer fence. We got onto the perimeter of the reservoir and spent an hour or more making a complete search of the area. We both realised that neither person nor body was to be seen, so together we left the reservoir and the park and called the civilian police from the nearest phone.

When the civilian police arrived we spent a further hour searching the park with them. Nothing was found. I was so confident that there would be a body that I went back to the park several times during the following week or so and I walked around the reservoir. Nothing was ever found.

The leg pulling, jokes and jibes were almost incessant, as you can surely imagine. The incident, of course, took the pressure off Froggy. In truth, I wonder to this day if he had any involvement with that occurrence in the park. After more than half a century though, I feel that it is unlikely we will ever find out.

A further fortnight went by and the jokes and jibes were beginning to ease a little. Again I had the Devonport beat, this time with a new but very staid character for whom I very soon gained respect. The beat passed off well, almost without incident. We had eaten our fish and chip supper and cleared the park. I must add at this stage that I was somewhat relieved that my new partner had not mentioned my previous experience whilst we were clearing the park.

At last, just another half mile to walk and then we would reach the Patrol Headquarters and be able to kick off those tiresome heavy boots. The weather had started to improve, and that particular night we had a full moon and clear bright sky. Again we had not seen a living soul since leaving Ma Merrin's shop. We were walking on a clear straight road, having left the park well behind us. At last we saw two people in front of us. We could clearly see their white caps and blue uniforms. They were two sailors for sure, and they were about ten paces in front of us when it happened.

Now, I have seen vanishing tricks in stage shows and in circuses where they put people into boxes and make them vanish, or even saw them in half and make one of the halves disappear. The incident I am describing was something entirely different though. Those two sailors disappeared in front of our very eyes and in the middle of an open road. I was about to stop and speak to my partner when I suddenly realised the possible consequences. If he had not seen what I was sure that I had seen, there was just no way that I would ever live it down after my previous experience at the reservoir in the park.

After the two sailors had vanished we must have walked a further three or four paces, surely the longest three or four seconds I have ever spent in my life. Then my partner stopped, turned to me and said, 'I am sure there were two sailors walking towards us.' I let out the deepest sigh of relief. 'Thank God,' I said, 'but I hope you realise that you will not be able to discuss this with anyone, because I will deny it ever happened.' He looked at me with a mixture of disbelief and incredulity. Then slowly his expression changed to one of obvious understanding as he remembered my recent experiences. I said, 'The fact that you saw them as well as I did alleviates both my concern and my worries.' Neither of us ever spoke of the incident again. He was killed in a road accident some months later. I wonder if he ever met those two ghostly sailors in his heavenly travels?

There really were some memorable characters in the Patrol HQ at that time, and one incident I often think about was when two of those characters had the job of surreptitiously trailing a surgeon lieutenant who was suspected of being a homosexual, which, at that time, was considered to be one of the Navy's most heinous crimes. They were sent out on a plain clothes job, and were instructed to keep a very close tab on him and to record all his movements and the description of all the people he associated with. The man in question had been quite a hero during an incident in the Far East shortly prior to this and I believe he had, in fact, received some sort of decoration for his bravery under fire.

Our two stalking heroes, however, were men who enjoyed their pints of beer and when they arrived in the first pub that their quarry visited they ordered their usual pints. The man who they were trailing ordered a half pint and soon left the pub, having drunk less than half of his beer. They both supped up their beer and left in hot pursuit of their quarry, who visited several other pubs, and virtually the same procedure happened in them all. It was obvious that the person or persons that their quarry was looking for were not in any of the numerous pubs that he had called at. Our two heroes had had a couple of pints in the Patrol HQ prior to commencing their surveillance duties, so by the time that they had drunk up quickly in the eighth or ninth pub, neither of them could find the handle of the door to get out onto the street. One of them was just sober enough to request the pub landlord to call the Patrol HQ, and a vehicle was sent to pick them up. They spent the remainder of the night in our 'drunk tank'.

I often wonder what eventually happened to that Surgeon Lieutenant. He was a big, well built, blond headed man that any woman would have been happy to wave her pants at, but, as I have already said, he was as queer as a nine-pound note. I suppose that it takes all kinds of people to make a world.

My knee problem that had led to the operation I had undergone on the hospital ship off the Korean coast was still giving me trouble, and it was suggested to me that there was a very good masseur who operated in a gymnasium on the Barbican, which was quite a well known area of Plymouth. I hobbled down to the Barbican one evening and was introduced to the masseur, whose name was Don; I never did discover if he had any other name. He worked on my leg, and almost right away I felt a great improvement, so the consequence was that I attended the gymnasium quite regularly. It was, in fact, a boxing gym and as my leg got better I started to use the punch bags and punch balls and the rest of the boxing paraphernalia. The chap who ran the gym could see that I knew my way around a boxing ring, and I was soon sparring with his 'stable' of boxers. In a very short space of time he was trying to talk me into taking out a licence to box professionally. Because of my determination never to box again as an amateur boxer for the Navy, I considered the invitation to become a professional boxer had a great attraction for me. There was also the fact that I had already boxed in fairground boxing booths, which, had that information been disclosed to the amateur boxing authorities, would have precluded me from ever boxing again as an amateur.

However, taking out a professional boxing licence was a problem for a person in HM Services. It was virtually illegal for a regular serviceman to become a professional sportsman. There were, however, numerous national servicemen in the Navy at that time who were professional sportsmen, some of whom were professional boxers, so I went to see my boss about this problem. He was a lieutenant commander, and, rather luckily for me, he happened to be the Naval provost marshal of Plymouth. He really was a helpful and obliging chap and must have spent numerous hours arguing on my behalf. His argument was that as there were several national servicemen who were professional boxers and were given time off, both to train and to box, it was therefore discriminatory and unfair to withhold such a privilege from me, a regular serviceman. I firmly believe that he enjoyed fighting the legal aspect of my cause much more than he appreciated the outcome, however, I had no qualms or complaints on that count.

My first professional fight was to be in St. Austell in Cornwall, where I was booked to box eight rounds against the local favourite there, who went under the name of Cliff Holbeck. In his previous fight, Holbeck had given a pretty sound beating to a good middleweight who had trained at the same gym as I had trained at, so in consequence Holbeck's large fan club were looking forward to a repeat performance against me. I heard later that the odds against me winning were rather astronomical. Unfortunately the low pay of servicemen at that time precluded me from taking any wagered advantage of such information.

I had spent weeks prior to the fight being tutored on the more professional punches such as hooks and uppercuts, and had been told to avoid, when possible, using the more elementary type of punches like right crosses, which could leave a boxer open to a counter-punch. The opening round of the fight was pretty even, but at the start of the second round I though, this man is showing me his chin ready for the obvious amateur-type right cross, so why not just give it one try. When I threw it, it landed spot on the button and he hit the canvas, from that moment on I knew that the fight was mine. He managed to get back onto his feet but with the next good punch, which was yet another right cross; he hit the canvas again and was counted out.

It was my first professional fight in the county and I had beaten the local favourite in two rounds. I knew that Cliff Holbeck had a very strong following of fans and I thought, *I hope those fans don't take their spite out on me because I had beaten their 'blue-eyed favourite'*. In fact almost the exact opposite happened, and his strong following changed their allegiance to me; the consequence was that I then had a ready-made fan club. The strangest thing to me though, was the fact that I had won my first professional fight with an amateur-type punch that I had been instructed to avoid if possible.

There were a few more fights in the West Country, which gave me little trouble, with the possible exception of the last one. This was against a character named Mike Kelly, who was known throughout the West Country as 'Cast Iron Kelly'. The reason for that was because more fighters had broken their hands on Cast Iron Kelly's head than could be counted on a Hong Kong shopkeeper's abacus. He was a red-headed, heavily-built Plymouthian of Irish descent. He had a very large chest and quite short arms. The consequence was that his method of fighting was to throw a series of short, powerful and rather deadly hooks from both hands. Mike and I were of the same stable; we trained in the same gym, and I had studied his tactics quite carefully. I was confident that I could keep out of trouble from those deadly hooks, but it needed a great deal of legwork on my behalf. So I just kept moving around the ring and jabbing away with my left hand, and after ten very hard-fought rounds, I won the fight by a reasonable margin of points, though I am sure, the following day I must have looked as if I had been in a train smash. The one great and thankful consolation was that I did not get my name added to the long list of fighters who had broken their hands on Cast Iron Kelly's head.

It was at this time that the Master-at-Arms of the Patrol HQ in Plymouth asked me if I would like to join his staff at the Royal Naval Air Station at Brawdy in Pembrokeshire, South Wales, which was where he was being drafted to. I felt quite honoured to be asked. The place was just a couple of hours away from where I lived. How could I have possibly refused? Despite the success I had had in the West Country with my boxing career, my heart was in Wales. My boxing manager in Plymouth was excellent about releasing me from my contract, and I signed with another manager who lived just outside Swansea, where my home was. Unfortunately this proved to be something of a mistake on my part, and I never saw eye to eye with that second manager. He was eventually imprisoned for some ticket swindle that he was involved in, but I think that was some time after I had thankfully dispensed with his services.

So, back to one of my favourite counties in the whole of the country. Since the first time I saw it, I have loved Pembrokeshire. It really is a green and pleasant land. It is now several years since I was last back there, but my memories of it are amongst the most wonderful held in my relatively meagre brain. The airfield at Brawdy had only recently been reopened and was, in fact, still being renovated to take more modern aircraft. I soon re-established contact with my old friend Ron Taylor who ran the boxing booth that toured that area. Very soon I was on the stand of the booth and taking on all comers. I really loved being with fairground people. It was smashing to walk around the fair and chat with them. They always seemed happy, and I think that they were amongst the most optimistic people I have ever met. They were always sure that today would be a better day than yesterday, and their humour was almost boundless. The boxing booth was somewhat of an asset to the fairground, and I know all the people working there appreciated it. One of the reasons for this was that if ever there was trouble of a violent nature, Ron would hustle all his boxers to the scene, and invariably the culprits would leg it at the sight of three or four rough-necked fighters bearing down on them. One of the consequences of this was that the booth boxers had something of a free rein, and when they were not actually performing in the booth, all the shooting galleries, coconut shies and the various rides and roundabouts were free to them. Perhaps today that may be interpreted as a sort of protection racket, though there were no financial gains acquired by any boxers to my knowledge.

Ron always seemed to get at least one good quality boxer to tour with him, and during this period he had acquired the services of a boxer named Al Brown from what was then known as British Guiana. Al was one of the best lightweight-cum-featherweight boxers in the world at that time, and he had put the skids under most of the British boxers of his weight. There were always some boys that we used to refer to as 'rough and tumble' fighters, who used to hang around the booth. They would invariably fight between each other when challengers could not be acquired for the more established boxers. This meant that Al Brown and myself would then box an exhibition contest to fill out the show. I used to look forward to these matches because Al was such a good class boxer, and the fact that he was much lighter than I was certainly improved my speed of both movement and thought. When challengers were available however, Al would take on anyone up to the weight of middleweight, which meant that he could be giving the challenger a weight advantage of up to two stones. Because I was often the heaviest boxer on the stand, anyone above middleweight was mine, and I invariably got the really big boys.

I was very conscientious at maintaining my fitness and I used to run five or six miles around the airfield six mornings a week. Due to the renovation work on reinforcing the runways, many workers were kept busy there, so by the time I started my run at about 7.30 a.m. they were hard at work. I used to wear some strange garb whist running. I was continuously fighting to keep my weight down so I always wore several jumpers, which would surely have made me look like some sort of fat teddy bear. I also wore an old trilby hat pulled well down over my ears. Thinking back now, I realise that I must have looked really idiotic, but at the time I gave it little or no thought at all. I do, however, remember some of the workers (who were mostly Irishmen) making remarks such as

'Paddy will murder the "eejit"', or 'That fat ole "eejit" won't last a round with Pat.' I never stopped to ask what the remarks meant, in fact I was never really sure if the remarks were directed at or to me, but I heard those kind of remarks several times when I was doing my morning 'roadwork' round the airfield.

Haverfordwest was the nearest reasonable sized town to Brawdy, and that was some twelve miles away. The annual fair in the town was called the Portfield Fair. It was a large fair that lasted a week, and it seemed to cover most of the town. One of the main attractions of the fair was the boxing booth. I have had some pretty good contests there over the years and the year in question provided some of them. There is one, however, that sticks in my mind, which is partly because of the incidents I wrote about in the previous paragraph.

Standing on the stand (or stage) of a boxing booth, some four feet above the prospective audience, one has a golden opportunity to study the crowd whilst the 'barker'(that is the man who ran the boxing booth) is giving his spiel, and on this occasion I was sure that I had a vague recognition of some of them. The men standing quite near to me were talking among themselves, and I could hear that they all seemed to have an Irish brogue. They were patting a man on the back and one of them was trying to hold the man's arm aloft. Obviously they were trying to encourage that man to challenge for a fight in the booth, and by the appearance of the size of the man, I was going to be the one he would be challenging.

It all now fitted into place. I had heard of a fighting Irishman by the name of Paddy O'Brien, who had been living in the area for some time. Everyone who had spoken about him had said that he was a very likable and popular chap, with an excellent sense of humour and a ready smile, and whose rugged good looks had charmed many of the local beauties. He was also reputed to be as hard as nails and had sorted out almost all the local so-called 'hard men' in bare-fisted fights behind one of the nearby hostelries. He was also reported to have made a considerable financial gain from wagers whilst doing so. I then realised that this must be the 'Pat' or 'Paddy' that the workers on the airfield had talked about as I was doing my 'roadwork' around it in the mornings. It seemed that I was going to be in for quite a night one way or another. The butterflies of excited anticipation started to tingle in my stomach. It was at times like that that you realised how big game hunters must feel when they face a large savage wild animal. That deep tingling sensation must be brought about by the adrenaline that makes idiots like me search for the savage challenges presented by such a barbaric sport as prizefighting.

The challenge was eventually made and readily accepted by the 'barker', and as Paddy climbed up onto the stand I realised that he must have had a weight advantage of almost a stone. I had suffered much larger weight disadvantages previously but I could see that Paddy had the marks of a fighting man, and if he was as good as I had been told he was, then this was going to be one hell of a fight. I took him round to the caravan we used as a dressing room and we had a very friendly little chat as he prepared himself for the fight. A couple of the 'rough and tumble' boys performed first, and then we were called into the ring. I entered the ring first, to be greeted by a friendly clap, but the welcome given to Paddy almost raised the top of the tented enclosure. It was obvious that he had many friends and supporters in the audience, so no underhanded 'boxing booth tricks' would be pulled by me that evening, no matter what kind of provocation I was offered.

We spent about half a minute of the first of the three rounds feeling each other out and exchanging left leads. His left was far from the fastest I had encountered, but when I took one on the top of my head I realised that it carried plenty of sting in it. It was going to be something for me to look out for as the fight progressed. He proved to have quite a good vocabulary of punches, and I soon realised that this was not a street brawler I was up against. He drove me back twice at the end of the first round, first with an excellent left hook, and then a short right swing that seemed to come from nowhere. Consequently I was not overly sorry to hear the bell denoting the end of the round.

The first half of the second round was pretty even. We caught each other with solid punches and it soon became obvious to me that the man had a chin of iron, the type that fighters could break their hands on. My corner told me later that they were signalling for me to lower my punching but I was experienced enough to know where I was going wrong, and I transferred my attention to his midriff. I managed to get a very hard right jab into the solar region and I could hear the heavy exhumation of breath as the punch sank in. I also smelled a distinct odour of beer. Paddy had obviously had a pint or two prior to coming to the fair. Just the invitation I needed, and within the next half minute I had managed to slip two or three of his left leads and got punches into his midriff. All my senses and experience told me that he was wilting. Several more punches and it must have been visible to anyone with a reasonable knowledge of boxing that I had found the key and he was being well and truly unlocked.

The bell came to Paddy's rescue at the end of the second round, and it needed the courage of a lion for him to get to the centre of the ring at the beginning of the third round. The once iron jaw was hanging very loose. His gumshield had long since dropped out, and a hard punch on the jaw could have done untold and totally unnecessary damage. To have let him leave his corner to resume the fight was sure proof of the total incompetence of the people who were seconding him. He was struggling to lift his hands to a defensive position when I just walked over to him and held him quite tightly; I then gently walked him back to his corner. Ron Taylor (the barker) announced to the spectators that they had witnessed a very courageous performance from a man who had given his all. Ron then offered to pay a large portion of the purse that Paddy would have received had he managed to last the full three rounds.

By the time that we had got Paddy back to the changing area and had given him a hot drink, he was obviously feeling much better, almost back to his old self. We sat and chatted for a while, and I realised what an open and likeable character he was. When he got up to leave he gave me a big masculine hug and said, 'You beat me fair and square, Dixie, and good luck to you for the future.' I said, 'That's wrong, Paddy. Tonight I beat the hell out of a few pints of beer. Nothing has been proved here today except that alcohol and fighting don't mix. I just hope that one day we can meet on equal terms, and I know that would be one hell of a fight.' He said, 'Perhaps one day we will.' There was a quick wave of his hand as he left. I am truly sad to say that I have neither seen or heard of him since.

In the days that I am reflecting on, the RN Regulating Branch (Police Branch) had several chores other than police duties and security work, and one of these duties was a responsibility for mail. In consequence I, as the most junior member of the branch at the Royal Naval Air Station, Brawdy, acquired a job as the station postman, which I found much to my liking because it enabled me to move around the area and keep in touch with my many friends. I also had to travel to Haverfordwest each morning and afternoon to both collect and deliver mail for posting. I was very friendly with all the staff in the post office there, in fact they were some of my staunchest boxing fans.

The next major fair after the Haverfordwest Fair was the Letterston Fair, in a large village some eight or ten miles from Haverfordwest. As the time for this fair grew closer, all the staff at the post office, and just about everyone else in the district that I met, would ask me if I would definitely be at the Letterston Fair. Back at Brawdy itself, I was asked many times a day if I was definitely going to be at the fair. Then the foreman of the transport section called to see me to tell me that he had organised a coach from the local village of Solva to Letterston for the fair and would be delighted to travel there via Brawdy to pick me up on the way. I thought, how smashing to have such good friends, and for that matter such a good fan club. My world seemed full of all that was good in life.

On the appointed evening of the fair, I was duly and promptly picked up as had been arranged, and the crowded coach seemed to be abuzz with a feverish anticipation that was virtually foreign to me. The excitement in the atmosphere seemed far above that which one would normally expect from a crowd of people going out to a local fairground, but all was very friendly and they were all very good and enjoyable company. The journey was quite short and I was soon bailing out of the coach and heading for the boxing booth.

The first show in the booth was a normal one with an average-sized audience. I was again delighted to be boxing with Al Brown. The show finished, and as that first audience dispersed, a huge crowd seemed to be surging towards the booth. They all seemed to be trying to get to the ticket entrance. I could never remember seeing such a large crowd in front of the booth. The really surprising thing about it was the fact that the second show had not even been announced. Challengers had not been asked for or accepted. Ron Taylor (the barker) was aglow with anticipation of a very full house, and he was soon in full voice with his spiel. Before he had really got into his full stride, however, a man at the back of the crowd had his hand in the air to make a challenge for a fight. The challenge was, as always, readily accepted and the man strode through the crowd to the stand and climbed the steps, and we, who were already on that stand now looked up at a giant. It was then that I realised how the Lilliputians must have felt on seeing Gulliver. Unfortunately my giant appeared to be erect and mobile, not lying immobile on the beach awaiting to be roped down.

A few days prior to this event, I had fought and won what I was told at the time was an eliminator for the Welsh Middleweight title. At the time of that fight I was 11 stone 4½ lbs (1,585 lbs). The man now challenging me must have been close on twice that weight. I had given away a weight advantage of four or five stones on several occasions, but I had never fought a man anywhere near this man's size before. I did ask him what he thought his weight was and he said. 'About 17½ stone'(245 lbs). I looked him up and down and thought, I *bet that you didn't have both your feet on the weighing machine when you got that answer.*

The normal procedure in the booth was to let a challenger go to the end of the second, or if you were very confident that you could take him quite easily and the fight was looking good, you could even let him go into the third round. It is obvious that the paying punters want to see some action, and if the fight is all over in a few seconds they quite rightly think that they are not getting their money's worth. This occasion was a totally different kettle of fish, though. I dragged Ron Taylor to one side and said, 'I am not going to hang around with this bloody giant, Ron. As soon as I get the opportunity, he will be on the canvas.' Ron replied, 'Take him as soon as you can, Dixie, because if he connects he will surely decapitate you.' It was possibly rather fortunate that I did not realise the meaning of the rather frightening word 'decapitation' at that time. It was surely one of the few occasions when my ignorance was an advantage to me.

Both of us were soon in the ring. Hell, the man looked awesome. He did not have quite as much hair as a bear, but he surely had the size. I cagily moved around him looking for an opening, but he was the one who made the first offensive move. I saw the big right hand coming in good time, and immediately put myself into position to ride the punch. Riding a punch is something like riding a rapid in a river; you just go with the flow. You take yourself totally off your forward momentum and ride the punch in the direction in which it was thrown. A boxer usually rides a well delivered punch for about a foot, but on this occasion I rode the punch right into the ropes of the ring, which were some three feet away. I thought, *hell, if this man catches me going the wrong way he really will do untold damage.* I realised that it was his right hand punch that he favoured, so I was going to have to bring him forward with that punch. I moved in closer. *Hell*, I thought, *this is surely like bear bating.* Luckily this bear was not allowed to bite me.

Again, the big right hand was thrown, but this time I slipped it over my right shoulder, at the same time I launched what I am sure was the heaviest punch I had ever thrown. It was a vicious right jab, and it landed plumb in the middle of his solar region. I could hear all the air expunging from his body with a kind of croaking sound. I then pivoted and transferred my balance to the ball of my left foot, and launched one of the most vicious left hooks I had ever thrown. It landed flush on his jaw, and the vibration of his collapse to the canvas was my first experience of anything resembling an earthquake.

I virtually staggered to the corner and hung onto the ropes. If that man had managed to rise from the floor of the ring before being counted out, then he would have surely become the victor. I doubted if I had enough energy left in me to mount yet another assault within the allotted ten seconds. The two punches I had thrown had expended more energy than any two punches I had ever thrown in my life. I had read about people performing virtually superhuman tasks when they were in some high degree of nervous tension, such as lifting a car off their injured child, but this was the first time in my life that I had experienced anything like this. Then another worry came to my mind. Was the man still breathing? 'Please God, don't let him be injured.' I walked slowly over to the prostrate body, I was sure I could see the chest lifting, though almost imperceptibly. *Thank God*, I thought. *Now please let the man stand*; and within a couple of minutes he was standing. Moments later he was standing quite erect and breathing normally. Ron Taylor came over to him and said, 'Now you will be able to see what kind of a man you were challenging, because you have the next two rounds to catch him with a good punch and he won't hit you.'

I often used to wish that I had as much confidence in myself as Ron Taylor had in me. He was, however, on a sure wicket in that case. That man knew that he had been well and truly beaten. Nothing would ever have restored enough confidence in him to challenge me again, or to have launched another full-blooded assault on me during that contest, even knowing that there would be no retaliation.

The coach was awaiting me after the last performance in the boxing booth, and I received something of a cheer as I took my seat. Almost all of the men were smiling and by this time I realised that quite a sum of money, in the form of bets, must have changed hands over my David and Goliath encounter. The one question for which I never received an answer was, why I was not told that I was going to face that Goliath when everyone else seemed to know? At first I thought they could have possibly considered that I might have chickened out on hearing of the size of the man.

Thinking back, they were possibly better off in retaining their secrecy. Judging by all the contented-looking faces I saw on the coach though, I am sure that the local bookmaker is still sticking pins in my effigy and, rather depressingly, I was the one who gained the least out of the encounter, financially that is.

I first put the last few pages of this biography together in the form of a short story, and shortly after doing so I saw an article in the Sunday Mail Magazine about Taylor's boxing booth, and was rather astounded to learn that Ron Taylor was still running it. In fact the booth had been at the Nottingham Goose Fair (one of the oldest and most famous fairs in the country) shortly before the magazine article had been written. So I wrote to Ron and enclosed some of my short stories that covered the boxing booth aspects of my life, which obviously included the one covering the previous few pages. I was both surprised and delighted to receive a phone call from him within a few days, thanking me and saying how much he enjoyed my stories. He told me that he was ninety-years-old on the last day of the twentieth century. He still holds his Heavy Goods Driving Licence, and drives a large lorry and trailer all over the country to the various fairgrounds. I could still sense the enthusiasm in his voice. It is now some fifty-four years since I first met him and by the sound of things Ron will last another fifty-four years.

In the letter to Ron, I mentioned that I had had some wonderful experiences and a very happy life to date, and that I had been lucky enough to meet some great characters. I did, however, and for the sole reason of not wanting to embarrass him, chicken out of admitting to him that he was one of those great characters. He was, of course, one of the most enduring of all the characters that I have had the good fortune to meet and enjoy the company of in my life. I have promised myself that I will go down to visit Ron and his wife in the not too distant future. My only hope is that he does not have a giant opponent lined up for me in his boxing booth.

I am sure I would dearly like to take my recently born great grandson Bran (I am pleased to say he was born in Wales) with me just to let him see where and how I spent some of the hard though pleasurable years of my prizefighter's apprenticeship.

Before I leave the prizefighting aspect of my life, I really should tell you of a man who I found to be the epitome of what is known in boxing circles as a man with the killer instinct. It is something that is so often talked about but fortunately, or unfortunately (dependant on what your views are), is so rarely seen. I first met Billy Doyle in the West Country Boxing Booth (Whitelegs). It was whilst I was serving as a leading patrolman and stationed at the Plymouth Patrol Headquarters. As I have already written, I spent as much time as I was able to in the boxing booth in the West Country, both to gain experience as a professional boxer, and to line my pocket. On a good fair, such as the Penzance Fair, I could make the equivalent of two months' Naval pay in one day, and being a newly married man, such an untaxed bonus was most acceptable.

The first time I saw Billy in action I realised the savagery within the man. He was totally ruthless and without any form of conscience. He was a powder keg just waiting to explode, and he had the physical ability to make such an explosion into a 'grand firework display'. At my first sight of him he was taking a challenger 'to pieces', or perhaps it would be more apt to say, he was pleasurably trying to destroy a fellow human being. Had the referee not stepped very quickly between him and his huge and powerfully built challenger, I feel sure that very serious physical damage would soon have been done. In all the time I knew him, I never saw him show any mercy. Once he knew that he had a man beaten, he would never let him off the hook. He was like a wild tiger that, once he had smelled blood, had to have his share of the spoils, and to him those spoils were to see that man lying at his feet.

After seeing Billy in action, I made it my business to swot up on his background, and I was most surprised by what I learned. I remembered seeing the man who had been voted 'The Boxing Prospect of the Year' during the mid 1940s. He was one of a famous boxing family, and he had been looked upon as the great hope of British boxing as he swept everything before him. When I saw him he was boxing as the chief supporting contest to a European title fight. He performed like the prospect he was considered to be, and his ability was such that I could see nothing but glory before him. That was until he met Billy Doyle. Billy took him apart in less than two rounds, and as far as I know he never fought professionally again. I also learned that Billy's behaviour had landed him in trouble on several occasions. He had served his national service in the RAF and had left that service under a cloud, though I was not able to find out exactly what had happened, despite the fact that I was quite a nosy copper.

Boxing booths were the nurseries of boxing, and most of our great champions came up through their auspices – Freddie Mills, Jimmy Wilde and Tommy Farr, to mention but three of the greats. Although the men standing on the 'stand' of a boxing booth would take on any challenger who appeared, challengers were not always available and in consequence there were often what we used to call 'gees' planted in the crowd. These were men known to the barker. In his early days, Freddie Mills, who later fought for the World Light Heavyweight Crown, often boxed as a gee.

As mentioned earlier, I first became interested in boxing booths in the 1940s and in those days all servicemen had to wear their uniform all the time. It was illegal for them to wear civilian clothes. When I boxed for the first time in the booth that covered the Plymouth area, and proved to the barker that I knew my way around a boxing ring, he then asked me if I would like to box as a gee. He then went on to explain that he preferred servicemen because the public would be less likely to think that it was a fiddle, or fix.

Please don't get the idea that a so-called gee fight was easy. When you take on a good professional boxer you have to know your stuff and bruises were often the order of the day.

One day Billy Doyle approached me. He said, 'Dixie, how about doing a gee with me?' I said, 'Not on your life, Billy. As far as I am concerned, being in the ring with you would be like embarking on a suicide mission.' He said, 'I promise you Dixie, if you gee with me it will be like a good sparring session, and I bet we will get good nobbins after it. (Nobbins is the money thrown into a hat which is passed around the audience after a good contest.) I will take this opportunity to explain that the name 'Dixie' was the standard nickname in the Navy for anyone who had the surname Dean or Dale.

For several weeks Billy was as good as his word. We had some really tough fights, and it was always a very hard contest to fight him because he was a real class act in the boxing world, plus the fact that he was about half a stone heavier than I was. I must admit though, I certainly tightened up my defence as a result. The barker was both surprised and delighted, and he mentioned to me on several occasions that he had believed that Billy would never be able to find a gee to take him for more than one fight.

As you have already been informed, I was a Naval copper, and one night I had the most dreaded beat of all the beats; it was on the notorious Union Street. One of the real trouble spots on that beat was a dance hall called the Paramount. I remember it once being referred to as the Royal Naval Academy of Ballroom Dancing. Some joke, it was the roughest place in the whole city. The dance hall was on the first floor and the approach was via a couple of flights of steep concrete steps. From about 10 p.m. we used to have to close onto the Paramount, because if there was going to be any trouble it was short odds that it would be in the Paramount, and the wife of the manager always indicated such trouble to us. Her method of signalling was to break a pane of glass, which invariably showered us as we stood in the street below. We would then charge up the stairs and hope that we were not going to be met by a boot in the mouth as we reached the top step. On this specific occasion the manager speedily guided us to a corner of the dance hall where there were possibly five or six uniformed males lying prostrate on the floor. There were only two people who were actually standing in the area. One was a girl, who was sobbing rather bitterly. The other (I bet you have already guessed it), yes, it was Billy Doyle. The manager hastily beat a retreat. He had obviously seen enough violence for one night, and he surely thought that if we could not sort it out he did not want to be the last line of defence, he having seen the damage that Billy was capable of creating.

My first and very obvious question to Billy was, 'What the hell happened here?' It was the young lady who replied. 'This man had his hand on the back of my chair, though he had not spoken to me. Billy thought he was trying to chat me up though, so Billy hit him, then all his friends tried to help him and now they are all hurt.' I had no jurisdiction over Billy because he was a civilian. I said to him, 'Billy, you know that with your record, if the police nick you, you'll go down for sure.' I then showed him where the emergency exit was and got him out of the place. The civil police were sensible enough not to attend, or perhaps just too hard-pressed to respond to the manager's request for their assistance. After helping with the casualties, we left the scene, there being no further necessity for our presence.

The next time I met Billy at the boxing booth he at least had the good manners to thank me for my assistance at the Paramount, but I rather stupidly failed to notice, after challenging Billy in the usual way, that the young lady he had been with in the Paramount was within the confines of the boxing booth spectator's area. From the opening seconds of the fight, I knew that I was going to have one of the hardest encounters of my life. Billy had obviously decided that he was going to show the new love of his life that he was a first-class boxer, and I was to be the demonstration dummy. I was fully aware that there was no way I could have given half a stone in weight to a fighter of Billy's class when the situation was serious, and this time it was very deadly serious. The barker, I am sure, had read the situation and the timekeeper had been tipped the wink so that the times of the rounds were reduced considerably. I still had all my work cut out to withstand the vicious onslaughts but I was determined not to surrender, though I did take a couple of counts. I was still more or less in the vertical position when the final bell sounded. I think it fair to say that I was bloodied but unbowed.

The barker could read my feelings; he and I had been friends for several years. I felt betrayed, and the barker knew it. He said to me, 'Dixie, he can hang around and take any straights (meaning normal challenges, not gees) but no one else will ever want to gee with him again.' I bet my last shilling that, in that booth, no one ever did.

By the middle of 1952 I had progressed quite well in the Professional Middleweight Boxing ratings and by that time I had moved back to South Wales, as I have already stated. I was again happy to be boxing with Ron Taylor's booth. I had married quarters, so my wife and I were living together for the first time in our married lives, and my whole world seemed to be a Garden of Eden. Then, disaster struck. Towards the end of 1952 I had won what I was assured was the final eliminator for the Welsh Middleweight title, which I won by a technical knockout in the fifth round. It was then decided that because I had not been born in Wales, I was not eligible to fight for a Welsh title. How times have changed. I was born just a few miles outside the Welsh border and the last time I did any research on reigning Welsh champions, two of them had been born in the West Indies.

Despite the title problem I was quite happy to be matched again with the man I had beaten in that supposed eliminator, if for no other reason than to prove conclusively that I was the better boxer. By the third round I was confident that I had the fight won. I said to my second that I would finish him off in the fourth round. He instructed me to keep boxing and forget the knockout idea and he said, 'We need a conclusive points win to demonstrate that you are the superior boxer.' In consequence of those instructions I was cruising along and building up a reasonable points score. Then in the seventh round my eye was damaged, and the fight was stopped in my opponent's favour. This defeat put my opponent back in line for a crack at the title, which obviously gave the Welsh Boxing Board a very easy way out as far as my claims were concerned.

A few weeks later I was again boxing, and again I suffered a damaged eye. My wife had been very upset because of the first eye damage, but when it happened for the second time in successive fights she became almost frantic. I must admit that it certainly made my face look even uglier than usual and it must have frightened the hell out of the kids.

At this point of my career I again though of Billy Doyle. Had I been drawn against the likes of him in a further contest, he would have cut my suspect eye to ribbons and my sight was, and for that matter still is, a very precious thing to me. This, plus consideration for my wife, were the two reasons I decided to call a halt to my professional boxing career. I carried on boxing in the booths, but meeting good class professionals when your eyes are in any way suspect would have asking for trouble.

As long as I could remember, I had had the ambition to be the Welsh Champion. I had always followed the Welsh boxing scene. I was steeped in the history of Welsh boxing. I had read and re-read the stories of the great Welsh boxers, such people as Frank Moody, who had fought five world champions, Johnny Basham, Jimmy Wilde, Freddie Welsh, Tommie Farr and 'Peerless' Jim Driscol, they were all my boyhood heroes. I had always held a special regard for Frank Moody though. I remember that during the serialisation of his life story in the Boxing News, I must have been like a person sitting on hot coals awaiting the next weekly instalment to be delivered.

Whilst I was stationed at RNAS Dale I went to Milford Haven several times and sat in the pub that Frank ran – I believe it was called the Royal Oak, and I just sat there for hours trying to pluck up the courage to speak to him. I would have happily fought any middleweight in Wales, but to me, just talking to Frank would have been like meeting God. So, apart from asking him for my half pint of shandy (and heavy on the lemonade please), we never did converse. What a wonderful opportunity I let go by, due totally to both my shyness and my stupidity.

I proved to be much luckier and less shy with Frank Moody's brother Glen, however, and he and I very soon became quite good friends. He worked on the airfield at Brawdy while I was there, and I found him to be a really likable character. Glenn had boxed all the big names in the heavyweights, and light heavyweights (including Bruce Woodcock, who he fought twice for the British Heavyweight title), in the mid forties.

During a boxing show at Brawdy, Glen offered his services to box an exhibition bout with me, and I have to say here and now that despite the fact that he was well into his forties by that time, of all the men I ever fought in the boxing ring, Glen Moody was the hardest man to hit that I ever met. I don't think that I laid one good punch on him during the whole exhibition contest.

There is one little insight into the character of Glen Moody that I would like to enter into these pages. He used to be in charge of a gang of labourers that did several pretty menial jobs during the reconstruction of the airfield. One day, one of his gang of workers ran to find him whilst he (Glen) was enjoying a cup of tea. He told Glen that there was a farmer threatening him with a shotgun and demanding that they should all get off his land. In fact the land had been taken over from the farmer many years previously and compensation had been paid to him, though the farmer had never fully accepted that fact. Glen quietly finished his cup of tea and then walked over to where the farmer was still brandishing the shotgun. As he walked towards him Glen said, 'You have two options, mate. You can either shoot it or drop it, but you had better think quickly about such options because when I get to you I will wrap that bloody shotgun around your neck.' The farmer very quickly dropped the shotgun and as far as I know he is still running.

I had heard nothing of Billy Doyle for more than ten years, and then in the mid 1960s I was travelling down from Scotland by train via Preston. I was nostalgically and rather dreamily looking out of the window as the train entered Preston Station and I was remembering the days, during the Second World War, when the good people of Preston used to run a free canteen for all the servicemen passing through their station, and we were able to eat as much food as we wanted, or at least as much food as the people of Preston could lay their hands on, keeping in mind that food was very strictly rationed. I was thinking, what a wonderful attitude prevailed in places like this during the times of that awful war.

Then I heard a once familiar voice, and bobbing up from right under my carriage window was none other than Billy Doyle. 'Hell, Billy,' I said. 'What in the bloody world are you doing up here?' Billy was bubbling, he looked to be full of the joys of spring. He had a big broad grin on his sunburned face and he looked very fit; he was obviously without a care in the world. 'I have just been released from prison,' he said. I thought, *I bet it was something pretty serious.* Then I asked him what had happened. 'I got in a punch-up and one geezer's head bounced a bit hard on the pavement after I knuckled him, so I got two years for manslaughter,' he said. Then the train whistle blew and my train started to move. 'You will have to look after yourself a lot better, Billy,' I said. He replied by means of two raised thumbs and his grin had become even broader, his voice inaudible over the sound of the train. That was the last time I saw Billy, and I have no specific longing for a further encounter with him. He was something of a stepping stone in my life, but I have yet to figure out why, or even what type. Someone once said to me, the best stepping stones in life are the ones you manage to avoid; and I can read a lot of sense into such a sentiment. I would nevertheless, like to add the comment, good luck Billy, wherever you are. He must be well past the stage of bouncing people's heads on pavements by now.

There is one virtually minute aspect of my boxing career that may be of interest to people with an eye to boxing history, and that was the wearing of gumshields. Several boxers did not even bother to wear them in my time, and several of us who did (I being one) used to make our own out of gutta-percha. The ones I made for myself were quite small, and when I was sparring, or sometimes when I was boxing one of the exhibition bouts in the boxing booth, during bouts of what they call infighting, I used to hang onto the fleshy part of my opponent's shoulder with my teeth and as I was wearing the small gumshield it would leave very little mark, and my opponent would hardly realise what I was doing. That was, as long as he stayed there, but he could not break away from the clinch unless I decided to let him do so. This practice was done a great many years before we had things like HIV to worry about. Anyway, I gradually, though unintentionally, formed a habit out of this holding on with my teeth idea, and during the fight just after the one that I was informed was an eliminator for the Welsh Middleweight title, some time about the fourth round, my opponent shouldered me. The referee immediately stopped the fight and proceeded to give my opponent a right roasting, telling him that if he tried that move again he would have a round taken off him. My opponent looked really perplexed and said, 'Well Ref, someone had to do something because he has been biting me for four bloody rounds and you have done nothing about it.'

The referee was quite an elderly little chap and obviously a man of vast experience. I did hear later that he had once fought the famous Jimmy Wilde, the World Flyweight Champion. He subsequently became a boxing referee and had acted in that capacity for many years. He had obviously never heard of anyone being bitten in a boxing ring. His jaw had just dropped and he looked completely nonplussed and utterly confused. I said, 'Sorry Ref, I promise it won't happen again.' The referee remained speechless and just waved us together again, and we carried on with the bout. My eye was damaged shortly after that incident so I lost the fight despite my opponent still having my teeth marks in his shoulder.

The Farmers' Ball

We'd been invited to a Farmers' Ball and were having a very nice
time,
Then a punch-up started beside the bar, it became quite a
pantomime.
There were bottles and glasses just flying around, so we hid behind
a chair;
They say Farmers' Balls are often rough, is it the coarse corduroy
trousers they wear?

The Jogger

My sex life had started to crumble, so I went down to see the old
doc.
'No wonder you're having problems,' he said, 'you look like a very
old crock,
You need to get yourself fitter, more athletic games you must play,
But first you'll need to start jogging, doing about five miles every
day.'

The doc said 'That's my diagnosis, now call me again in a week.'
So I pushed off to get myself fitter, to try and get back to my peak.
It's hard when your body's gone haywire and you're sadly
overweight,
But I persisted for a week with my jogging, just hoping my will
wouldn't break.

After seven days of the jogging, I once again phoned the old doc,
I was very happy to tell him, 'I'm no longer an unfit old crock.'
He said, 'Where the hell are you? Your wife has been on the phone.'
I said, 'Tell her I'll see her much later, because I'm thirty-five
miles from home.'

Mouse Droppings

I promised the wife before going to bed,
I would sort out the mess in the garden shed.
It was very untidy; I am forced to admit,
The place was festooned with a large pile of mouse *droppings*.

Mousetraps and poison I'd tried once before,
But the little sods tossed them out of the door.
I can't let these vermin rob me of my wit,
Despite that my shed is now full of mouse *droppings*.

The vermin must go, there is no other way,
Or the wife will leave home the very next day.
If she goes to the shed, she'll have a blue fit,
To find that the place is still full of mouse *droppings*.

How can I get all the vermin to go?
Who is the best man to answer my woe?
Ah, the jossman's the one with both courage and grit,
Yes, he's surely the man to shift all the mouse *droppings*.

But the jossman refused, I was silly to ask.
Moving mouse droppings was not part of his task.
He suggested that I should then dig a big pit,
And there I could bury the pile of mouse *droppings*.

I'll have to practise a lot and do better next time,
And try very hard to get those last lines to rhyme.
This poem is a failure; I'm forced to admit.
In fact I would say, it's a load of bull *droppings*.

Doggy Do Do's

I hope you enjoyed my poem about the mouse droppings I found
in my shed,
But I've now got a much bigger problem to sort out before going
to bed.
My wife recently bought a wee puppy, but I'm sure I will soon
have a fit,
I don't mind the odd little puddle but I hate having to clean up
dog mess.

We invited some friends round one evening for drinks and a bit of
a snack,
But I omitted to mention the puppy, now I'm sure they won't
want to come back.
It happened just as they were leaving, one guest had a very bad slip,
His feet glided right underneath him and he landed head first in
dog mess.

The embarrassment really was awful, our relationship became very
sour,
I took the guest up to our bathroom where I hoped he would
enjoy a shower.
When he arrived in the bathroom, the first thing he did was to sit,
But the pup had used the bath stool before him, so he sat himself
down in *dog mess*.

Well, I found him a clean pair of trousers and I got out my bottle
of rum,
I apologised for all that had happened and hoped he would still be
my chum.
His mood improved with the spirit and his cheeks reddened up
quite a bit,
But as he walked over to top up his glass, he once again slipped in
dog mess.

Our guest was now really furious; it was then he stormed out of
the house.
I too was getting annoyed with the pup, but my wife was as quiet
as a mouse.
The guest didn't switch on the porch light, so alas, the front path
wasn't lit,
I am sure you will never believe it, but he once again slipped in *dog
mess*.

So our guest is now threatening to sue us, for every penny we've
got,
But all we have left are our pensions, so he's not liable to get such
a lot.
We've been advised to sell all our assets and try to acquire some
back-up,
So in view of this liquidation, will someone out there buy our
pup?

Battle Scars

Lord Nelson stood on the quarterdeck; he knew that the battle was
    near.
He said, 'Send me up my trusty steward, I want to see him here.'
The man arrived quite promptly and stood at Nelson's side,
'I am always proud to serve you, Sir,' he said with glowing pride.

'Then get below, my trusty man, and bring my tunic of red,
You will find it on a hanger by the foot of my bed.
So hurry my good fellow and return with all good speed,
I don't want the men to notice if I receive a wound and bleed.'

The steward returned to Nelson's side, with his tunic ready to
    change.
He said, 'I must tell you now, Sir, before the enemy come in
    range,
When I was in your cabin, Sir, and I hope you won't think it
    treason,
But I put on my brown trousers for a very similar reason.'

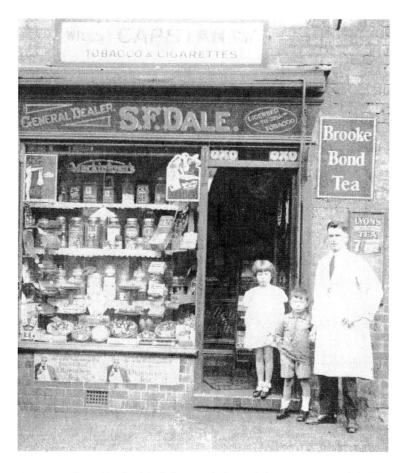

A very serious Fred with father and sister, Margaret, around 1932

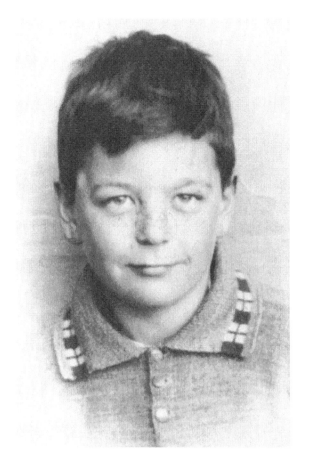

Fred in the late 1930s

Top: Fred as a boy seaman in 1944
Bottom: Fred with three friends, waiting to go shore in the Orient, 1945

Top: Fred and Betty on their wedding day, 1950
Bottom: Fred and Betty with friends in Malta, 1961

Top: Master-at-arms Fred Dale. Could even a mother love him?
Bottom: Fred just before his first professional fight, 1951

The Jolly Jossman takes a tumble in the first round

Last round. The punch looked good but the energy tank was rather empty

Master-at-arms Fred Dale on board HMS *London*, (arrow points to Dale)

The re-commissioning of HMS *London*, (arrow points to Dale)

Top: HMS *Devonshire*, after three of her main turrets were removed after I left her
Middle: HMS *King George*
Bottom: HMS *Duke of York*. A really lovely old lady

Top: I was in Korea on this frigate. The only ship I disliked and I will not name her
Middle: HMS *Apollo*. A very fast girl
Bottom: HMS *London*. One of the great loves of my life

Top: Field gun wheel carriers crossing the chasm, late 1990s
Bottom: The author in a nostalgic mood in the field gun mess, 1990s.
On the wall are photos of previous crews, including the 1948 crew.

Top: The author today
Bottom: The author's great-grandson,
Brân Holley, already showing a love of water

CHAPTER SEVEN

I had, fortunately, never suffered from the delusion that I had enough talent or ability to make a fortune from boxing. Therefore, long before the problems with my eyes, which were due to my boxing activities, I had sought opportunities to attain promotion in the Navy, and whilst I was at RNAS Brawdy I requested to take the course for regulating petty officer. I duly did the course and passed the necessary exams, and was consequently promoted to that exalted rank. I found several obstacles along the way, such as a Master-at-Arms who was totally useless at his job but managed to convince the Commander of the air station that all his numerous mistakes were due to the incompetence of his staff. That Master-at-Arms had always advocated the suppression of coloured people, and because of his love for the principles of apartheid, he emigrated to South Africa after he was pensioned off from the Navy. I really wished that he had come onto the ship of which I was the Master-at-Arms when, much later, it visited Cape Town. I would have taken great pleasure in personally throwing him off the ship, and I am sure that I would have had a good cheer from all the other Naval personnel who knew him. Unfortunately such luck was not to be mine.

The Royal Navy, like any seagoing service, is awash with great characters. The sea just breeds characters that want to be different in some way to the people with whom they are living in such close proximity. Individuality is something that some people are even prepared to give their lives for. I just love to recall the many people who have crossed my path, whose lives have enriched my memory and whose friendship I have held to be a very precious ingredient of my own life. One I can recall is a character by the name of George Bramwell. His name came to the forefront of my mind this very morning and it must be fifty years or more since I last saw him.

I was the duty Regulating Petty Officer on the main gate of the Royal Naval Air Station Brawdy in the early 1950s. George had arrived there on draft from Plymouth; he slid open the hatch window of my office and announced that he was George Bramwell and that he had been drafted there as the GI (Gunnery Instructor). I looked at the broad smile and took an instant liking to him. He had had one hell of a journey that had started in the early hours of the morning; he had needed to change trains on several occasions, refreshments were almost unobtainable, yet here he was with the widest grin on his face that I had ever seen. He had been travelling, virtually unwatered and unfed, for some fourteen hours, and yet he was totally at peace with his lot. Almost everyone else arriving under the same circumstances would have been full of moans and complaints and displaying the sourest of faces, but George was full of smiles. I thought, *Hell, I wonder if I have someone here from one of those strange Eastern religions*, then I thought, *perhaps I should get hold of the Master-at-Arms.* But I remembered in the nick of time that the Master-at-Arms was a devout Roman Catholic, and I could therefore be creating more problems instead of solving the one I believed I already had. It seemed that the best bet was to take the bull by the horns. I was about to be temporarily relieved for a meal break, so I told George that I would show him where the petty officers' mess was and I had one of my assistants help carry George's kit to the mess, but George picked up the two heavy bags and seemed quite happy to carry them himself.

On arrival in the mess George immediately ordered two pints of beer. Because I was on duty I courteously refused the one he had ordered for me, so George very quickly quaffed them both. I thought, this certainly means that my Eastern mystic religion idea is out of the window, and I happily left him there, where I believe he quaffed a fair quantity of ale, and in fact, as the mess was almost empty, he had a virtual one-man party.

George very soon proved himself as a first-class gunnery instructor. The sailors in his charge must have thought that they had been hit by a thunderbolt, but he would always demonstrate how the thing should be done by first performing the task himself. Whenever I could afford myself the opportunity to see him instructing a class I did so. His dedication and enthusiasm were a revelation that one could best describe as infectious, but his humour was the thing that shone through in everything he did. He always wore a big smile-cum-grin that seemed to totally disarm any malcontent or complainant, not that there were many of them. They would have received short shrift from George in any case.

The accommodation on the air station was pretty primitive, as it had been built as an emergency airfield during the Second World War, and little in the way of improvement had been made since then. The sleeping accommodation was a series of Nissen huts that were often wetter inside during a rainstorm than they were outside, and the bathrooms were some two hundred yards walk away. Not a big problem in the summer but the winter was rather horrid. The bathrooms were even more primitive than the sleeping accommodation; they consisted of a long bench, a couple of coat hangers and two showers, which rarely produced hot water and often failed to produce water of any temperature.

I was enjoying my shower one evening with the rare delights of warm water when George appeared in the next shower. I was mesmerised to see all the scars on his body; it literally looked as if he had been used as target practice in a spear-throwing contest. There just was not a reasonable-sized area on his body that was unmarked by a scar, and when he turned around I could see that there was a scar at the bottom of his spine that could possibly have been made by someone using a shovel. I used a series of expletives, the lesser of which was the word 'hell'. 'What in the world has happened to your body, George, and how did you get all those scars?' He said, 'The Japs intended to starve me to death and I decided that that was not the way I wanted to die. So I became a rather brazen thief and I stole their food at every opportunity, often from right under their noses. I am not the best thief in the world and they sometimes caught me; anyway, that is the reason I bear so many scars.'

I had not realised that George had been a prisoner of war of the Japanese. He seemed so fit and healthy and his constant smile-cum-grin had conveyed to me that his life was blissful and full of joy, and that he just loved the job he was doing. That he had endured the total deprivation that was inflicted by the Japanese on the people they had under their control as prisoners of war, to me, it was just staggering.

George had been taken prisoner of war after the sinking of his ship during one of the earlier sea battles of the war, and I had met several of the survivors from the same ship who had also survived the harsh imprisonment by the Japanese. I was still in contact with some of them and was able to question them about George. He was obviously held in high regard, but each one I spoke to seemed to be holding something back when they spoke about him. It was as if there was a secret that was reluctantly held between them and none of them seemed to want to talk about it. I knew in my heart that none of them had made a pledge of confidence, but people who have undergone such deprivation and survived must feel that they owe all their fellow survivors a confidence, if such a thing were needed.

Many months after George's arrival at the air station, I was drafted to a ship as the acting master-at-arms. I enjoyed two rather happy years aboard the ship, and she visited several parts of the world that I had not been to previously. I think that the meeting I am about to describe took place in the Danish port of Copenhagen, but it could have been almost anywhere in Scandinavia. I was attending a civic function with several people from another Royal Naval ship that had accompanied us to the port, and we were really being well looked after. Scandinavian beer has a very pleasant taste and it was flowing quite liberally. I was sat at a small table with a Petty Officer from the other RN ship, and during the ensuing conversation I found out that this Petty Officer had survived the sinking of the same ship as George, and had been taken prisoner of war at the same time as him. I was delighted to hear that he had known George quite well. Then I sensed that undertone of secrecy again which I had encountered when I had made previous enquiries. It seemed that this Petty Officer was making a purposeful effort to change the subject. I was now totally wrapped in curiosity and there was no way that he was going to get off my hook. Fortunately the drink kept flowing and tongues loosened a little more. The Petty Officer's voice, however, became much lower, as if he was reluctant for anyone else to hear any part of our conversation.

I was told of the savage beatings that George had undergone because of his acts of stealing food from virtually under the noses of the Japanese guards, and how he had been left for dead on at least two or three occasions, and how it seemed that it was always the same two guards who meted out the beatings and the bayoneting in a most sadistic way. I was told that there were occasions when they would pick out George for a beating just for the sheer pleasure of doing it.

The prisoner of war camp in which they were incarcerated was eventually overrun by the American Marines, but unfortunately the ex-prisoners were unable to be moved for at least a week because of difficulties of transportation and the reluctance to subject men, many of whom were very ill, to a long and uncomfortable journey until they had been adequately fed for a reasonable period. The Japanese guards were naturally disarmed and put into a compound, but as there was no place for them to escape to, there were no guards posted to cover them. After about five days the whole of the lower part of the camp was inundated with the most awful smell, and after a short search it was discovered that two of the former Japanese guards had been killed and their bodies had been thrown down a manhole. Five days in the hot sun under a metal manhole cover had created the most obnoxious of smells, and the remaining Japanese guards had the task of recovering the bodies and burying them. It was no surprise that the bodies were those of the two former guards who had so willingly meted out the beatings to George. Everyone was sure who had done away with the guards, but it was not spoken about among the former prisoners and there was no inquiry about the killings.

It is about fifty years since I last saw George and he will be into his late seventies, perhaps his eighties, if he is still alive, which I sincerely hope he is. He, in my opinion, deserved a long and happy retirement. He was some character. Or, as the Yankee Marines put it, some cookie.

By 1953 I had replaced my boxing career with a liking for the game of rugby, though, as it was rather late in life to be actually starting to play the game, the chances were not very high of me ever reaching a reasonable pinnacle of the sport. I was, however, selected to play for the Fleet Air Arm on a tour of Eire, only to be withdrawn because of injury a few days before we were due to leave for the tour. The person who took my place came to see me on his return from the tour and said that he had enjoyed the trip immensely and was subsequently chastised by me for adopting such a gloating attitude.

I found rugby very satisfying from several aspects of my nature. For one it worked off the natural aggression that any former prizefighter had to have, and it kept me reasonably fit and healthy; and in my opinion there was a much better camaraderie amongst its players than in any of the other team sports, which I think was its greatest asset and attraction for me.

My favourite position in a rugby team was as a front row forward, or what is known as a prop forward. It seemed the ideal spot for a man of my build, weight and personality. By that I mean that the front row is where a lot of the aggression takes place. I had rapidly gained several stones in weight after packing up the boxing. In the days that I am now reflecting on, prop forwards were virtual 'battering rams', and all the forwards used to refer to the backs (or three quarters, as they then liked to be called), as the 'fairies'. Forwards were rarely in a position to score tries in those days, but their physical battles were perhaps even more horrendous than they are in the modern day fifteen men, all-running, all-scoring, rugby.

I remember playing a game at a town called Whitland, where the mud was so deep that one of the opposing props had to be carried off the field to be given mouth-to-mouth resuscitation, but he nearly died before they could find someone without a sense of smell who would do the resuscitation job because his breath was so bad, and all his teammates had refused to do it. One of the oldstagers there told me that several seasons before, the mud was so deep and thick that it filled all the forwards' ears and they could not hear the whistle to signify the end of the match, and in consequence the forwards were still playing rugby fifteen minutes after the match had finished and the ball had been removed from the field. The 'fairies' had all bathed and changed into their normal gear ready for the usual booze-up, and were enjoying the demonstration of forward-play that was still happening on the field, when one of the embarrassed forwards noticed that there was no ball on the pitch. I played against the prop forward who was reputed to have needed resuscitation, and I can still remember the smell of his breath in the set scrum, but I feel that the game going on fifteen minutes without the ball is a little over the top for even my dull, prop forward-type brain to accept. A few years ago I had cause to travel by road to Pembrokeshire and found that Whitland now has a very good bypass skirting the town. There at the side of the bypass was a brand new rugby ground. It even had a posh stand for spectators. Rugby there could never possibly be as entertaining as it was when the ground was by the side of the river, which regularly flooded it.

As I mentioned a few paragraphs ago, it was back to sea for me, and this time I was to join a fast minelayer. As stated, I had by this time been promoted to Regulating Petty Officer, and I was to be the senior member, nay, the only member of my branch on the ship. You might say I was the acting Master-at-Arms (Chief of Police), though I did not get any extra pay for the position. The ship was capable of a speed in excess of forty-five knots and in consequence she very often had the job of rushing the Commander-in-Chief (Home Fleet) around Europe to carry out visitations of various ports and to other seagoing ships of his fleet.

In other words she was very often what is known in the Navy as the flagship. I was quite young and also very junior as an RPO at the time. I was blessed with the confidence of youth though, and virtually devoid of any worries about the situation or the responsibilities. Years later I realised that there must have been numerous RPOs who were much senior to me, who were breaking their legs and pulling all sorts of dodges to avoid having to join the ship I then found myself on. I took it all in my stride and did not have even the slightest worry about the situation. Oh, how I envy the young me, that devil-may-care attitude, as I now sink speedily and just a little worryingly into my dotage.

I suppose that I really have to admit that at this stage of my career, I was somewhat immature to be acting in the capacity of a ship's master-at-arms. I was in my mid-twenties. In fact, I was at that time one of the youngest petty officers on the ship. From the time I had first gone to sea, I had always looked upon the master-at-arms as a very mature figure whose word had invariably carried the day in any discussion on the Naval Discipline Act or Naval law in any capacity. In other words, he was looked upon as something of a sage or a ship's wise man. Here was I, a virtual upstart in the eyes of almost all the ship's company. My predecessor had been a very mature RPO, whom I had known for many years and for whom I had always had a great deal of respect. The question was now, could I do my job? Or to be more precise, could I rise high enough to accept the challenge that had been offered to me?

Because the ship had such a good turn of speed, other than often acting as flagship, she was assigned to a variety of rather unusual jobs, many of which were not the most pleasant. One job I remember in particular was at the time of the combined fleet manoeuvres in the Arctic during a particularly nasty winter. We had the job of remaining behind in Scotland for twenty-four hours after the remainder of the fleet had sailed, then we picked up all the personnel who had missed their ships, due to occurrences such as lateness of trains etc. We then had the task of transporting them all back to the fleet and spent some forty-eight hours dodging around the Arctic distributing the personnel to their various ships by means of jackstay transfers (a pulley system rigged between two ships whilst they are ploughing through the water, beam to beam and some twenty or twenty-five metres apart). I had the pleasure of having to complete all the necessary paperwork, which had taken me almost the whole of the forty-eight hours that the ship spent in reaching the fleet. Each of the jackstay transfers (of which there were about twenty) took something like two hours or more, and I had to be on the upper deck virtually the whole of that time to ensure that the right paperwork went with each transfer. By the time we had completed this task I was almost past the point of requiring sleep and was surely due to become a registered zombie. My eyes had taken on the appearance of organ stops in reverse.

During our often long sojourns at sea on the many exercises that the ship took part in, the previous paragraph being an example, I decided that, although my office was not allocated a typewriter – because, at that time, all my records and reports were all submitted in handwritten form – it would surely not be long before the twentieth century started to catch up with us and we would have to submit such reports in the typewritten idiom. For this reason I decided to teach myself to touch-type. I had always got on well with the other members of my mess, and one particular member that I had been very friendly with was the Petty Officer Radio Telegrapher. His department had almost all the typewriters on the ship, and they were firmly ensconced in his office. He willingly leant me a typewriter on condition that he could have it back at the rush if it were needed. I gladly accepted his conditions, and having purchased a book on touch-typing during my last venture ashore I was 'all stops go' on the self-tutorial roll of touch-typing. The book I had purchased was Pitmans' book entitled *Touch-Typing Made Easy*. I found it very easy to follow and within about six weeks I was quite proficient at the art, and by that time I had got to the stage whereby I was typing a lot of my letters to my wife and family.

One day I was typing away happily, and because by that time my typing had become almost totally of the touch typing mode, I was possibly looking at the far corner of my office whilst composing the letter I was typing. At this very moment the Communications Officer was passing the door of my office. He stopped and came in and asked me if I had previously been a member of the Communication Branch and therefore been taught to touch-type during my initial training. I told him that that was not the case and that, in fact, I had taught myself the rudiments of touch-typing from a book. He left my office muttering, 'I will keep this in mind.'

Several months later I received a message from him stating that I was required to attend an Emergency Cryptographers' Course the next time we were in our home port of Devonport (Plymouth). I was really annoyed about being nominated for such a course because I was the only member of my branch on the ship, so if I was away doing any other job I still had to put the time in on keeping my own job up to date, and this would obviously have to be done in my off duty time. I complained to the Executive Officer, but we found that the Communication Officer had cleared my appointment for the course with the Captain before submitting my name, which meant that I would be working late into the evening almost every day I was doing the course, and there was nothing I could do about it.

I have got to admit that the cryptographers' course was very interesting, mainly because the course was on the KL7 Cryptography System, which was still in the process of being introduced into the Navy. We were in fact almost the very first course to work on the KL7. I was glad when the course was completed, and was quite pleased to return to my own job on the ship.

The Communication Officer came to see me a few days after the cryptography course was completed. He had a large form with him and he proceeded to ask me several questions about my security clearance. I asked him what he was talking about and he said, 'Well, being a Regulating Petty Officer, you must surely have a high security clearance.' I cottoned onto it in a flash. 'Sir,' I said, 'you have sent someone on a course that involved the KL7, the latest and most secret cryptography system in the Royal Navy, and that person does not have even the basic security clearance.' His face turned as red as beetroot. He knew then that I had him by the short and curlies. I was wearing my broadest of smiles when I said to him, 'You won't be sending me on any more courses, will you Sir?' He looked very sheepish as he left my office, and he kept very much out of my way for the remainder of the time we served together. I don't think that I ever did get the full security clearance, but it is a bit late now for me to think about selling my secrets to the Russians, as all that happened nearly fifty years ago. I should imagine that the KL7 has, no doubt, been submitted to a museum long since and is possibly kept in the same glass case as the Enigma coding machine.

I was happily typing away in my office one day when the Petty Officer Steward came into the office and he asked how I had learned to type the way I was typing, so I told him about the book I had used. He said that the next opportunity he had he would get a copy of the book and start the touch-typing course himself, because he was in possession of a portable typewriter. Several weeks later he came to me and said that he had not been able to acquire a copy of the book whilst he was ashore and he asked whether, as I was now proficient at typing, I would sell him my copy of the book, which I willing did, for the same price I paid for it. In other words, learning to type didn't cost me a penny. Incidentally, I distinctly remember that the price of that book was three shillings and six pence (eighteen pence).

During another one of our long periods at sea, whilst on the fast minelayer, I spent a great deal of my leisure time devising what I considered to be a much more streamlined method for the recording of the Naval discipline process. By that I mean the making out, method of use and method of recording of charge sheets and their insertion into the ship's daily record of offences, and also the method of recording those offences in a man's service documents. I put dozens of hours into it and I tackled the problem from several angles, such as time saved, amount of paperwork saved and the efficiency to be gained. When I thought I had laid it out in an acceptable manner I showed it to the Captain's secretary, who was a lieutenant. He was a person I necessarily had to work very closely with, as our specific jobs overlapped considerably. Fortunately he and I got on very well together, and we more or less always seemed to see eye to eye. After he had been in possession of my folder for some twenty-four hours, he brought the folder to my office. He was full of praise about the work I had put into it and he said he had also shown it to the Captain, who was also very impressed about the methods I was suggesting. He did make some suggestions for minor alterations and left the folder with me. Unfortunately, I had a rather hectic 'run ashore' in one of the Scandinavian countries shortly after having the folder returned to me, and having put so much work into it I was beginning to hate the sight of the thing, so I am afraid the folder received the 'float test'. In other words, it found its way over the ship's side.

Two or three years after the above incident, the Navy introduced a completely new method for the discipline process, which was considerably less efficient than the one I had suggested in the study I had carried out. Over several of the following years further amendments were made, but even when I left the Navy many years later, the method in use was still not as good as the method that my system had suggested. I wish, even to this day, that I had submitted my suggestions to the Regulating School. The one snag about that would have been that, had they liked the method I was suggesting they might have had me drafted there for instructional purposes, and I know that that would have been a job I would have hated. I suppose, if for that reason alone, it was really just as well for me to have let sleeping dogs lie.

We made several pleasant visits around Scandinavia shortly after the Arctic manoeuvres described in previous paragraphs. By that time my eyes were beginning to lose their sunken appearance. My accommodation on the ship was in the petty officers' mess, and we certainly had some great characters in that mess. One very memorable character was a petty officer named 'Tank' Windsor. He was invariably at the foundation of any skylark that occurred in the mess, but there was one particular incident that rebounded on him. The ship visited one of the ports in Norway and the mess laid on a guest evening. Tank attended this mess function with the ugliest woman that any of us had ever seen. 'Hell, Tank, I hope you are not intending to bed that one,' said one of the mess members. 'Listen,' said Tank, 'all you blokes, with your good-looking women, might think that you are doing all right, but in a couple of weeks you will be down at the sickbay getting your penicillin injections. The thing is,' said Tank, 'if you pick a real ugly one, no one else will have touched her.'

A fortnight after that specific visitation to the Scandinavia port, only one of the ship's company had reason to visit the sickbay with a sick sex organ, and please don't expect prizes for getting the right answer. Had it been any other member of the mess, they would have probably either dived over the ship's side through embarrassment at having boasted that nothing would happen to them because of their ability to read the female types. Or they would have locked themselves away somewhere until the fuss blew over and the laughter ceased. That was not Tank's way, however. He brazened it out to the very end, and in fact it is possible that he enjoyed the joke as much as anyone else on the ship. It will need a very deep grave and a heavy-duty coffin, or if buried at sea it will need a well-sewn shroud and a very deep ocean, to stop Tank Windsor laughing over a mishap, be it to himself or anyone else. He really was a great character to have as a mess member and we certainly never went short of laughter when he was around.

I am reminded of another one of Tank's pranks here. We really enjoyed a good and entertaining tour of Scandinavia, and at our first or second port of call, our Petty Officer 'Officers Steward' had met a really beautiful woman, typically Scandinavian, long blond hair, blue eyes and beautiful shape all round. She certainly had it all. Good looks, nice house and plenty of money. She asked what the ship's next port of call was to be and was duly informed. There she was on the jetty awaiting the PO Steward on the ship's arrival. This pattern carried on for the remainder of the Scandinavian tour. Before we left that last port of call in Scandinavia, Tank had obviously had a quiet word with her and as she waved goodbye to the PO Steward for what he thought would be the last time, she shouted, 'Goodbye Darling, see you in Plymouth.' The PO Steward's facial colour turned very pale. He was a native of Plymouth and he had a house there; each time the ship berthed there he was always met by his wife.

Because of the many duties that we had to perform, it was several weeks before we actually returned to Plymouth. By that time, the PO Steward had lost at least a stone in weight through worry. In fact, I don't think that he was ever quite the same man again. The only woman to meet him on our eventual arrival in Plymouth, however, was his wife. I remember Tank chuckling as he watched the PO Steward kissing his wife, whilst he sneakily and rather sheepishly looked over her shoulder at all the other guests. Fortunately for him, none of the other guests had any particular desire to see the PO Steward.

The Navy did not take many national service people during the 1950s but what few they did take were distributed between the few ships that were permanently in the Home Fleet area, which of course included *Apollo*. The ones we had were invariably very good and enthusiastic people. Due possibly to the fact that we took so few; the Navy had something of a pick of the best. Tank Windsor used to get a bit wound up about the national servicemen working on his part of the ship. One of his main points, with which most of us had to agree, was that national servicemen only got about half the pay that regular sailors got and quite honestly some of the national servicemen were twice as good as the poorest of the regular servicemen. One of the national servicemen we had was an international yachtsman and a brilliant seaman, which emphasises my point very well.

We did occasionally get the odd exception, and Tank was the person who got him. He was a chap in his late twenties who had joined rather late in life as a national serviceman because of the time he had spent in formal education. I later found that he had about three or four degrees, one being a Masters, and he was entitled to put a whole string of letters after his name. The one snag with the man was that he just had not the slightest idea on any practical subject. He had a wonderful brain but could hardly tie his own shoelaces. Eventually Tank came up to my office and pleaded for me to take the man into my office as a messenger. He

said, 'If he stays on the upper deck he will kill someone,' so I took
him and found him to be an excellent person to have in the office,
though he was hardly the person you would ask to make the tea
because he would be bound to make a mess of it.

Just prior to one of our Scandinavian tours we took on board a
Petty Officer Radio Telegraphist of a specialist sub-branch that we
used to refer to as the radio warfare branch. They specialised in
covert listening devices, and we had taken this man on board
because the ship was expected to go up near the northern Russian
border. He and I were chatting in the mess one evening and the
conversation got around to language and communication in
general, and he mentioned that he had an interest in Esperanto, the
international language. He showed me a couple of books that he
had with him, and I really became interested in the subject. The
next time we were back in the UK, I bought a 'teach yourself book'
on the subject, and I found it reasonably easy to gain an
understanding of the language. I was rather surprised by the sheer
simplicity of it, and was most surprised that the language had not
really caught on, and that a large portion of the people of the world
were not speaking it. The language is completely phonetic and it is
therefore almost impossible to misspell in it. There are twenty-
eight letters in the Esperanto alphabet, and each one can only be
pronounced one way. The greatest asset of the language, however,
is its twenty-six prefixes and suffixes, which always mean the same
thing. This means that an Esperanto dictionary is much, much
smaller than its equivalent in any other language.

During one of our several tours of Scandinavia I sought out
Esperanto speakers and was very cordially received by them. At
one period I attended a meeting of Esperanto speakers and there
were representatives from twenty or more countries present. I had
not been speaking the language very long at that time and was
therefore not very adept at it, however I was struggling on in a
conversation with one man, and he was helping me with the odd
word but keeping strictly to the Esperanto language. The last
question I put to him was, what nationality are you? He then told
me that he was an American, but he had been determined not to

break into our joint national language, a point with which I was in full agreement, and I thanked him for his patience and his help. I always found Esperantists to be really fine people with great ideals. Their obvious intention was that if ordinary people could talk together then international animosity would fade.

The great pity about Esperanto is that it seems to have been overcome by English, mostly because of the fact that the computer age is upon us and that the USA virtually controls the world of computers, so almost everything that means anything in computers virtually has to be recorded in English. I truly believe that the world has missed a golden opportunity. The true idea behind the Esperanto bubble was that if everyone in the world were taught two languages, their own native language and the very simple international language of Esperanto, then the whole population of the world could easily communicate with each other (dream on, Fred).

Back to Scotland after our pleasant sojourn in Scandinavia and we had a few days in Musselburgh, which is virtually a stone's throw from the city of Edinburgh. We were all delighted at the opportunity to have a good gander around the Scottish capital. The ship's company were a pretty reasonable lot and gave very little trouble whilst they were ashore. I think that we only had one offence of any consequence during the whole of our visit to Musselburgh, and that was a Leading Engineering Mechanic who decided to have a wee in the middle of Princes Street, and to assist the police in directing traffic with his disengaged hand whilst he was doing so. A police report soon arrived at the ship but unfortunately by that time it was at sea and the offender was denying the incident ever happened. I think he would have been better off if he had pleaded insanity, or even, perhaps loss of memory due to an alcoholic fog.

By the time that we were able to get the police constable down from Edinburgh to attend as a witness (the not guilty plea making it necessary to have the witness there in person), the ship was in London and the constable had to make the journey down there by train. Once he was on board the ship, I gave the constable the necessary briefing on the procedure at the 'captain's defaulters table' (which is very much on the same lines as a field court martial in the other two armed services). After my spiel I fortified the constable with a couple of tots of rum, which he soon seemed to acquire a taste for. There were no problems at the captain's table and on conclusion of the proceedings the constable was duly thanked by the Captain and we both (meaning the constable and I) repaired to my mess, where he proved that he really had acquired a taste for 'Nelson's Blood', and he sank several more tots. Getting him to the railway station was not the easiest job I have ever had and I remember that I was the one who paid the taxi fare, due partially from the fact that the constable suffered from the notorious Scottish disease of short arms and very deep pockets, though by the time we had arrived at the station I don't think that he could even remember if he had any pockets. I have to admit that I really was very relieved to see the train pull out. I bet he slept all the way to Edinburgh, or perhaps even through to Aberdeen.

Many months later the ship made a rather rushed and totally unannounced visit to Musselburgh to pick up a rather urgent package. Only one person, other than the high-ranking brass, was obviously privy to the secret information about our visit and he did not disclose to me how he acquired his information. He did, however, drink my tot, after which he left the area in a police car. I hope that he did not wee in the middle of Princes Street on his way back to the cop shop.

The Home Fleet had one of its many gatherings at Invergordon in Scotland, and the part of it that involved me was the Home Fleet Rugby Cup. We were included with the fifth frigate squadron in all the sports that took place during the visit, and I was chosen to represent them in the front row of the rugby scrum. There was quite a lot of rugby played during the visit and most teams played twice a day to get through the extensive programme. Our team got to the finals, and I scored the winning try. I think it is the only try I can ever remember scoring. One very memorable thing about the try was that the team captain gave me a rollicking over it. His theory was that a prop forward should not allow himself to get into a position whereby he could score a try. Times have certainly changed in the half-century that has passed since the times I am writing about. Anyway, I was very proud of my try. The rest of the team (with the exception of the miserable team captain) got me well and truly pissed, but had the good manners to carry me back to my ship.

One quite funny incident that I was informed about some time after the rugby final was that the team were lugging me up the brow of my ship whilst I was in the aforementioned very high degree of inebriation, and they were accosted by the Officer of the Watch, who was a young sub lieutenant with a very strange temperament and an even stranger and very officious attitude. 'Who is that drunk that you are bringing aboard my ship?' said the Sub Lieutenant. 'It is your bloody jossman and we have just come aboard to put him in his hammock,' said the huge lock forward whose shoulder I was drooped across at the time. The Sub Lieutenant evidently took a good gawk at me and said, 'I don't care who he is, he ought to be placed in the capstan flat because he is drunk.'

'Myself and the rest of the bloody team are going to put him into his hammock, Subby,' said my huge bearer, in a very authoritative tone.

'Who do you think you are?' said the Sub Lieutenant.

To which my bearer replied, 'I am Lieutenant Commander W M Nonsuch of HMS *Impossible*, (Thanks a bunch, Billy, and I won't print another bloody word about you, or the incident. I promise.) The next morning I awoke in a neatly slung hammock, but oh, what an awful brain-festering hangover I had.

After doing my usual checks, I made my customary morning report to the Executive Officer (Ex O), and he smiled as he saw how I was trying to hide my eyes from the light, then he said, 'Congratulations on the victory in the rugby final. I was unable to attend, but I hear that you scored the winning try.' I replied, 'Yes Sir, but there was a long period last night when I wished I had not done so.'

'I heard about that too,' he said.

It is very important that the master-at-arms (or the senior regulator on the ship) should have a good rapport with the Ex O. I seem to have been very lucky in that direction. I suppose that was one of the reasons why I was eventually selected for promotion to fleet master-at-arms (more of that in later chapters). The Ex O of the ship in question was a lieutenant commander, though all my future Ex Os were of commander rank.

The officer in question was quite a nice chap and very easy to work with, though he always seemed to play his hand very close to the printed rules. With the exception of the deviation I am about to describe, I just don't remember him ever straying from the strict Queen's Regulations.

Shortly after the major sports meeting at Invergordon, it was down to Devonport (Plymouth) for Easter leave. A ship's dance had been arranged prior to the ship's company proceeding on leave, but as the time spent in our home port is always a busy period from the regulating point of view, such as arranging leave passes, travel warrants etc. I was rather up to my neck in paperwork, and in consequence I was very late arriving at the dance. As I walked through the foyer the Ex O, who was leaving the building, passed me. I was also most surprised to see that he looked a little unsteady. I noted that a young sub lieutenant was with him, who, I was rather pleased to see, had read the situation and was obviously intending to put him into a taxi to get him back to the ship. The incident was most surprising to me because I knew that the Ex O rarely partook of drink. My suspicious copper's-type mind was alerted and I quietly stalked around the dance hall to see if I could account for the strange behaviour of the Ex O. Within a few minutes, bingo; I saw two stokers swilling their beer back whilst laughing most profusely at some obviously very funny situation that had recently happened. Fortunately I was quite friendly with a couple of the people sitting at the next table to the two stokers, so I surreptitiously plonked myself down at that table and soon got the gist of the recent happenings from the conversation I overheard. I was soon fully aware of why the two stokers were displaying such merriment. They had apparently slipped the Ex O a 'Mickey Finn' into his glass of soft drink. A mental note was firmly plastered onto my meagre brain.

I had spent the remainder of the evening watching my own drink very carefully in case the two stokers fancied getting a further, though lesser, scalp to pin to their belts. On my return to the ship, I heard that the Ex O had returned on board okay, and there had been no other untoward incident.

Because of my late arrival at the dance, I had had very little to drink, and when I went to the Ex O's office to make my usual report the following morning, I was full of the joys of spring and quite chirpy, but oh dear, the Ex O looked like something the ship's cat had brought in. Having made my report to him, which I don't believe really registered, I then informed him that there were several requestmen and one defaulter for him to see. He said, 'Oh dear, RPO, is it really necessary that I deal with these cases this morning?' I told him that unfortunately the cases could not wait, so he reluctantly made his way up to the after flat where such people were seen. I recollect that I virtually had to push him up the ladder we had to negotiate. Nevertheless, he was there and he did his job. We had a short discussion afterwards, but neither of us mentioned the happenings of the previous evening. I saw very little of the Ex O during the rest of the day. That Mickey Finn must have been pretty powerful.

The next morning I again repaired to the Ex O's office to make my usual report, and this time I was in an even more chirpy mood than I had been on the previous morning. On this occasion the Ex O's expressions were back to normal. I said, 'I hope you are ready for the presents I have for you this morning, Sir.'

The Ex O's face took on a look of quizzical surprise; he even turned to look at the calendar, obviously thinking that he had forgotten something like his own birthday or some other special occasion. He said, 'What the hell is so special about this morning, RPO?'

I replied, 'Well Sir, I know, and you know and in fact, I can tell you that the whole ship's company knows, that you were slipped a Mickey Finn during the ship's dance.'

'I don't think that we need to go into that any further, RPO,' said the Ex O.

I said, 'I can imagine that it is something that you would prefer to forget about, Sir, but the reason I brought it up was because of the presents I have here for you.'

'Look RPO, this mystery of yours is beginning to confuse me,' said the Ex O.

'In that case, Sir,' I said, 'you had better look carefully at the presents I have brought,' and I placed two charge sheets on the desk in front of him.

'Is this some kind of a bloody skylark of yours RPO?'

'I can assure you sir,' I said, 'this is gold tipped genuine. Stokers Bloggs and Smith (I wish I could remember their real names) were absent from their place of duty yesterday morning and when the duty stoker PO went to look for them at about nine o'clock, he found them still in their hammocks, which had been slung in an out of the way, and little used compartment.'

The Ex O snatched the two charge sheets off his desk, rushed past me, and it was as much as I could do to keep up with him on our way to the upper flat where he held his 'defaulter's table'. 'Call the two of them up to the table together,' he said. This was totally contrary to the Naval Discipline Act, but as the Ex O was just as conversant with that act as I was, I decided that the situation was going to be much more interesting if I were to keep schtoom and obey the instructions he had given. I read out the two names and then the charge of 'absent from their places of duty'.

'Well, well, well,' said the Ex O, 'we met quite recently at the ship's dance, and I recollect that we had some merriment. I must tell you both that due to that merriment, I had to exercise quite a deal of willpower to set about my work the following day, but I did so.' He then turned to me and said, 'Is that not correct, RPO?' I obviously had no option but to agree, in fact I was more than pleased to confirm that the statement he had made was totally truthful. 'You two could not make it though,' he said, 'in fact, it is obvious that the merriment created at the ship's dance was too much for you. The consequence of your inability to get to your place of duty is that I am awarding each of you fourteen days' number nine punishment.' (That was extra work and other restrictions.) I then gave the order, 'On caps, right turn,' and marched them away.

When they were both well clear of the upper flat, and their Divisional Officer and the Officer of the Watch, who were necessary spectators, had left, I turned to the Ex O and said, 'Hell, Sir, you know that the maximum amount of number nine punishment you can award is seven days. How the hell am I going to square this in my daily record of offences?'

By this time the Ex O's face had taken on one of the widest grins I had ever seen him wear. He said, 'Listen RPO. You know that I can only really award seven days' number nines. I know that I can only award seven days. The only other person on the ship who knows that I should only award seven days is the Captain's Secretary (A lieutenant of the secretarial branch), so before your daily record gets to him, for later presentation to the Captain for his perusal and signature, I am sure that you can make those fourteens look like sevens.' My silent answer was given in the form of a grin that possibly surpassed that of the Ex O's, but no further words were spoken on the subject.

I think that the above incident was one of the greatest laughs that that ship's company ever had. The general opinion was that there had been a very great display of poetic justice. By the time I had returned to my office, the whole ship had heard about it and I am sure that those two young stokers had the ribbing of their lives. I never felt any pangs of conscience about the incident, and I am sure that the Ex O likewise would have retained few regrets. One thing I do remember, though, was the smile that the Captain's Secretary gave me when he handed me back my daily record of offences after the Captain had signed it. It is my belief that even the Captain was in on the joke, but nothing further was ever said about it.

A big breakthrough in relationships between the Western powers and the Soviet block had come about during this period, though I am sad to say it did not have long-lasting consequences.

Several ships of the Home Fleet were invited to visit Leningrad, as the city was then known (since renamed with its old title of St Petersburgh) and in reciprocation a Soviet cruiser visited Portsmouth. My older readers may remember the incident in Portsmouth when Buster Crabb, the former Naval officer, was drowned. It was believed that he was trying to gain some information about the Russian cruiser and was believed to have been diving below her. The mystery has never been solved, despite numerous theories having been put forward as to what actually happened and why. I have no intention of putting forward a personal theory about the matter, but all the senior divers I spoke to about the incident seemed not to have had a very high opinion of Buster Crabb, as a man, a former Naval officer, or his abilities as a diver. I would also emphasise that he had only held a temporary wartime commission and as far as I know he never had any formal diving qualification.

We had the job of taking the Admiral of the Home Fleet to the Russian city. It was quite an experience for all of us, and a great insight into life behind the Iron Curtain. One day during our visit I joined several other senior NCOs from our ship, and we were taken to a Russian destroyer for a lunch party. The party was very good and the spread of food that lay before us was quite fantastic. The Russian NCOs looked about, as surprised at the layout of the meal as we were, so we soon realised that it was far above their normal fare. One incident that remains quite distinct in my mind is the fact that because none of us spoke a word of each others' language we were doing a lot of arm waving and gesticulating, and I for one worked up quite a thirst. I saw a water bottle, at least I thought it was water, on the table so whilst still waving my arms about and trying to stress a point in the difficult and virtually wordless conversation, I poured myself a large glass of water from the bottle. I was still gesticulating profusely whilst taking a large slug of the supposed water. It was, in fact, neat and very powerful vodka. From that point on in the lunch party, it was just as well that speech was of little use to us because my voice box was bruised for several days afterwards. The state of that Russian destroyer was rather a surprise to us Brits though. I for one would not have liked to have to gone to sea in it, and I think it could have best been described as a 'rust bucket'. I also attended the Lord Mayor's reception and we were well furnished with champagne of a type, and lashings of caviar.

The locals of Leningrad looked very drab and poorly dressed, and I thought the place looked similar to what parts of the UK had looked like in the early 1920s. Everyone was quite pleasant to us and the visit went down well, but the general impression amongst the ship's company was 'if that is Russian Communism they can keep it'. The Russians were still very wary about security at the time, and in consequence all the RN ships were instructed that they were going to have to leave the port and put to sea during the hours of darkness. The reason was obviously that the Russians did not want us to see the layout of their Naval installations during our exit from the port. The Admiral of the Home Fleet had gone down to Moscow to meet the top brass of the Russian Navy, and then sent a signal to us to say that he was unfortunately delayed and could not get back until the early hours of the morning. The other three or four RN ships in company with us had to sail during the hours of darkness and leave us lying there in the harbour awaiting the return of the Admiral. Before the ships sailed however, each one of them with Naval photographers on board drafted them to us with all their camera equipment secreted in their kitbags and suitcases. All the porthole glass along the upper deck was cleaned and polished and as we sailed out through the port, under a rising sun, our photographers snapped away merrily. That was but one of the cat and mouse games that I encountered between the Russians and us; others you will learn about in later pages.

After yet more confounded exercises at sea it was into Gibraltar and there the first major sporting contests were all water sports, which were to be followed by a boxing contest. For the purposes of the sports our ship was paired up with a large depot ship, and we were to compete against two frigate squadrons and a destroyer squadron (or flotilla, if you want to be more technical). I am a reasonable swimmer and have played some fair games of water-polo over the years, but when I saw what ability was available to our team I just knew that I would be far down the list of possibles, and I soon withdrew my name from the list. One particular player caught my eye, and he was a member of our own ship's company. He was a young electrical mechanic, he stood about six foot four inches tall and he was built like a tank. When he was in the water it was like watching a shark swimming with sprats. He just swam over the top of the opposition as if they were not there. I had never seen a more aggressive polo player in my life. I thought, this man was surely going to be an international water polo player before very long. Our team won the Home Fleet Water Polo Cup very easily. The truth of the matter was that this young electrical mechanic virtually won it on his own. I remember watching him get out of the water after one of the matches and I looked at his feet. He had the largest pair of feet I had ever seen. I thought, no wonder he swims so powerfully with feet that size! It was akin to a normal person having flippers on. I asked him what size his feet were and he said, 'I can get a pair of size fifteens on at a pinch.'

The Physical Training Petty Officer (They are always known as 'Clubs') on the depot ship and myself had been friends for many years and it was good to re-acquaint. He knew, as did several people involved with the boxing, that I had boxed as a professional, so I would have no chance of slipping myself in as a ringer to try and swell our points total. We were able to gather together some rather reasonable boxers, and the depot ship had a smashing heavyweight who really showed promise. The training had gone well, then, a few days before the contests were due to take place, a disaster struck in the form of an accident to our heavyweight hope. The accident occurred whilst he was working in the engine room; in fact he had slipped and broken his jaw on a piece of machinery.

Although the boxing contests were to be a four-part affair, our spy organisation had informed us that there was only one other team with a heavyweight boxer who would be entered into the competition. We then sat down and worked out the odds and the possibilities. If the boxers from our team gained the achievements in the lower weights that we anticipated, we would still be two points short of the overall points target to win the competition. The loss of our heavyweight had created a problem, and my mind wrestled with the dilemma for many hours before I at last flashed onto an idea. We had possibly the biggest and best water polo player in the Navy on our ship, and he was also one of the most aggressive characters I had ever seen in a water polo game; surely if this aggression could be transferred into the boxing ring we would have a great chance of winning the Home Fleet Boxing Championship Cup.

I realised that the task in hand was going to need all my silver-tongued persuasion, and we were very limited by the fact that the boxing contests were but a few days ahead of us and, as I have said, we just had to have a substitute for our fallen participant in the heavy weight stakes or the cup would be lost to us. I called the young electrical mechanic to my office and sat him down in a comfortable chair in the corner. I first complimented him on his great achievements in the water polo competition and assured him that it was, I felt sure, the most accomplished performance I had ever seen in the field of water sports. Now, I said, we had only one hurdle left before we could proclaim that we had truly swept the board of the Home Fleet Sports. That hurdle, I proclaimed, was the Boxing Championships Competition. His whole countenance changed and he seemed to shrink into a shell. It was reasonably obvious that boxing was not a sport he wanted to participate in, or for that matter even to talk about. To transfer this man's aggression from water sports to the boxing ring was going to be one of the most challenging tasks I had ever set myself.

Remember that we had but days to go before the Home Fleet Boxing Championships were to take place. I had a large, quite intelligent, and ultra obstinate prospective heavyweight boxing challenger whom I had yet to talk into becoming an aggressive heavyweight boxer. I spent hours getting him to the stage of even sparring with me, and when I did so I found it almost unbelievable that a man who was so aggressive in the water was so totally lacking in aggression in any other event. My youngest daughter could surely have punched holes in him. I think it would have been best just to think of him as a fish out of water. The thing was that this man was a virtual giant in stature, and had proved to the entire Home Fleet that he was a formidable athlete, so it seemed that psychology was going to be our only method of promoting his boxing abilities, or rather in covering up his total lack of them.

I knew that any further attempt at sparring was a waste of time, and I went over to the depot ship to have a word with Clubs. He was rather surprised to learn of the snags I had encountered in trying to convert our aggressive swimmer into an aggressive fighting machine on land, but he listened intently to my psychology idea that I hoped would circumvent our problem. He was rather sceptical of it at first, in fact, as he said to me at the time that he thought it smacked a little of cheating by deception. I must admit that I played a bit on his word little, and soon I reduced the said adjective to 'minute'. From that point on it was reasonably easy in talking him into assisting me in giving my idea a try.

The night of the boxing competition arrived, and by the time the middle weights were boxing it was obvious to both Clubs and to me that things were working out very much as we had both predicted, and my psychology ideas were going to be the only chance of us lifting the Home Fleet Boxing Cup. After the middleweights got into the ring we knew that there would be two more bouts before our further participation as seconds would be required. The heavyweight who was to compete against our giant 'shark' was already down near the ringside and awaiting his coming contest. Clubs and I walked over separately and very slowly; we were lucky to find two seats right behind him. We started to talk between each other about the different bouts, without any hint to possible listeners to the conversation as to which team we were a part of. Then Clubs said that he had heard that the heavyweight on the depot ship who had had his jaw broken was lucky to get away without even more serious injuries after sparring with the shark. I could see the ears of the shark's pending opponent prick up. 'Got him,' I thought, and now we can lay on the psychological banter that is about our only chance of picking up the Home Fleet Boxing Cup. I then told Clubs that I had heard that the shark's father had been pressing to get his son out of the Navy to box as a professional, and several managers were vying to sign a contract with him. Clubs then went on about his hope that the referee was switched on enough to realise the power of the shark's punching, and that he would not let his opponent take too much damaging punishment before he stepped in and stopped the fight. He then added a lovely little rider that he was glad it was not him who was boxing the shark. Luckily the shark's coming opponent had not looked behind him during our conversation and we both quietly got up from our seats and departed to the dressing rooms once again.

After the usual wait, we at last had the two heavyweights in the ring, and I was delighted that the shark did just as I had instructed him to do without any further prompting from me. I took his robe from him as he got into the ring. He then sized up to the corner post with a little sparring session, which he followed by flexing his chest muscles; it really was quite something to see. He truly was a very large and well developed man. I was even more delighted when he looked over to the opposite corner and did the only officious act that I had been able to inculcate into him. He snarled menacingly in the direction of his opponent, which he followed up with further flexing of his huge chest muscles. I sat him down on his stool and told him that I wanted just one big right hand swing from him as soon as he got within range of his opponent, and I told him that I was confident that that would be just about all that would be needed from him.

The bell for the first round sounded and I knew that my part of the dastardly plot was over. If the psychological snarling and the big right swing did not do the trick, as I expected them to do, then my plan would have been consigned to what many would have considered to be our just rewards. Another big flex of muscle from the shark as he strode to the centre of the ring to meet his opponent. Hell, I thought, the man was carrying the psychology lark to the ultimate. Then he swung the big right hand as he had been instructed to do. I am confident that it missed his opponent by at least half an inch, nevertheless, down his opponent went as if he had been pole axed. He lay quite rigid on the canvas; there was surely no chance of him beating the count. When the count was over, he had to be carried to the corner, and in fact he was stretchered from the ring.

If any medals for acting had been awarded that evening then the shark would have been totally out of the running, his opponent would have won the Oscar hands down. Our team, however, won the Home Fleet Boxing Cup and the shark was feted as the Home Fleet Heavyweight Champion. It is true that he threw but one punch in anger, but I can assure you that it did not land. Perhaps we ought to have named him The Unconnected Champ.

There was one other happening in Gibraltar before the fleet left there to go about its normal business again. On the last night of the Home Fleet gathering there was to be a fleet concert in one of the larger theatres on the Rock. Each ship in the fleet had been expected to submit one act for the concert, and I had talked our ship's company into laying on a little one-act pantomime. In consequence of having talked the cast into it, I naturally had to take part myself. Sailors don't like taking the more feminine parts, even in a pantomime. I suppose it is because of the reflection it might have on their masculinity, so when it was realised that there was a part in the pantomime for a Fairy Queen, I was nominated with a 100 per cent show of hands. After several hundred fights I look about as feminine as a bull elephant, in consequence I could not have cared less about any strange reflection it might have had on my character or reputation.

Fortunately I had a very small part in the show, as my appearance consisted of a couple of waves of my magic wand and then a little fairy-type dance prior to departing via one of the wings. I must emphasise that our part in the show was to be a comedy pantomime so we had to make ourselves look like the comedy part we were to play, and to make the Fairy Queen look truly ridiculous, I went to the newly crowned Home Fleet Heavyweight Champion, the Shark, and asked if I could borrow his size fifteen boots (I normally wear size eight) just for the show, to which he readily agreed.

This period of reflection was one during which I had only relatively recently got into the habit of drinking alcohol, and in consequence my capacity to hold such drink was still rather limited. As already stated, the concert took place in a rather large theatre, which was an ideal layout from the normal sailor's point of view because right at the back of the theatre, behind all the seating, was a large bar. Standing with our backs to the bar we could see everything that happened on the stage. Our ship's pantomime was to be the last of many acts in the show so, as the weather was rather warm and I had plenty of time to wait, I went to the bar to partake of a half of beer. Unfortunately my arrival at the bar coincided with the arrival of Clubs (The Physical Training Petty Officer from the Depot Ship). Two large beers and two large brandies appeared on the bar. Then several of our respective ship's companies saw us both standing there and came over to congratulate us on our team winning the Home Fleet Boxing Cup, and many of them accompanied their congratulations with more brandy for me.

I shudder to think how much I had had to drink before I realised that I had but minutes before I was due on stage. As I rushed to the dressing room to get changed, I realised that my gait had taken on something of a wobble, which, unfortunately, did not augur well for my forthcoming fairy dance. I made it to the stage in the nick of time and I fortunately remained sensible enough to avoid putting the boots on until the very last minute prior to my entrance.

This was the first time in my life that I could remember having a pair of inanimate objects taking complete charge of me. This was virtually Cinderella in reverse. I bent my knees to lift my boots but they dropped down only where and if they wanted to go there. I did manage to wave my magic wand around as was scripted, but unfortunately the dance consisted to two totally unscripted pirouettes, the second of which carried me right off the stage and landed me in the empty orchestra pit. Fortunately, and undoubtedly due to the excessive amount of drink I had partaken of, I was relatively uninjured. I saw a small trapdoor leading under the stage and I thought to myself, *I must get the hell out of here while I can.* I seemed to have been in total darkness for an eternity as I crawled around on my hands and knees under the stage, and I surely bumped into every object that had been stored there; by the amount of dust and dirt I was swallowing it must all have been under there since before the First World War. At last, a light; I made my way towards it and was soon dragged out of there by a pair of very powerful arms. The Shark was possibly there to make sure that nothing went amiss with his boots, and I was never more pleased to get rid of a pair of footwear in my life. As I gladly removed the boots I was grabbed by several more pairs of arms and again hoisted up onto the stage. I think that we took four, possibly five curtain calls, after which there were shouts of 'We want the Fairy Queen'. If they had any intention of trying to get me to repeat my aerial display, they certainly had to forget it, though I don't think that I ever will.

It was rather sad leaving that fast minelayer; she had been a great ship from my point of view and I would have been quite happy to stay aboard her for another year or more, but time marches on and we all have to march with it. The chap who relieved me aboard that ship was much older than I was and he was a real worrying type. In the two or three days that I had to turn over to him I tried hard to put him at his ease, but I have to say that I really foresaw some kind of disaster pending. Then low and behold a few months after I left the ship there was a mutiny on board. Because it was months after I had left her, I am not in a position to make a true and fair judgement on the matter, except to say that I know in my heart that if I had been on the ship at that time, that mutiny would not have happened. I believe the trouble started in the stokers' mess, which was right below the Regulating Office, and I know that I would have been down there in a flash and sorted out the ringleaders. At the subsequent court martial the Regulating Petty Officer was cleared of any blame, but he was on that ship in the capacity of the ship's master-at-arms, and he should have known what was going on and stamped it out whilst it was still in its embryonic form. I do not believe that it is possible for a ship to have a mutiny on board and the master-at-arms not to have some part of the responsibility in the fact that the mutiny is not properly and satisfactorily quelled. Any master-at-arms worth his salt would, I am sure, feel the same way as I did about the situation.

Alas. Now a dead end job ashore for me.

Police Observations

We were staggering down to the local pub to buy ourselves more
  beer,
When we saw a copper sat up in a tree, I thought, hell that looks
  rather queer.
I said to the girl who was with me, 'What's he sitting up there for,
  Blanche?'
She said, 'He's either as drunk as we are or he's part of the Special
  Branch.'

The Little Bird

A migratory bird really sealed its fate
When it started its southerly journey late,
With ice on its wings it was forced to yield,
And it fell from the sky to land in a field.

A passing cow (in grass munching mode)
Lifted its tail and dropped its load.
This covered the bird, turned its fortune about,
As the heat of the dung thawed its body right out.

The bird was now singing and tweeting with glee,
Which attracted a cat in a nearby tree.
'Twas a one-sided struggle, there could be but one winner,
And the cat had the poor little bird for its dinner.

Here's a moral for everyone, old and young,
Being late can land us all in the dung.
Not everyone crapping on you is a foe,
But this is the thing that you really should know:
Not everyone pulling you out is a friend,
If you're in the crap, keep quiet and avoid a sad end.

Our Billy Goat

I hope you enjoyed my poem about the antics of our little pup,
Well, at long last we managed to sell it, to save any further cock-up,
But the wife is a true animal lover, she wanted a pet for the house.
I suggested we buy something cuddly, like a kitten, or perhaps a white
mouse.

But the wife had been raised in the country, a farm animal she had in
mind.
I said that we hadn't got room for a horse so keeping one would be
unkind.
She said that I need have no worries because our garden is nicely
remote,
Then she sprung an awful surprise on me and suggested that we buy a
goat.

I argued for a long time to stop her, but I knew that I hadn't a chance,
I was sure that the goat would upset all our friends and lead us a right
merry dance.
We visited some country markets; at last she found a goat that looked
bright
But I was sure from the first time I saw him that our future would not
be all right.

Now the wife is a very keen gardener who grows a variety of posies.
One day she invited the vicar around to inspect her large bed of roses.
The vicar bent over the rose bed and remarked that the petals were
sparse,
It was then that the goat decided to act, and butted him right up the
buttocks.

Our milkman was a very nice fellow but we warned him to look out
    for our goat,
And to be careful when he's bending over to take more milk out of his
    float.
But he laughed aloud at our warning; he said the goat being
    dangerous is a farce,
The next time he bent over to pick up milk, the goat butted him right
    up the buttocks.

A burglar climbed into our garden, with intentions to break into our
    house.
The man was obviously a well-practised crook, he moved as quiet as a
    mouse.
He crawled slowly up to our back door and peered through a panel of
    glass,
But as he bent over to lock-pick the door the goat butted him right up
    the buttocks.

We then called the police to arrest him; they didn't have to come very far,
We very soon saw the flashing blue lights on the top of their Panda car.
The copper bent to inspect the damage where the burglar had broken
    the glass,
But whilst carrying out this inspection, the goat butted him right up
    the buttocks.

The copper looked badly shaken so I helped him to get back to his feet.
I then poured him a large glass of brandy because his face was as white
    as a sheet,
Then I made the mistake of bending to pick up his torch from the grass,
And before I could straighten myself up again, the goat butted me
    right up the buttocks.

My wife stooped down to help me and assist me to reach the back
    door,
She saw that the goat had butted me hard and knew that my buttocks
    were sore.
But while she was trying to help me she slipped on the broken glass,
By then the goat was charging again and he butted her right up the
    buttocks.

Now the milkman and the vicar are suing and soon we'll be going to
    court.
I'm really pig sick at these happenings and the poor wife is awfully
    distraught,
So when all these troubles are over, we're going to move out of this
    street,
But before that happens I must ask you, does anyone out there like
    goat meat?

CHAPTER EIGHT

So, I was ensconced as one of the Regulating Petty Officers in charge of the security on the Main Gate of the Royal Naval Barracks in Devonport. It was a real dead end job that I think had been specially designed for people who were totally without ambition, and of exceptionally low intellect. It was one hell of a comedown for someone who had recently been the master-at-arms of the flagship. The only good point about it was the fact that I was able to get home to Swansea every other weekend, so most things in the garden seemed quite good as long as I was not going to have to hang onto the job for too long. After just a few weeks I returned from a weekend leave to be told that I would soon be on my way back to RNAS Brawdy; a pleasant and most welcome surprise.

There had been many changes made since I had left the place more than two years previously, and they were pretty much changes for the better. The accommodation had been almost totally renewed, and the old messes had been knocked down and really posh buildings put up in their place. I was therefore able to soak in a bath for as long as I wanted, and to have all the hot water I desired, a most dramatic change from the first period I spent there.

The roster for married quarters was rather disappointing, however. It seemed that my wife and I were in for a long wait before we were to occupy our first married quarter. We had been married for seven years and had never really had the opportunity to live together before that time, so it was something that we had both been looking forward to very much. Then, at last, the chap who was one ahead of me on the list was moved into a quarter. My name was now on the top of the list. Perhaps in a month or so it would be our turn. Within days of that predecessor on the waiting list moving into his quarter, he was killed in a helicopter crash. So my wife and I took the quarter that he had been in for less than a week. It is an ill wind that does not blow some good to somebody, as my lovely old granny used to say. I would have preferred the circumstances of my getting the quarter earlier than anticipated to have been more pleasant though.

All the regulating staff at Brawdy had changed during my period of absence from the place. The complement for the place was one master-at-arms, two regulating petty officers and three leading patrolmen. The other Regulating Petty Officer was a very old stager who had originally changed over from Yeoman of Signals because of failing eyesight. He really was a very strange character who had had a lot of disappointments in life and it certainly reflected in his personality. For several weeks he would be of a really nice and friendly disposition, and then he would hit the bottle for several days, during which time he would be the most obnoxious person you could imagine. The master-at-arms changed a couple of times whilst I was there, and I also requested for and successfully completed the course for master-at-arms, though at that time, the anticipated waiting time to be promoted to master-at-arms was about ten years.

Rugby again was my biggest sporting enjoyment, and I turned out for Brawdy often twice a week during the season. I also boxed in the boxing booth when it was in the area, and I kept myself in reasonable physical shape. I bought my first car a few months after my arrival, and it was a 1939 Austin Eight. It was pretty clapped out and had hardly any flooring on the front passenger's side, but it was our first car and we treasured it as if it had been a Rolls Royce.

The Church of England Padre on the station was an Irishman and he was the secretary of the Brawdy Rugby Club. He was the Rev. Black, and he was quite some character. All the rugby players used to call him 'Bish'. I think the name Bish was short for Bishop, which in itself was a joke because he would have been the last person in the whole world to be made a bishop. Oh boy, could he sink the pints of beer, and his vocabulary of uncouth words and songs was renowned throughout all the rugby clubs in the area. He never turned out in a dog collar when attending anything to do with rugby though, in fact he used to wear a really tatty old sports jacket that I think he must have stolen from a tramp.

I remember that we had played rugby against Tenby Town one Saturday and after the game we all mustered in their rugby club for the usual singing of the coarse rugby songs and the quaffing of large amounts of beer and, as is usual in rugby clubs, both teams intermingled and I was sat at a table with several of the Tenby players. One of these players asked me what the chap that we all called Bish did on the air station, and I quite rightly told him that he was the station Padre. Everyone around the table burst out laughing; to them, it was evidently the funniest joke that I could have told. Nothing could ever have convinced them that I was being serious with my answer. I have often wondered if anyone ever did get around to convincing them that I was telling the truth.

My youngest daughter was born whilst we were in the married quarters in Haverfordwest, and my wife and I decided that because of the prospect of many more family moves we would call a halt to the size of our family. We were lucky to have very good neighbours whilst there, and we became very close to one family living next door to us; in fact I am still in touch with the husband of the family, though I am sad to say that both he and I have lost our wives of that time to cancer.

The neighbours mentioned above received a draft to Malta after about a year, and I thought that I ought to try for a foreign accompanied draft myself; I was most surprised when I phoned the drafting office to be offered a draft to Malta. I naturally accepted it with open arms, and we were soon happily packing all our accoutrements to go by sea whilst we awaited a flight.

It seems that I have spent a large part of my life being in some way involved with Malta. I must have been in and out of Malta at least fifty times during my life, and I must say that I have always had something of a soft spot for the place. I have got to admit that when I first called there in 1946, I knew that it had had quite a blitz during the war, and it showed on the bomb scars around the place, but it has never looked any different. Areas of Malta still look as if they have been recently bombed, but that is the way the Maltese are and you have to take them or leave them. Personally I like the Maltese people, and then again, who is without fault? Or as one of my Maltese friends, whose command of English was rather limited, once said to me, 'Let him who is without stones throw the first sin.'

I had a great job in Malta; I was working at the civil airport at Luqa. The job mostly involved attending to and sorting out all the Naval passengers passing through the airport, who were mostly from air trooping flights. We were also given a few headaches trying to get flights for Naval personnel being sent home on compassionate grounds, like a serious illness of a near relative. We worked very closely with the Army and the RAF, and it was the first real insight I had into the workings of the other two services. The work was interesting without being too demanding, so it was possibly the best of both worlds.

My family enjoyed Malta every bit as much as I did and within weeks of our arrival both my daughters could swim quite well, and it was great that they should enjoy their swimming because I had always loved being in the water. In fact it is still one of my great loves in life. When we arrived in Malta I was very surprised to hear from my wife that she could not swim. The fact that she had been born within sight of the sea and could not swim was really astounding to me, and after a lot of nagging on my part, she eventually bought a bathing costume and within an hour I had taught her to both swim and float on her back in the warm buoyant water of the Mediterranean. She soon grew to love the water and never looked back after that one lesson. I was also lucky enough to have the opportunity to take the ship's diver course whilst I was stationed in Malta. I had to forfeit a week of my leave to do so but I nevertheless considered it worth my while. I think that the course lasted three weeks; the third week was spent mostly doing night dives, which I found to be particularly interesting.

There are some rather interesting wrecks around Malta, in fact I think that Malta is one of the best places in the world for diving on wrecks, and I know that we were very lucky that the Royal Navy had a diving school there. Some of the wrecks around the islands had been there for more than a thousand years. The fact that the Mediterranean is virtually non-tidal is an obvious help to such preservations, particularly of the ones close inshore. The fact that diving is becoming much simpler now, with the introduction of the more sophisticated (though very easy to use) compressed air diving gear, it now means that more people are able, and can afford, to go diving. Unfortunately this can create a problem from two aspects, the first being that irresponsibility and the lack of adequate training of a diver can lead to would-be rescuers having to risk their lives in a rescue attempt. The second is that some so-called 'divers' are often nothing more than vandals and create unnecessary damage to wrecks that are virtually under water museums. When I took the diving course, the Navy used neat oxygen bottles with their diving equipment, which could be dangerous unless you knew exactly how to handle them. I had to do a conversion course later to be able to use the compressed air equipment, which was obviously much simpler and far safer to use.

I had the idea at one time that my wife did not realise what was meant by a diving course. I got that impression some time after the course was finished when we were out in a boat and she mentioned a wreck in the water, and I told her the name of the ship that was down there. She asked me how I knew and I told her that I had dived on it one night. She produced quite a look of surprise at the information, so I asked her what she thought I was doing during the nights that I had left the house to go diving. We both had quite a laugh about it. I never did get a sensible answer to my question though.

There was no television within the Malta area at that time but there was a forces radio station covering the area, and the Naval Physical and Recreational Training Officer for Malta (P&RTO

Malta) occasionally broadcast about any forthcoming sporting events that concerned the Navy. I was listening to him one evening and he was speaking about a forthcoming boxing event. It was to be the Naval Championships of Malta, and he went on to say that the big disappointment this year was that the reigning Heavyweight Champion from last year would not be boxing, as there were no challengers for him.

The next morning I went into work at the airport, and I had a call from the Master-at-Arms of the authority that covered our department. He and I were quite good friends, and he said that he had just spoken to a very good personal friend of his who was the P&RTO, and he had said how disappointed he was at not being able to get a heavyweight to take on the present incumbent of the heavyweight title. He went on to say, 'He knows you used to box as a professional, but he is really desperate to have a good show this year and not having a heavyweight contest robs the show of a lot of its pulling power.

My reply was, 'Harry, you are a smooth-talking bastard, and you have just talked me into it.' Hell, I hope that I am not still as gullible as I was during that part of my life, though I fear that in fact, I am.

At the time of that suicide mission that I had rather foolishly volunteered for, I was well into my thirties and rather overweight, especially from the boxing aspect. I was doing a lot of swimming at the time, but the type of fitness required for boxing is very much different from that needed for swimming. The boxing tournament was but a few days away however, so it was much too late for me to think about boxing training. If I could not do it by the ability and experience I had acquired over the many pugilistic years that had preceded it, then I felt that it was not going to be done by me. The question on my mind at that moment was, what the hell have you let yourself get talked into on this occasion?

The big night came, and I met my opponent for the first time. I don't think that he was much above my own weight, but unlike me he was carrying not an ounce of fat on him; he was a couple of inches taller than me and obviously had a reach advantage. He was broad round the chest and slim round the waist. In other words, his shape was in complete contrast to my own. He was a leading engineering mechanic, and I should think that every member of the engineering branch in and around Malta must have been there to support him. I had no more than six or eight supporters there, one of them being a very good friend of mine, Will Caruana, the Maltese police sergeant who worked on the same shift as I did at the airport. He was a huge man of about twenty stone, and I thought at the time that I wished I had his weight, but preferably without the fat. My opponent was announced first, and he got a rousing cheer. Then I, being a copper, when my name and rank were announced I got a rousing boo. I thought that this did not augur well if there was a close decision in my favour, (a possible proof that I still had some of the old confidence hanging around, or was I just being over optimistic?).

The bell sounded and I was rather surprised when my opponent rushed across the ring and started to throw punches at me from all angles. It was evident from these first moves that he had taken a good look at my shape and decided that I was going to be easy meat to him, and he intended to finish the job off quickly. I was managing to pick off most of the hooks and swings on my forearms and then I noticed that he did a quick step-back movement with his right foot; and as he replanted the foot on the canvas he almost simultaneously launched a right cross. Fortunately I realised what was happening and reacted with but a split second to spare. It was too late to slip or avoid the punch and my instinct and experience acted virtually as one. I took myself off all forward motion to ride the punch. Because of the sudden onslaught that my opponent had launched, I was still virtually in my own corner and obviously close to the ropes. I had not realised that the ropes were, in fact, not very tight and that there were not the usual holding guides between the three ropes to stop them from parting in an upward or downward direction. The consequence was that I rode that right cross clean through the ropes, between the top and the middle one in fact, and right out of the ring. I bounced once on the apron of the ring and then landed neatly in the laps of three of the ringside spectators. I distinctly remember smelling a feminine-type perfume so one of those three spectators must have either been a woman or a rather gay man.

From the time you are knocked down you have ten seconds to get back to your fighting position, even if that knock-down involves you being ejected from the ring. I think I made it on the count of eight. I was told later that the remainder of the first round was a pretty masterful exhibition of defensive boxing on my part though I do remember getting my left hook working quite late in the round.

Towards the end of the second round my opponent really knew that he was in a proper fight, and I had the feeling that he was beginning to realise that the fight was slipping away from him. His vocabulary of punches was rather limited but he did have that advantage of fitness over me, and he was just about as game as they come. He had but three minutes to show his many supporters how much he wanted to win that contest. It was now physical fitness verses experience and determination, with that most necessary ingredient of all yet to come into play and that ingredient is pride. All the experience or physical fitness in the world is as nothing if you don't have the pride to lift you off the deck when all the odds seem to be stacked against you. I possibly pulled a couple of old pro-type tricks in that third round, like the odd elbow follow-through, but it was nothing too serious and I was not cautioned for a misdemeanour at any time during the fight. I could virtually feel the frustration in my opponent's actions during that last round. All the physical advantages were his but I had tied up his most effective punches, and though I was fast running out of energy he was even more bereft of ideas of how to regain the physical dominance. I could virtually hear his brain ticking over in an effort to produce a new plan of campaign when the bell thankfully called a halt to the exhausting proceedings. I think my opponent still had quite a bit more left in the tank but I had been running on empty for at least a minute. Thank God for the few shots of 'upper cylinder pride and determination' that had been injected in there to keep me going.

I got the verdict and it was greeted with a rousing cheer, which I thought at the time said a lot for the attitude of the average sailor. I suppose the fact that I had been knocked out of the ring in the first round and then crawled back to narrowly win the fight, had gone a long way to getting the spectators on my side. It had been a really hard, relatively close and fairly contested fight and there was not a great deal of point's difference at the end. My opponent came over and embraced me and said, 'I certainly learned something tonight, and it was the hardest fight I have ever had.'

I said, 'If you are going to stay in this sport, son, you are going to find strange donkeys like me raising their heads all along your path, and you have unfortunately just fallen to one at virtually your first hurdle.' I don't think that in the heat of the moment he realised what I had said to him and the most awful and frustrating part of it was that that was the last time I saw him. I would have loved to have explained my thoughts to him and given him my opinion of his abilities. I never heard or saw anything of him after that fight. Perhaps if he reads this he may get in contact with me. I really would love to know how his life progressed after our encounter. The most frustrating part of this incident is the fact that I cannot even remember his name.

The social life in Malta was excellent and we really did enjoy our time out there. We had some smashing Maltese neighbours and fitted in well with the local populace. The Maltese people are really very easy to get on with and we still have quite close friendships amongst them that have reigned for almost half a century. I have been back there and enjoyed many holidays and swum at the same beaches that I have visited for almost sixty years. May it long remain so.

There was one incident that recently came to mind in relation to my shore commission in Malta, and that was that during one of the many social occasions that my wife and I attended, several of the wives stated that they had heard a lot about 'the Gutt' in Valetta but none of them had, as yet, had the opportunity to visit it, or for that matter even to know where the place was. The ladies won the day, or perhaps it would be much more apt to say won the night, and we were soon Valetta bound. We had to park our cars outside the city walls and walk down towards Straight Street, which was the proper name for the Gutt. There were, fortunately, several HM ships in Malta at that time and the Gutt was throbbing with excitement. There was also something of a big ceremonial occasion due to take place the next day and for this reason one of the Army's most famous Scottish pipe bands was in Malta.

Our venture into the Gutt with our ladies justified the warnings we had given them, and several of them had had their bottoms pinched rather hard even before we got to the first bar. A couple of drinks in some of the more notorious bars and then on to the 'Egyptian Queen' and upstairs to the dance floor. One young sailor must have heard my wife talking, and recognising that she was Welsh, he came over for a chat with a fellow national. He eventually asked her to dance but she chickened out on that score, and he then said, 'Well, if you won't dance with me I will ask this young lady in front of me.' The supposed young lady he was talking about was one of the pipe band, who was dressed in his full uniform, which obviously included a kilt (hence his description of 'young lady'). The piper in question must have surely been the biggest piper in the band (possibly in the whole of Scotland) and when he stood up I could see that I was right in the line of fire. In other words, if that big Scotsman had hit the young sailor he would have landed right in my lap. I was shuffling my chair as far out of the possible path of trajectory of the young Welsh sailor as I possibly could, then the huge piper grabbed hold of him, he put his right arm under the sailor's left arm and hugging him to his chest, he then danced him round in a circle dangling like a puppet, his feet being some six inches or so clear of the floor. After a complete circuit of the dance floor, which, fortunately for the young Welshman, was quite small, he was then plonked back into his seat fighting for breath because of the pressure that had been exerted on his chest. Then there was the sound of breaking glass and I saw a chair being lifted above someone's head, so we hustled the women to the stairs and out. That was the last guided tour of the Gutt that our ladies requested to make.

We were eventually due to return home to the UK in the August and I had heard that several people who were able to travel in the summertime had ventured back to the UK by car. My family were very excited about the idea and we discussed this possibility with a friend of mine who was due to return home at the same time. He was a petty officer physical training instructor named Fred Prosser, and like me he had two young children. To save expense we decided that the best way to go about the accommodation aspect of our journey was to take a tent and use the many campsite facilities that were available on the Continent. Luckily both families did some practice camping runs in Malta and ironed out a lot of possible problems. Eventually we said all our goodbyes and boarded the ferry that would transport our cars and our families to Sicily, where the three thousand mile adventure would begin in earnest. It really was the holiday of a lifetime, and the four children of the two families were enjoying every minute of it. We had not intended to travel all the way back to the UK together, in fact we had intended to part company in northern Italy.

Italy is not the easiest place in the world to drive, particularly when you are driving a right-hand drive car on the right side of the road. Italian drivers are world-famous for not giving way to anybody, and these were the two major factors that brought about our parting. It actually happened in Naples. I turned off to the right and Fred Prosser kept on going, and I have not seen hair or hide of them since that time. I know that they got back to the UK okay but I have not seen them in the flesh since that day. The strange part about it was that on many of the days of the week or so that we had spent getting to Naples, we had on several occasions had each other's children in our cars, but as luck would have it, at the time of our unplanned parting both families were fortunately in the right car.

Rome, oh beautiful Rome, that was the first time my wife and I had seen Rome and we both fell in love with it on the first day we were there. It is still my favourite city and I am sure it will always remain so. We were to have stayed in and around Rome for two days but found it so hard to drag ourselves away from the place that we stayed a week. On to Florence, and our planned one-day stay turned into three days, though both my wife and I vowed to return to Florence one day to see the many wonderful things we felt we had missed (We were both lucky enough to have fulfilled that vow long before my wife succumbed to the dreaded breast cancer). On and up through Italy via Pisa.

At the Brenner Pass (between Italy and Austria) we had quite a problem. On the day prior to our arrival at the pass, the Austrian customs officers had been on strike and the border had been closed, so in consequence there was still a long queue to cross the Austrian border at that point. This meant that we were in a traffic queue all the way up the mountain pass, which is 4,495 feet high. The problem that this created was that by the time we actually got to the top, the clutch of my car was screaming like a hyena. Down the other side of the pass and into Austria and across Switzerland, Liechtenstein, up to northern Germany and down through Holland, Belgium and northern France. Our car was then loaded onto an aircraft, and we all flew across the channel to land back in the UK. A long and very rainy drive up to my parents' house in Cheshire. We had travelled three thousand miles, and enjoyed every minute of it. The clutch was still very noisy but the old VW Beetle plodded on for another couple of thousand miles before my eardrums demanded that I do something about it.

I then started my four-year Father Christmas act. That means that for the following four years I moved on a draft just before Christmas. By the time of the fourth and last move to coincide with the festive season, my kids were convinced that Father Christmas came in a suitcase. My first move was to Abbotsinch just outside Glasgow, which at that time was a Naval air station. Within weeks of my arrival we were informed that the place would soon be closed down and be rebuilt as Glasgow Civil airport.

Abbotsinch was not the best draft that I ever had, but I was lucky enough to be able to hire a nice bungalow quite near to Hamden Park Football Ground in Glasgow, and I can still remember hearing the Hamden Park roar when Scotland scored a goal. My wife and I had several Scottish friends who we had met over the years, so our social life was reasonably good. I remember that I had a speeding ticket when driving to work one morning. I was not doing much over the limit, but when the policeman realised that he had stopped a regulating petty officer he really had a good chuckle about it. He was obviously an ex-Naval man who had possibly been put on a charge by some RPO during his service, and he seemed to take great delight in handing me a ticket. I was a bit annoyed that several vehicles passed us going faster than I had been travelling during the time that the policeman was happily writing out my ticket. Thankfully though that was in the days long before licence endorsements, but it did cost me a few pounds in the form of a fine.

One thing that delighted my wife was the wonderful variety and quality of the meat that we were able to buy in Scotland. The Scottish beef in particular was always beautifully presented and most succulent to eat. During the time we had lived in Malta we were not able to get fresh meat anywhere near the quality of the meat we had in Scotland so we were a little gluttonous during the first few weeks.

After the Christmas at Abbotsinch I made enquiries about the possibility of me taking my qualifying dives to keep my diver's logbook up to date. I think that at that time the rule was, each diver had to do at least one hour's diving every month to retain his status as an active diver and to retain his diving pay, which at that time was four shillings (twenty pence) a day. He also had to submit his diver's logbook every quarter for checking by the diving officer. I found that there were several divers serving on the airfield, and I was soon happily on my way to the Gareloch (one of the lochs just outside Glasgow that is used almost exclusively by the Royal Navy) to carry out my dive. I had been very lucky up until that time and all my diving had been carried out in the ideal conditions of the Mediterranean; but the dive in question was to be carried out in January, and January in Scotland is usually very cold. The day in question was no exception; in fact that winter was one of the coldest winters for many years in Scotland. When we had changed into our diving suits and walked to the ladder that we were to use to get into the sea, I noticed that there was ice around the ladder. When seawater freezes it really is cold, and the fact that I had recently returned from the Med meant that I was virtually a tropical flower. I did the dive okay, but had a really hard time clearing my ears when I got to about thirty feet. I spent several minutes holding onto the shot line at that depth, and tried all the known methods of clearance. At last I seemed pretty clear but I was still rather uncomfortable. After getting back onto the ship that we had dived from, I took my hood off to enable me to hear what the other divers were saying and when I did so, blood just seemed to ooze from both my ears. It was naturally a very uncomfortable journey back to Abbotsinch, though by the time I got there the bleeding had virtually stopped.

The Medical Officer had already left the air station by the time we returned from the Gareloch so it was the following morning before I could see him. After the medical staff had spent some time removing the dried blood from my ears the doctor poked his spying instrument in there. He then diagnosed that I had two perforated eardrums. An appointment was made with an ENT consultant ashore in Paisley Hospital for the following week, and I duly kept the appointment. By that time the blood had totally cleared and he had an unhindered picture of the inside of my ear. He proclaimed that the ears were not perforated and that I had had a 'reversed ear', which means that as I removed my hood after returning to the surface, the hood had worked like a toilet plunger in reverse and the action had burst tiny blood vessels in the ear.

I was quite happy with the consultant's findings, and happily returned to Abbotsinch to inform the doctor there that my problem was fortunately not as serious as he had thought and that I had not had eardrum perforations. The doctor was a very tall, dour Scots surgeon commander. His reply to my jubilant news was, 'If I said you had perforations, perforations you had.' I still have a 'hurt certificate' claiming that I had two perforations, so I was not over-worried at the time that I could not do any more diving in that cold loch. They do say, fools rush in where angels fear to tread.

My next move was to HMS *Ganges* near Ipswich on the east coast, which was still operating as a boys' training base. My whole family really enjoyed our time there, as all the families were afforded the use of the facilities such as the swimming pool etc. My first job at *Ganges* was something of a dead end job, as I was in charge of security on the main gate of the establishment. Then after a few months the only RPO who was senior to me left the place, and I took over his job as the Discipline RPO and also President of the mess. From then on I really enjoyed my time at *Ganges* and would have happily spent the rest of my Naval service there.

There was one rather unpleasant task that went hand in hand with the job of Discipline RPO and that was the delivery of the cane to the unruly boys whom the Captain had decreed should receive such punishment. It was only awarded for quite serious offences such as theft, desertion and bullying and was administered in a very formal manner. Having been awarded the punishment, the boy would first be medically inspected. The sentence would be carried out in front of his Divisional Officer, the Master-at-Arms and usually one other senior officer. It was a very formal occasion, almost in the same category as the decapitation of the historical royals that one often sees on the TV, with the exception that the person executing the punishment did not wear a mask. There was a huge oak chair frame that was placed in the centre of the room where the caning took place, and two RPO's used to cross their arms across the offender's back to ensure that he did not move. As the Discipline RPO laid on the strokes of the cane the Master-at-Arms used to count them off until the punishment was completed. The offender was once again medically examined and then sent away to join his class. It goes without saying that he invariably, though one would hope only privately, bared his bottom to the rest of his class to let them see what a neat job I had done.

I had endured such caning myself at the training ship I was on prior to joining the Navy. The caning was just as hard, even if the execution was not quite as formal as it was at *Ganges*. At that time, I could never have possibly dreamt that I would ever be in the position of giving that cane myself. I think that I received the cane on three occasions at that training ship, once for fighting, once for smoking, and for the life of me I cannot remember what the third time was for. The strange thing is that now I am able to smoke without hindrance or punishment, I have no desire to do so and in fact now hate the smell of tobacco smoke.

Caning, as it was done at *Ganges*, although well controlled and carried out very formally and with all due decorum, I still consider rather barbaric, and I was glad that the punishment of caning was withdrawn shortly after I left there. I was, at the time, and for that matter I still am, anti-corporal punishment. I considered it degrading, not only to the people who received it but also to the people who carried it out. However, I do have a very strong opinion on the offence of paedophilia, though I do think that such an offence warrants a much more appropriate sentence than corporal punishment. Paedophilia is in my opinion one of the most hideous crimes imaginable, and its perpetrators ought to be castrated and their testes sewn into a fluorescent plastic bag which should then be strung around the necks of the perpetrators, never to be removed.

During our time at *Ganges* my wife had to go to her parents' home in Swansea for a period due, I think, to a family illness. Whilst she was there she went into the post office to draw her family allowance. The man behind the counter said to her, 'I see from your book that you normally draw your money at Shotley Gate,' which was the post office nearest to *Ganges*. He then went on to tell her that his son had just been discharged from the Navy and he had been serving as a boy at HMS *Ganges* and had had the cane just prior to being discharged. He went on to say that he would like to get his hands on the person that gave him that caning because his bottom was still black and blue when he got home. My wife said that she mumbled a little and then exited as quickly as possible. She obviously knew full well that the post office clerk was unknowingly referring to her husband. A truly very strange coincidence.

There was one incident during one of the canings that I think is worth the recall and that involved one of the two RPOs who, I have already mentioned, had the job of holding the offender whilst the punishment was carried out. The RPO in question was a chap by the name of George Lawrence (know to us as Porky). He really was quite a character, he was the type of person that could keep you alive with the laughter he used to create out of even the worst of circumstances. I had cautioned him on a couple of occasions about looking in the direction that the cane was coming from whilst he was doing his restraining job. The reason for this was because the cane would sometimes bounce and I was afraid that it might catch the restrainer's face. My advice to Porky had obviously fallen on deaf ears as the next time a caning occurred Porky was again facing in the direction of the cane. Then, about halfway through the punishment, one stroke of the cane bounced as I had said it might. The end of the cane caught Porky's glasses just where the hinge attaches to the lens, and the glasses went flying up in the air. Fortunately the cane had not touched Porky's face. The crafty devil asked for, and received, a brand new pair of glasses because of the incident. It certainly had the desired effect of making him face the right way at any future canings though.

Whilst on the subject of Porky Lawrence, he eventually left the Royal Navy on a transfer to the Royal Australian Navy, and because he was in the Naval police branch he was transferred to a civil police ranking system. When he died some two years ago he had reached a very high rank within the police organisation there. I was always sure that he was the type of person who could talk himself into or out of anything, and before he popped his clogs he proved me right. However, I should explain how he came to acquire the nickname Porky. As a boy seaman he was sent out to South Africa on one of the Union Castle liners to join an HM ship in Simon's Town, which is just outside Cape Town. As he was travelling as a passenger he dined with the rest of the civilian passengers and sat with the families, most of whom were travelling with children. Porky always had a very good appetite and during the meal, if any of the children sitting at the table that he was sitting at failed to eat any item of their food, Porky would dig his fork into it and soon polish the food off for them. After a short while the kids got wise to Porky, and by sheer determination they would force their food down rather than see it vanish off their plate and into the ever-open door of Porky's mouth. The parents were delighted with this sudden turnaround in the appetites of their kids and soon other parents were bribing Porky to sit at their table and help in the improvement in their kids' appetites.

Promotion came my way after ten years as an RPO. The exalted rank of master-at-arms was to be mine at last. The promotion was also accompanied by a draft from *Ganges* to the Joint Service Air Trooping Centre in London, which was to take place some four or five weeks after my promotion. The Master-at-Arms who was resident at *Ganges* saw his chance to take all the leave he could fit in during that last month that I was there. I had no grumbles over his scheming however, as it was good for me to get the feeling of being the 'master of my own destiny', as one might say.

Ganges, being a training establishment, was very formal from the point of view of parades and such. Sunday was the biggest parade of the week and was known as 'Sunday Divisions'. Everyone that was still alive attended the Sunday Divisions. There was first a formal inspection, and then a march past which was conducted to the beat of the Royal Marine Band. During the formal inspection the Master-at-Arms led the Captain round all the platoons that were formed up. The dress was also very formal and the Master-at-Arms and all the officers on parade wore their swords. There was a group of seats behind the dais that was taken up by families and visitors, and on the first Sunday Divisions that I acted in my capacity as the master-at-arms my wife and the Commander's wife were sitting together. They were both quite friendly, as they were members of the same wives' club. As I marched up the steps of the dais to report to the Captain that the parade was ready for his inspection, my wife quietly said to the Commander's wife, 'I hope he does not trip over that sword and ruin our married life.' Unfortunately the Commander's wife had a very raucous laugh; the result was that, on hearing her laughter, I almost did trip over my sword. After that incident I think I must have seen the Commander's wife two or three times before I eventually left the place, and each time I noticed the hint of a smile crossing her face. I could not resist returning the smile because I knew what she was smiling about.

Shortly after taking over as the president of the regulating mess I was approached by one of the mess members and asked if I would consider giving my approval to the Royal Marine Band Sergeant joining our mess, as he was not getting on very well with the members of the petty officers' mess. I knew the Band Sergeant and he had always struck me as a pretty good character, so I certainly had no objection to the proposal being put to the mess members at the next mess meeting, and his membership was unanimously accepted. Robbie, the band sergeant, was a good mess member and great company to be with, but there was one very comical incident that will remain for ever in my mind when I think of him. He was one of the world's great practical jokers, and he had pulled several jokes on members of the band, including the Bandmaster. Robbie was a big man and always smartly turned out. He used to lead the band as the drum major with the mace and I have never seen a person who could do the job better than he could. As I have already said the band used to play during divisions, and as the last platoon marched past, the band used to march behind them off the parade ground; they would then wheel to the right and then make a second wheel to the right, led, of course, by big Robbie bearing the mace.

On this one memorable occasion Robbie executed the two right wheels but instead of the band following him in the second right wheel they just marched straight on. It was obvious that everyone in the band was in on the prank and I am sure it was originally dreamt up by the bandmaster, but to see the immaculate Robbie, now carrying his mace in one hand and his topi (pith-helmet) in the other and running to catch up with the band, it was surely one of the funniest sights I have ever seen in my life. I know that several quite senior officers must have seen the incident and I bet they almost split their sides laughing about it when they eventually reached the seclusion of their cabins, but no further comments were made about the incident. Suffice to say that Robbie's practical jokes eased off for several weeks after that incident.

And so on to London, and the Joint Services Air Trooping Centre (JSATC) at what was left of RAF Hendon. The place was already closed as an airfield and it was then used as transit accommodation, a museum and JSATC, as already stated. There was quite a large number of service personnel actually working there in various capacities. The Master-at-Arms was classified as a warrant officer and as all commissioned and warrant officers used to have to do duty orderly officer, I was part of that roster. One of the duties of the orderly officer was to go around the dining hall at meal times and ask if there were any complaints. I had not even an inkling of what I would have done if someone had complained about his meal, so thank the devil that no one ever did. The ceremony of morning and evening colours when the RAF flag was hoisted and lowered, was also quite a funny occurrence too. On several occasions when I was the orderly officer, the duty non-commissioned officer would be an army sergeant. So an army man would hoist or lower the RAF flag whilst a sailor (me) would stand there in charge and do the necessary saluting. It certainly had all the hallmarks of a 'rag-tag and bob-tail' organisation.

After a few weeks of waiting I was given a married quarter just outside of the airfield, and as there was a very good social life and a very friendly atmosphere in the mess. I was quite happy to be there – though I was sure my stay would not last for very long, as there was surely a ship somewhere on the horizon with my name on it. My job was taking charge of what was known as the Inbound Traffic Office. I had a staff of about six, possibly seven. They were all men and taken from all three services. Apart from the staff that cleared the paperwork for flights in and out of the country, there were three watches (or shifts) operating from JSATC Hendon, which both met and despatched flights from the two major London airports. Each of these shifts was led by an RPO, and all the shifts operated from the Inbound Traffic Office, so the shifts obviously spent more time in my office than my staff and I did.

Shortly after my arrival at JSATC, I returned to my office one morning to find that all the office stapling machines had vanished, and as staples were a very necessary method of keeping our paperwork together I was infuriated. The next opportunity I had to get the three shift leaders together I gave them a right rollicking and told them that I wanted all my office stapling machines back in the office by the following Monday morning, and that in future no stationery or office implements were to be removed from the Inbound Traffic Office. I further decreed that any further problems of a similar nature would result in the shift leaders running their shifts from outside in the corridor.

I had had a very enjoyable and affable weekend and I returned to my office in a rather joyous mood on that Monday morning, only to be met be a relative mountain of stapling machines in the centre of my desk. I soon realised that every desk and organisation in the two major airports must have been totally denuded of their stapling machines.

The three RPOs were all very experienced policemen and they were all fully aware of the fact, and no doubt elated, that they had put one over on the master-at-arms. However I left a note (grudgingly hinting at submission on my part) suggesting that the stapling machines should be returned to their rightful owners. My desk was, fortunately, soon denuded of the said machines. I have had many drinks and a whole heap of laughs over that incident when I have again met the culprits (the shift leaders) in the years that followed. In fact I still have a pang of conscience when I look at the stapling machine that adorns my desk as I type this story. It was on the top of the said pile of machines on my desk at Hendon. I often wonder if, at times, it now feels lonely, having been on its own for almost forty years and having once enjoyed the company of such a large number of its relatives.

Unfortunately it was not long, however, before a very much bigger fly landed in our 'ointment jar'. The RAF Movements Section in Aden began to get rather nasty problems. Insurrection had broken out in the Aden area and 'revolutionary gunmen' were popping up everywhere. Aircraft were even being fired on as they took off and landed, and in consequence flight manifests first became illegible and then often non-existent.

I sent several signals in an effort to alleviate my problem, but the situation became even worse. I eventually saw the Station Commanding Officer. He signed and sent a signal in his name, but no noticeable improvement occurred. The Commanding Officer was a wing commander RAF; he was originally from Australia, and because I had been to North Sydney where he had once lived, we had had several friendly conversations. There was a pretty good social life at RAF Hendon between the officers' mess and our mess so I often met the CO socially, and he really was very good company. This was certainly luck on my part because he must have had a problem trying to pacify the airlines, who by now were owed several hundred thousand pounds, with an obstinate master-at-arms refusing to pay them, or at least to clear the documentation that would have enabled them to get paid.

Things were fast getting worse in Aden, from the fighting aspect that is, and the paperwork from RAF Aden was now virtually non-existent. The television news was full of the armed insurrection. One of the rebels' favourite ploys was apparently to throw grenades into army and RAF trucks, and several people were killed in that manner. One day I received an urgent phone call from the CO's office, and I was instructed to present myself there forthwith. On arrival, the CO said, 'I have thought of a way of solving our Aden problem, Mr Dale.'

I said, 'That will be a great relief, Sir, how do you propose to do it?'

'I am going to send someone out there to sort it out,' he said; 'I want you to go and pack a few things and we will get you onto a flight that will be leaving for Aden in three hours' time.'

I was living in an RAF married quarter that was fortunately within a few hundred yards of the CO's office. I dashed home and asked my wife to help me pack enough gear for a week as I was off to Aden post-haste. Having just watched the news and seen what a problem there was in Aden, she merely sat in a chair and laughed, thinking that I was pulling a great practical joke. I spent several minutes explaining that if this was a practical joke, it was the CO's joke, not mine.

It is a long haul flight to Aden, and in my case it was not the most comfortable. The anticipation of me, a sailor, travelling around the Aden Protectorate lecturing the RAF on flight passenger manifests filled me with a foreboding bordering on dread. It seemed akin to me receiving a lecture on rope splicing from an RAF policeman. It was rather fortunate that I had had a previous job working with the RAF. At least I had some idea of the possible pitfalls. Nevertheless, I looked on it with great trepidation.

The 'jungle drums' went to work almost as soon as the plane landed and within minutes I was met by the Master-at-Arms of the Naval Shore Patrol, who was able to transport me to the Services Transit Accommodation. As we boarded the Landrover he said to me, 'If I say jump, get out of the vehicle as soon as you possibly can.' I replied, 'If somebody throws a hand-grenade in here, Wiggy, I guarantee that you will be the second bastard out of this bloody vehicle, my old mate.'

The reception I received was somewhat better than I had anticipated it would be, with the possible exception of the Air Commodore. He had the rather rare ability of being verbally pleasant whilst looking down his nose at what, to him, was a maggot on a piece of rotten cheese. Fortunately my time in his presence was limited by his busy schedule, and I was glad to leave his office. I was pleased that I would not have to submit the final report on my conclusions to him.

My visit afforded me some comprehension of the problems that the RAF staff had in trying to sort out a passenger problem whilst often under sniper fire, and I must admit to holding back a smile when they promised to do better in the future. I left after about five days, and I think that the visit could best be summed up by the way things went at our flight boarding. I was the last to board the flight, which had to be done at the double (running) for obvious reasons. The rushed goodbyes were accompanied by the presentation to me of a rather tatty large brown envelope. *Joy*, I thought, *masters-at-arms rarely get farewell presents.*

After being shown to my VIP seat (that should have raised some strange suspicion in me at once, because there were several passengers on board who were senior in rank to myself). I spent a few minutes getting my breath back. Then I opened the large brown envelope and there I found a very scruffy and dog-eared list of passengers. There were a lot of crossings out and alterations, and pinned to this list was an obviously hurriedly handwritten note which said, 'You are the Officer I/C Flight. Sorry we were unable to complete and verify this manifest, we would appreciate you checking all the passengers on the flight during the passage to the UK and make any necessary amendments to the list. Much appreciated, thanks' (signed with a totally illegible signature). In other words, 'We have no idea who the hell we have thrown onto this bloody aeroplane but we would like you to sort it out for us.'

Two hours of work and the personal checking and identifying of everyone on the flight ensured that I was able to place in my office in-tray the first totally correct manifest to have arrived from Aden in many weeks. The said in-tray had filled to capacity, nay, overflowing in my absence and it kept me busy for several days. During the week after my return three flights had arrived from Aden, and the manifests were in a worse state than the one that had been handed to me prior to my flight home. The CO of Hendon obviously wanted to know how things had gone during my trip to Aden, and if I was finding any improvement in their documentation. I assured him that all was fine and I cleared every Aden flight post-haste. I thought, *hell to the bloody paperwork, the last place I want to go back to is Aden.*

Within a few weeks of my return, I received notice of my pending draft to a missile destroyer. Further enquiries established that the ship I was due to join had been allotted the 'joyful' task of leading a flotilla of ships whose job was going to be to cover the Aden area for a period of at least three months whilst all British forces were being withdrawn, and then to turn the place over to a government made up of the local populace. In other words, they were being given their independence. Anyone who has been to Aden knows that I must have enjoyed that part of the seagoing commission in the same way I would have enjoyed attending a party in a cage full of lions. I well remember standing on the bridge of the destroyer, watching the last of the aircraft taking off and wondering, *what poor bloody fool is going to sort out their passenger manifest?* Perhaps I could have saved them the job by firing one of our missiles at the airfield runway. Then all the personnel would have had to go home by sea and, as the Suez Canal was closed during that period, there would have been plenty of time to get their manifest right as they sailed round the Cape of Good Hope. Some bloody hope!

There was a very sad happening on my last duty as the duty orderly officer at RAF Hendon. In the early hours of the morning I received a phone call from the civilian doctor who covered the medical aspect of the place. He told me to get around to the Commanding Officer's house as soon as I could, but he would not tell me over the phone what the problem was. I had never met this doctor, but his plea had sounded very urgent. I decided to run to my house and get my own car to go to the CO's house, which was about a mile off the airfield. When I got there the civilian doctor was waiting for me at the front door of the house, and he said, 'The CO woke up about half an hour before I arrived here and found that his wife was dead alongside him in the bed. He phoned me and I have pronounced her dead, but I have several more calls to make, so as you are the orderly officer the problem is now yours.' He then got into his car and left. I walked into the house, and the CO was sitting in a chair in the living room. He was sobbing profusely and because the room was rather cold he was shivering. I had no idea of the heating facilities of the house, so I went up stairs and into the bedroom where the CO's wife was. I took the bedclothes off her, carried them downstairs and wrapped them around the CO to keep him warm. I then put the electric kettle on and made him a hot drink whilst thinking of my next move. My head cleared a little, and I phoned the RAF Hendon telephone exchange, and asked if they had the phone number of the Squadron Leader who was the Second-in-Command of RAF Hendon. My call to him was, 'Sir, this is Master-at-Arms Dale, the orderly officer of RAF Hendon, speaking. I am requesting that you get around to the CO's house as soon as you can get here.' All he replied was, 'I will be there within minutes, Mr Dale.' He was as good as his word; he actually did get there within minutes, and I turned the problem over to him on the doorstep in much the same way as the doctor had turned it over to me.

I drove back to my house, parked the car outside in its normal parking space and walked back to the orderly officers' room. I tried in vain to sleep off the couple of hours that were left of my duty, but all to no avail. After doing my job at Morning Colours and then turning over to my successor, I walked around to my house to find that my wife was in a state of deep apprehension and nervous tension because she had seen our car being driven away in the early hours of the morning. We had no telephone in the house at that time, so she had had one of the most miserable nights of her life and had not been able to contact anyone. She was also obviously too scared to venture outside. By the time I got home she was almost at the stage of a mental breakdown. Fortunately she was a person with very strong powers of recovery from such incidents.

My departure to join my ship occurred just a couple of days after the above incident so I was not able to see the CO again; I really would have liked to have conveyed my condolences to him personally, because he was one truly very likeable person. I did, however, receive a phone call from his deputy thanking me and commending me for what he considered was very sensible, tactful and sensitive action that I had taken. I replied that I considered the CO to be a friend, and any friend of mine deserved, and would always receive, any help and consideration that I was able to give them.

Bowel Movements

Doctor, I've got a big problem, and I'm now in a worrying state,
I have a bowel movement each morning, just after half past eight.
The doctor said I was lucky, regular bodily functions are fine.
'That's not so in my case,' I told him, ''cause I never get up until
nine.'

Beer Reservations

It was a crummy old pub he had stopped at but he needed to use
their loo,
He thought he would order a pint whilst there as they sold his
favourite brew.
The clientele looked a rough lot so he thought of a good idea,
He left a note by the side of his drink, saying, 'I've spit in this pint
of beer.'
He returned to find another note which said, 'I'll be honest and tell,
Whilst you were away relieving yourself I spit in your beer as well.'

Henry the Hunter

A gorilla escaped from the circus,
And he'd climbed up a very high tree.
There was only one man to sort it all out,
And that had to be Henry McGee.

Henry arrived with his little dog, Dan,
A shot gun and a big heavy net.
He asked the constable to hold onto the gun,
Saying, 'It isn't needed just yet.'

Henry said, 'I'll climb up in the tree,
And I'll shake all the branches I can.
When the gorilla falls down from the treetop.
It will then be up to Dan.

'Dan will grab the ape by its testes,
I can assure you he will never let go.
Until you have trapped the ape in the net
He'll hang on and withstand any blow.'

'Does the dog ever fail?' asked the copper.
Henry said, 'Well he's never failed yet.'
'Then tell me, what the hell is the gun for,
As well as the dog and the net?'

'I'll tell you what you need the gun for,'
Said Henry, his expression agog.
'If I am the first to fall out of the tree,
For heaven's sake, shoot the dog.'

English Confusions

English as it is spoken is truly a very strange tongue,
No wonder that other nationals so often get things wrong.
For instance, just take sweetmeats, they are nothing to do with meat,
In fact the meats in question are sugar-coated sweets.
Sweetbreads, you must all agree, just don't hold bread at all,
They're made from the glands of little calves, as I do recall.

The plural of tooth, as the English know, is the familiar word of teeth,
So why is the plural of booth not pronounced as beeth?
I would like to double up on an order I've just placed for a goose,
But if I used the plural gooses that would be no use.
The English language certainly has some very strange uses,
When you realise that the plural of mongoose is actually mongooses.

When the stars are *out* they twinkle and the sky is glowing bright,
But we can't see a hand in front of us when *we* put *out* the light.
The temperature is also confusing, we say it is *hot* or *cold* as hell,
And our nose is sometimes running whilst our feet can often smell.
And if vegetarians eat vegetables and never turn to meat,
For heaven's sake please tell me, what do humanitarians eat?

CHAPTER NINE

Joining the missile destroyer HMS *London* was truly the highlight of my Naval career. I considered that I really had reached the pinnacle of everything that I wanted in life at that point. She was the ideal ship from a master-at-arms's point of view. She was 6,200 tons, and had a ship's company of a little over 600 officers and men. She could not have been better from my point of view even if I had had the pleasure of designing her myself. My cabin was well laid out, and tucked away in a secluded part of the ship just aft of the operations room. The combined regulating and mail office was in the canteen flat, which was virtually the centre of the ship. The ship was really well air-conditioned, though I will stress that the main reason for the air conditioning was to hold the ship's internal air pressure above the external air pressure in a defence against nuclear fallout. Nevertheless, it served to make the atmosphere in the ship very comfortable to live in.

Almost as soon as I reached the top of the gangway, the Master-at-Arms that I was to relieve ushered me into the Captain's cabin to be introduced to the Captain. I was later told that he was the first non-British born man to have made the rank of full captain in the Royal Navy for many years. The reason for that was that as a very young Naval officer in the Polish Navy he had taken over a Polish destroyer and escaped to the UK with the ship from virtually right under the noses of the Nazis who were occupying his country. After that daring exploit he then evidently had an excellent war record during the whole of the Second World War.

It struck me as very strange that the Captain should want to see the master-at-arms almost before he had stepped onto the ship, but I should have realised that the Captain had had my predecessor court-martialled whilst the ship was in South Africa only weeks previously, and that master-at-arms was subsequently demoted to leading patrolman. The master-at-arms who was on the ship at the time that I joined her (who happened to be a good friend of mine) had been sent out on a very temporary basis, virtually just to bring the ship home.

The very first thing that the Captain said to me was, 'I see from your records that you were on HMS *Apollo* (the fast minelayer). Was that when she had the mutiny?'

I said, 'No it was not, Sir, and had I been aboard her at the time, I am confident that that mutiny would not have occurred.'

To which he replied, 'That is very good, Master-at-Arms.' He asked me several more questions, and I believe that I gave the kind of answers that he wanted to hear. During that rather short interview I gained an almost instant respect and liking for the man, and although we only served some six or seven months together I was sure that the feeling was reciprocal. I was really sorry to see him leave the ship. He figures very high on my list of good captains. He was later promoted to rear admiral but unfortunately given the 'golden bowler' (retired from active Naval service) at the same time. It was a great pity; I am sure he would have made a very fine admiral of the fleet.

I had similar luck as far as the Executive Officer was concerned, and I knew almost as soon as we met that we would get along well together. He was of commander rank, which was warranted because of the size of the ship's company. He had joined the ship very shortly before me, so we virtually leant on each other for our first couple of weeks aboard. The second day I was on board, the Commander said he was about to swot up on how to form a welfare committee. (Fortunately he was fully aware that it was his duty to be the chairman of such a committee.)

I said, 'You can forget that, Sir; the rules concerning such committees are contained in the Queen's Regulations and

Admiralty Instructions, and I am the one whose job it is to organise such elections.' He was no doubt relieved at having that chore taken off him, and I must say that organising a welfare committee proved to be something of a laborious task. In several of the messes there were no volunteers putting their names forward, which meant that I spent a lot of time finding out who the more 'gabby' members of those messes were and then talking them into volunteering to join the committee. After a couple of weeks the committee had been fully formed, and I proudly presented the list of members to the Commander. He was quite jubilant, and told me to organise a meeting for the following Friday, at which I should be there in attendance. I was most surprised by this instruction, and stated that I considered that I would be one of the last people that the committee members would want to see. The Commander said, 'Look, Master-at-Arms, you were the one who organised this committee, so I want you to be there to see that it gets off on the right footing. You will not need to speak, but you should just view the proceedings.' I think that the four and a half hours that the meeting lasted was one of the most boring periods of my life, and I could see that the Commander was fully aware of my feelings. So from that moment on, if the Commander and I had a small difference of opinion, his face would invariably break into a smile and he would say, 'Any more of that, Master-at-Arms, and you will be attending a welfare committee meeting again.' He knew that he had me over a barrel on that one.

We headed south, first for a short stop in Gibraltar and then on down the west coast of Africa bound for Cape Town. Just off the Western Horn of Africa we cruised through the largest shoal of hammerhead sharks that I have ever seen. It must have been the mating season for sharks, and there seemed to be nothing but sharks as far as the eye could see. The one thing for sure was that 'Hands to bathe' was out of the question at that time. The reason we were heading for Cape Town was because we were making our way to Aden, and at the time the Suez Canal was closed due to the fact that it had been filled up with wrecks during one of the Arab – Israeli wars.

My very first visit to South Africa, and we actually berthed at the Naval base of Simon's Town, just a few miles outside Cape Town. What a lovely and friendly reception we had there. It was during the time of apartheid in South Africa, and we were all warned not to discuss politics and apartheid principles in particular. We had about three or four ratings on board with brown-coloured skin, and I was quite concerned as to what the situation would be towards them. I am pleased to say that my concern soon acquired a ready-made answer. A messenger arrived at my office door virtually within minutes of the ship securing to the jetty. The messenger was from the Officer of the Watch who was at the head of the brow, and he was escorting a very large coloured man. The messenger said, 'The Officer of the Watch asked if you could help this gentleman, Master-at-Arms.' After a very warm and friendly smile and very firm handshake, the gentleman introduced himself as the foreman of the stevedores and asked if there were any coloured sailors on board. I told him that I had several and if he would like to meet them I could quite easily get hold of them for him. His smile broadened and soon he was chatting to my entire ship's compliment of brown-skinned sailors. They were all invited to his club, and he assured them that they would really enjoy themselves. They evidently all took him up on his offer, and after we had left there and were well on our way to Aden, each of them called at my office and told me that they had had the time of their lives. It made me feel rather jealous and disgruntled about the pasty-coloured appearance of my skin.

So, on up the east coast of Africa and on to Aden. I am sure that the period whilst the ship was there at the closing down and British withdrawal from the Aden Naval base was the busiest period of my entire Naval career. I worked some sixteen hours a day, every day, for the whole period of almost four months that we were engaged on that task. Sailors, like anyone else in the world, can be very troublesome when they are bored, and troublesome sailors are the ones that cause a great deal of extra work for, and a bad reflection on, the master-at-arms, so I made it my sworn task to keep them occupied in some form or other. I have yet to mention that the ship was equipped with closed-circuit television (black and white only though) with one TV set in each of the messes. This meant that we could run TV quiz shows, interviews and all the other stupid programmes that one saw on the TV at that time. The ship's company must have got really fed up looking at my face on the TV though. Their bad luck on that score was even further compounded when they ventured onto the upper deck only to find that I was running a tug o' war or some other outdoor activity.

There is one little point about Aden that I ought to mention at this stage, and that is that when I was there on my visit from JSATC Hendon I had spoken to an RAF helicopter pilot who was stationed there, who had offered his car for sale at one of the local garages and was willing to let it go for a pittance of its actual value. The garage owner had stated that within weeks, the local population would have all the cars they wanted, when the British left and were unable to take their cars with them. The pilot said to me, 'they are going to have to do a lot of climbing if they want to use my bloody car after I leave Aden.' Sure enough, whilst we were monotonously churning up the sea off Aden (the ship was acting very much like a guardsman outside Buckingham Palace), through our binoculars we espied a car perched high on one of the mountains. It could have only got to that position if it had been dropped from a helicopter. I had a wry chuckle to myself when I realised what that pilot had meant.

One of the hundreds of quiz questions that I asked during this monotonous period of time outside Aden was, how did the British try to cover up their use of radar during the Second World War, so that the Germans would not realise how advanced our radar actually was? I had acquired the question and the answer from some rather tatty and very old quiz book. The supposed answer was that the information fed to the Germans was that all our aircrews were fed on carrots, which were reputed to enhance their night vision. This simple question and subsequent answer raised more debate than any of the other anti-boredom projects in which I took part. I believe that someone even wrote to the BBC in an effort to get an authenticated answer to settle the dispute, but a reply was not received. Perhaps the powers that be are still debating it.

After being continuously at sea for a period of four months, at last our sojourn covering Aden came to an end and we headed for, and secured to, a mooring buoy in Mombasa harbour in Kenya, for the benefit of a 'self-maintenance period'. Each watch was to be given five days' local leave. Once ashore, a group of some eight or nine of us hired a minibus and off we went around the National Parks and the foothills of Mt. Kenya. During our passage through one of the National Parks, we had a slight mishap whilst crossing one of the several rivers, as the supposed ford was rather deeper than we had anticipated; unfortunately this resulted in most of our food being spoiled. However, we were able to rescue all of the canned food, although the cans had suffered the misfortune of losing their paper labels due to the soaking they had received (paper labels were the only ones in vogue at the time). After visiting Nairobi we started the long drive back to Mombasa, and as evening fell we decided to stop and cook our remaining food. As we started to open the label-less cans, someone had the bright idea of throwing all the contents into one pan – in fact it was the only one we had, it was a large billycan. The resulting concoction was to have been a sort of pot-mess, but as we carried on opening the cans we could see that most of them contained baked beans. It was beans, beans and even more beans; however the fresh air had sharpened our appetites, and every morsel was eaten. Unfortunately, and despite all the windows being open, the flatulence created by such a large quantity of beans made the atmosphere inside the minibus almost unbearable as the overworked alimentary canals of all the passengers joined together in a noisy and very smelly chorus.

Most of us in the minibus were able to drive, which meant that after about an hour of driving we could then sit back for several hours and enjoy the scenery as passengers. The roads in the area were pretty awful and as I took my turn at the wheel darkness had begun to fall. For the first time during our five-day journey, the cloud base had completely covered the moon, throwing all around us into pitch darkness. The lights on the minibus were almost non-existent; their weak beams strained to penetrate the overwhelming darkness of the road ahead. Unable to drive with confidence I therefore slowed to walking pace, albeit slow but sure. As to what happened next I cannot give a logical explanation. There we were, in the middle of the jungle, surrounded by impenetrable darkness, when I was overcome by a feeling of extreme unease. I just felt that there was something on the road in front of me. I switched off the engine then got out of the driving seat and stepped down onto the road. I strained both my eyes and ears to give some credence to this feeling of trepidation. I could hear or see nothing, so slowly and uneasily I climbed back into the driving seat. My stomach was still virtually churning with a feeling of apprehension. Inside the minibus the dozing passengers were beginning to stir. Someone shouted, 'We are still in the middle of bloody jungle, so what the hell have we stopped for?' Several other even more factious remarks were made and totally disregarded by me. I just could not release myself from the deep feeling of apprehension, nor could I bring myself to switch on the engine and drive on any further. I just sat there wrestling with that strange feeling. Then the moon suddenly broke through the cloud and we were once again able to see the road ahead of us. Standing in that road was a most magnificent bull elephant with his herd around him. He then nonchalantly turned to his right and quietly led his herd back into the jungle. Everyone in the bus was fully awake by this time and we were all in awe at what we had seen. Someone said, 'Surely you must have seen or heard something?'

I know that I had had no visual or hearing perception of the presence of that herd of elephants, and had no physical intimation of anything untoward. I had had nothing other than a very strange feeling that something was amiss. What scared the hell out of me was not the fact of the elephants being there or the possibility that there could have been a very tragic accident, but the fact that something that I could not account for had, for some reason, stopped me from being a part of that possible accident. I am not a man of strong religious beliefs but whichever way I look at it, I feel sure that some divine act of providence raised a hand that evening. However, I felt it best to keep those thoughts to myself, and to hold my tongue and not dwell on the matter.

Shortly after our return to the ship, the 'radar and carrot' question came to prominence once again. Those who had been in the minibus claimed that if there was a specific vegetable that was able to enhance vision, carrots were out and baked beans were in. Thereafter, that became a standing joke on the ship, up until she 'paid off' many months later.

To sea again, this time back down the east coast of Africa and yet another most welcome visit to Simon's Town on the Cape. A few of us took advantage of a weekend leave and went upcountry for a camping weekend on one of the large farms. I think it would be really more appropriate to have called it a large vineyard as their main crop seemed to be grapes. It was owned by an English couple, and she had been quite a famous broadcaster in the UK, but for the life of me I cannot remember her name. The foreman on the farm was a Boer (Afrikaner). He was well into his seventies but was still a large and powerfully built man; he was a smashing chap to us, but oh how badly he treated the coloured workers on the farm. He carried a stick with him at all times and certainly did not hesitate to use it on the workers. Having seen such behaviour, it makes me wonder how South Africa managed to achieve such a peaceful transition from apartheid to democracy. The white population of South Africa certainly have a lot to thank Nelson Mandela for.

Across the wide Atlantic, and yet another visit to Bermuda. I think that during the five or more years that I spent on board HMS *London*, we must have visited Bermuda at least five times. It is, nevertheless, a nice place to be, but as a master-at-arms I found one very big problem from the aspect of discipline. That was the fact that it was so easy to hire small motorbikes there, and most of the sailors on the ship took advantage of that mode of travel. I remember seeing an American film called *Mister Roberts*, starring James Cagney and Henry Fonda. James Cagney was the captain of a US Naval supply ship, and when, after a very long period of sea time, he reluctantly gave shore leave, several of the sailors returned on motorbikes and rode them right off the end of the jetty and straight into the water. There is a very strong possibility that the person who wrote the script for that film was in Bermuda during a visit by HMS *London*. I think he really should have contributed something to our ship's welfare fund for acquiring the basic idea from our sailors.

The Royal Navy's liaison with the civilian police in Bermuda was always very good, and if any sailors committed an offence ashore whilst we were there, the police would turn them over to the ship to be tried by our captain. The consequence of that was that my typewriter would be red hot with the work I put it to on producing charge sheets. It was times like that when I thanked my lucky stars that I had had the good sense to teach myself to touch type during quieter times in previous years.

Several of the civilian police in Bermuda were British police who had been seconded there for a period of a few years, and they would invariably come on board when the ship was there in Hamilton harbour, if for no other reason than to acquire a pint of British beer in our mess. I think that it was the first time that the ship was there when I was warned about the civilian postman by the police. In those days homosexuality was considered to be a very serious offence, and the civilian postman who liaised with our own postman on all aspects of mail was a known homosexual. I warned our postman about the problem, and consequently thought nothing further about the matter. At the time in question homosexuality had taken on a very serious connotation in the Navy, because shortly prior to the time I am writing about there had been a serious case of espionage by a British member of the embassy staff in Moscow, who had been blackmailed into giving away very vital British secrets after being compromised by the Russian KGB, who had obviously acquired photographs of him involved in homosexual acts.

Several months after I left HMS *London* I learned that several of the sailors who had been in Bermuda on the ship, had been arrested and were under investigation by our own Special Investigation Branch. Evidently the flat of the civilian postman in Bermuda had been raided by the police there, though I did hear that the offence for which the raid was made was unrelated to his homosexuality. The consequential search had produced wads of photographs; many of them were of sailors in compromising situations, and several of the sailors were men from HMS *London*. I remembered all the sailors who I was told were involved, and none of them were homosexual. In truth they had all gone to the flat under the promise of free booze, and were obviously all shot away with the booze when the photographs were taken. The one aspect of it that rather annoyed and upset me was that one of the sailors concerned was our former ship's postman. He was not the one that I had cautioned about the civilian postman and had, in fact, taken over the job long after I had issued my caution, but I never thought to continue carrying out the warnings during the following years when we visited Bermuda on several occasions. In fact I had virtually forgotten about the warning I had received years previously.

There were about ten or twelve sailors involved in those investigations (not all from HMS *London*) but no charges were made against any of them. They were just unceremoniously thrown out of the Navy. A couple of them were only a few years away from going out on pension. They were all discharged from the Navy as 'services no longer required'. I was surprised that none of them got around to appealing against the action that had been taken. To my knowledge, none of them did. They possibly considered the embarrassment it would have caused to their families had they done so, and considered it better to let sleeping dogs lie.

Some weeks after the above incident, I had a phone call from our former postman, who asked if he might come to see me on a subject that he was not prepared to talk about over the telephone; I said that I would be happy to see him at any time convenient to himself. He had been an excellent postman whilst he had been part of my staff on HMS *London*, and I had felt all along that he had had a raw deal over the way he had been thrown out of the Navy. I found during the interview, his problem was that he had applied for a job with British Gas, but because of the way he had been just thrown out of the Navy, he had no record of previous good conduct to produce at the job interview. In consequence, I wrote him a glowing, and totally truthful, report that he had been very good at his job and had proved himself to be both honest and reliable. The report was made to look very pukka because it bore the official stamp of the fleet master-at-arms. Several weeks later I received a phone call from him thanking me for my efforts and informing me that he had been accepted for the job he had applied for and was then undergoing a course with British Gas. That was the last time I heard from him. I sincerely hope that all went well for him from that time on.

Returning to the HMS *London* period of my Naval career. I had been to most parts of the world, including several parts of South America, but by some strange chance I had never been to the United States. I am delighted to announce that that omission was now to be rectified, and we put into the US Naval base at Charleston in the state of Carolina. We were in that area to cover the West Indies during the period in question, and I suppose that our visit to Charleston had some NATO connotation; but that aspect mattered not the slightest to the sailors on our ship. We could not have been better received by the local populace. Invites came from all and sundry and the whole ship's company surely enjoyed themselves. The chief petty officers' mess in the base would have been better described as a first-class club; it had a wonderful restaurant and all the other accoutrements needed for a high standard men's club, making us Brits feel like really poor relations.

The first night that we were in Charleston, our mess invited several of the more senior members of the US Navy chief petty officers' mess and their ladies on board our ship for drinks. It was a most enjoyable occasion and greatly enhanced our already firmly held relationship.

The following morning I was sitting in my office and reflecting on the wonderful atmosphere created so far during our visit, when the President of one of the ship's chief petty officers' messes came to the office and asked to speak to me privately. I cleared the office of the staff and asked him what the problem was. He told me that one of his mess members had acted in a rather disorderly manner in the chief petty officers' mess ashore in the base the previous night, and that he had ordered him to return to the ship forthwith. He had furthermore instructed him that, because of his behaviour, he would be on duty on board for the remainder of our time in Charleston.

Not one of our sailors had put a foot wrong, the only snag we had had was from a chief petty officer. I was furious about the situation, however, the President of the mess who had come to see me was a first-class man and out of respect for him I decided not to speak to his offending mess member. I did decide, however, that I should go to see the President of the chief petty officers' mess in the base and convey my apologies personally.

By the time that I had cleared my problems of the morning it was almost noon, so I hurried ashore with the express purpose (to use an American idiom) of 'eating crow'. At this point in the story, I will make the bold statement that at that stage of my life, I very rarely partook of alcoholic drink, and never drank during the day. (All right, things have changed a little since then). The President of the chief petty officers' mess in the base was a most affable fellow who seemed to wear a permanent smile, or perhaps one could better describe it as a 'chuckle'. The whole mess committee was called over to be introduced to me, but before I had shaken hands with the last committee member, the bar in front of us was full of drinks. I then realised that I was way out of my league as far as the drinking was concerned. I just wished that I had had the good sense to bring the buffer (Chief Bosun's Mate) with me, knowing that he was the one man who could have held his own in such company. However, one has to show willing and after quaffing a fair quantity of the drinks and then making a whole bucketful of excuses, I returned to the ship with a slow and rather unsteady gait. I felt that I had climbed a mountain when I eventually reached the chair in my office and I was happy to collapse into it like the proverbial sack of crap. One of the staff asked me a question, but try as I might, I could not formulate the words to make a comprehensible reply. I then scraped enough sense together to realise that I might make something of a fool of myself by sitting in the office, so I was straining again to acquire an upright posture in order to retreat to my cabin when the office phone rang. The call was from the Commander, who stated that he wanted to see a defaulter on a case that had been stood over for several days awaiting a piece of vital evidence that had now become available.

I instructed one of my staff to get hold of the defaulter and his defending officer, whilst I descended to my cabin to sluice my face with cold water. On my return to the office, the defaulter, his defending officer and the appropriate charge sheet were awaiting me, and I sallied forth with dread to meet the Commander. The defaulter was called up to the Commander's table, and I used every ounce of my willpower in an attempt to pronounce the words in the charge properly, but it seemed that the harder I tried the worse I sounded. I can remember the defending officer looking at me out of the corner of his eye. I was sure that it was a look of complete disdain.

The appropriate punishment was awarded, and I walked slowly away from the Commander's table, expecting him to say something, but he did not speak. I got back to my office and slumped into my chair. I was thinking of the certain rollicking I would deservedly receive the following morning. I threw the charge sheet into a drawer and was about to leave the office when I was met at the door by the Surgeon Lieutenant. He pulled me gently to one side and quietly said, 'If you are going up to see the Commander, you can forget it, because we brought him from the officers' mess in the base about half an hour ago and I can tell you that he will not be resurfacing for the rest of the day.' I said, 'Well, someone had bloody well better tell the Commander that, Doc, because he finished his defaulters' table about two minutes ago.'

The doctor's jaw dropped almost to his knees. 'Hell,' he said quietly as he walked away. 'I have never seen him drink as much as he did today, he must have a sponge in his bloody stomach.'

The following morning I made my usual morning report to the Commander and noticed that his eyes were about as bleary looking as the ones above the chin that I had shaved that morning. Not a word was spoken about the previous afternoon.

A sad departure from the US and the ship then strove on around several of the West Indian Islands, mostly to just show the flag. I have to say that I used to love travelling between the West Indian islands. I think that we all used to enjoy the friendly atmosphere there, though some of the islands were much more friendly than others. I have to say that Jamaica could present problems, and one had to be especially careful there during the hours of darkness. Barbados was always one of my favourites. I remember one incident in the most famous nightclub on the island. The club was called Harry's Nightery, and it really was a hot club with a truly great and friendly atmosphere. One night the club was full almost to bursting point, and I would have thought just about all our ship's company, with the exception of the duty watch, were there that night. We were all sat around at the tables in the normal clubbing fashion, just anticipating the start of the cabaret. Then, at last, on they came. They consisted of a troupe of women dancers. They were all of a deep brown skin colour, with huge thighs and breasts. They kicked their legs in the air and we all began to fear that the vibration from their rather weighty thighs might cause the stage to collapse. They each wore nothing but a G-string. And at the end of this troop of dancers came the cabaret's *pièce de résistance* in the form of our ship's Chief Petty Officer Telegraphist. He was doing the high kicks almost to the same standard as the troupe of girl dancers, but he was in the complete buff. Not a stitch between him and his maker.

The novelty of the performance went down like a house on fire, with a terrific roar of appreciation, and people were virtually falling off their chairs laughing about it. He did not stay on the stage too long so as not to spoil the novelty of the occasion, and he soon retreated to the dressing room. Unfortunately that was where he struck a major problem, because the girls in the dance troupe had hidden his clobber. Fortunately before the joke wore too thin they all had a great laugh about it and presented him with his clothes. I would hope that he had earned quite a few drinks from the management. He certainly looked to be wearing quite a hangover when I saw him the next morning. I also heard that some young midshipman was walking past him and was stupid enough to pass the remark, 'I saw you performing last night, Chief'. The Chief Telegraphist grabbed him by the collar and drew the middy towards him and with his mouth about an inch from the middy's ear he shouted, 'Well, keep your bloody mouth shut.' I don't know if the chief gained any satisfaction from that incident and I bet it bruised his hangover almost as much as it bruised that young middy's eardrums.

After the joys of Barbados we called into the island of St. Vincent, which was virtually torn apart several years later by a volcano – many of the population were killed, whilst almost all were made homeless. They were such a warm and friendly group of people. It seems such a pity that mother nature has to make such choices as to where she is going to strike her most savage of blows. On the occasion in question, we were having a nice quiet weekend alongside a very newly built jetty. I was sat in my office just after eating a very enjoyable Sunday lunch; I was staring at my navel and contemplating descending to my cabin for forty winks, when I received a phone call from the Chief Electrician. He asked me if I fancied a good walk on the island. A great awakener, I thought, and agreed to join him. His arrival at the office coincided with the arrival of a young electrician of his division, who said that he believed he had left his identity card ashore. He was unfortunately unable to proceed ashore without having a card, as it had to be produced to the duty Petty Officer before he could leave the ship. He was asked if he was sure that he knew where he had left the card and he answered in the affirmative. The Chief Electrician and myself thereby decided to escort him to the place where he claimed that the card had been left.

When we arrived at the address, I looked at the young electrician and said, 'I hope to hell that you did not sleep with a woman in this place.' The place was just a mud hut, with pigs, hens, dogs and several other animal species running in and around it. We walked inside and there was a pile of rags in one corner, and an exceedingly fat and ugly woman was lying amid these rags. She did not say a word, she just held up the young electrician's ID card. He snatched it off her and the three of us did a very quick exit. As soon as we were clear of the hut the young electrician was violently sick, and I said to him, 'Right son, you now have your ID card so you are ashore legally, but my advice to you is, you should get back to the ship as soon as you can and have a very good shower, but first you ought to rub yourself down with neat Izal' (a very strong disinfectant). I did keep my eye on the sickbay attendance list for some weeks afterwards but he was not on it. He must have been one of life's really lucky people.

The Atlantic decided to have one of its carnivals during our return to the UK, and the sea lifted to a force ten or more. I suppose it just wanted to show us that it was the boss. This would not have been much of a problem in normal circumstances, but by that time we had been away from the UK for about nine months or more. Although we were able to take on fuel oil and normal lubricant oil quite easily from the fuel depots and fleet auxiliary tankers that are strewn around the world, the special lubricant oil for our stabilisers was not always readily available and by that time we were virtually out of it. So, in the middle of the Atlantic in a force ten or twelve sea, we had to switch off our stabilisers. Boy, did that lovely lady jump around. I don't think that there could have been anyone on the ship who did not have a fair smattering of bruises during that Atlantic passage. They were a lovely class of ship but were rather top-heavy, a fault that was normally easily overcome by the use of her stabilisers. Life proved to be sheer hell without them.

The actual return to the UK after a lengthy period abroad was always a very hectic period for the master-at-arms and his staff. There were some times when I thought that the MAA ought to be cut into a dozen pieces and shared out amongst all the people who needed his attention. There was the customs clearance to think about, for which the MAA was responsible, and he had to ensure that every man on the ship was seen by the customs officers. There was invariably a large amount of mail just waiting on the jetty, which needed to be sorted and distributed. This kept one of the staff busy for several hours, and thereby reduced the working capacity of the staff quite considerably. There were always people who needed to leave the ship as quickly as possible for such things as compassionate reasons. There were invariably people who had to get away urgently to commence a course that was due to start yesterday. People joining the ship seemed to block up the passageways and tended to look like lost sheep, whilst visitors seemed to flood everywhere. I always asked my wife not to attend our homecomings and to expect me to arrive at my own home a long, long time after the ship had actually berthed.

After some well-earned leave and the replenishment of several items that had gone in the path of the devil – an expression that was often used at that time when an item of equipment failed to stand up to the rigours of the wear and tear that sailors used to put it through – we were ready again for our next sojourn to lands afresh. I am going to wind forward again here to but a couple of years ago. It was whilst I was at one of my branch reunions. That particular reunion was great for two reasons. The first was that it is always a pleasure to meet old and trusted friends, though I must admit to imbibing a little too much of the wicked brew. The second was the fact that I got an answer to a question that had been bugging me for more than thirty years. That question was, who had bestowed Chopper Lea on me? The answer turned out to be my old mate Ken Etheridge (the sod). I regret to say that Ken 'crossed the bar' (died) quite recently, after quite a period of illness; we will all miss him. He was a very likable character, and always first class at his job as a master-at-arms.

Ken was, at that time, the master-at-arms of the detention quarters in Portsmouth dockyard (a type of prison known throughout the Navy during that period as DQs. It was closed several years ago and the offenders are now sent to Army DQs). I was, of course, the Master-at-Arms of the missile destroyer HMS *London,* and halfway through a seagoing commission. One day I received a telephone call from our Commander, informing me that we had been assigned a 'DQ trusty' by the name of Lea, and that he would be drafted to our ship. I knew of Chopper Lea; he was the reigning Heavyweight Boxing Champion of the Navy. The reason that he was doing a long DQ sentence was because he had tried to leave the service to box as a professional. The Captain of Whale Island (HMS *Excellent,* the gunnery training establishment, which was a shore establishment in Portsmouth) had refused to grant his request to leave the service, so Chopper took what he then considered was his only alternative route, which was a right hook aimed at the Captain. He really was a big lad and must have needed a hell of a lot of restraining. The consequence of this was a long stretch in DQs for Chopper but no ticket to 'civvy street', which had obviously been his aim. Good behaviour in the DQs, however, ensured his early release and I won the raffle to get him, Ken having volunteered me. My name was obviously on every bloody raffle ticket.

The ship was bound for Sweden the day that Chopper arrived on board, and he seemed to settle into the ship's routine quite well. We eventually arrived in some rather outlandish port in northern Sweden, which unfortunately had little to entertain sailors. I detailed the ship's postman (they are always known as 'Postie') to latch onto Chopper and accompany him on his run ashore. Postie was a rather small but very popular member of the ship's company. Fortunately Chopper was quite happy with the situation of being chaperoned in that way. It was quite funny to see them walking down the brow. Chopper was about six foot three, and Postie was at least a foot shorter and possibly less than half of Chopper's weight. I found out later that Postie had guided them out of the normal sailors' bars area and had chosen some quiet bar off the beaten track. They were both enjoying their drink when Postie decided he needed to visit the loo. On his return to the bar he saw that some six or eight leather-jacketed yobs were sitting at the same table as Chopper, despite the fact that the bar was virtually empty. The atmosphere was looking rather trouble-laden. It was then that Postie gave a signal to Chopper to leave the bar and he stood up to do so, but obviously the leather-jacketed yobs had no intention of letting them go. Then one of them made a rather silly mistake; he took a swing at Chopper. Postie later told me that the first three were dropped with one punch each but the fourth one needed two punches, for which Chopper was very self-critical. The rest of them legged it quickly. Postie, Chopper and the barman were attempting to render first aid to the casualties when the police arrived. The sergeant in charge asked who had done the demolition job.

Chopper said, 'I did it but I did not start the fight.'

The sergeant replied, 'My friend, we have two other bars in this town that I would like you to visit, and I will pay for all the beer and spirits you can drink.' Postie sensibly hurried Chopper back to the ship before any further incidents occurred.

It was the following morning when I got the full story of the above incident. As I had pre-arranged a boxing tournament to take place during our return passage to the UK, I sent for Chopper to reassure myself that no harm had befallen his hands. On arrival at my office, he immediately went on the defensive and proclaimed that he was not responsible for the incident in the bar ashore. I put him at his ease by telling him that I knew all about the incident, and that he would hear nothing further about it. I later heard from the Petty Officer in charge of Chopper at his place of work that he (Chopper) had stated to his chums that he now believed that he could do nothing wrong on board this ship. He said that he had been involved in a punch-up and then thanked by the police. When he got back to the ship, he was summoned to the master-at-arms office, only to have his hands inspected and told that all was well.

As already stated, I had organised a boxing tournament to take place during our return passage to the UK. The obvious reason for this was that it seemed a waste of entertainment value to have the Navy Heavyweight Champion on board and not to let the ship's company see him perform. There was, however, only one man on the ship who was stupid enough to take him on. Before I go so far as to waste any expletives on this virtually mindless stupidity, let me say here and now that people entering their forties do some very silly things. I can honestly state that this incident must be classified as one of my silliest. Or put another way, if I am ever guilty of doing anything more stupid than the act I am now about to describe, then I truly ought to be certified as completely bonkers and locked away in a nut house for ever and ever (Amen). To start with, Chopper was some five inches taller than me. He was also about three stone heavier and virtually in the prime of youth, whilst I, as stated, had already reached my two score years.

Within the first minute of the fight, I was spreadeagled over the bottom rope of the ring. I can distinctly remember shaking my head and saying to myself, *If you don't get up from here, you will never be able to face the ship's company again.* I knew that my pride was, and for that matter still is, one of the most precious things that I possess. I had had possibly as many as five hundred fights during a long career, first as an amateur, then as a professional, many in the boxing booths of both South Wales and western England. I had never once been humiliated. Pride can be a heavy taskmaster and it sure as hell lifted my arse off that bottom rope before the count reached the dreaded ten.

The bell to end that first round was a joyous sound. Hell, how I needed that minute break. If someone had been stupid enough to ask me how long I thought the interval between rounds ought to be, I think my answer would have been 'forty years'. I really needed to get that pugilistic brain of mine working and utilise all those years of experience that had seemed to have deserted me and to have gone completely by the board in that first round. I must admit at this point that some of my experiences, particularly during my boxing booth days, were not what one could describe as very savoury. I hope that I have never damaged another fighter to the point that he could not recover from the injury. However, when you are in a situation of 'it's him or me', who could ever predict what damage one might inflict? It is unfortunate that pride can often make a man walk tall, with his head held high, when, in truth, his injuries can sometimes be quite horrendous.

Again the bell clanged and we rose for the second round. Hell, the man looked awesome. I knew that I had to get inside that long left and the right cross that had created such havoc in the first round. I managed to slip a right cross and got in a really heavy left hook. I felt that I had backed him off a little. At last I had been able to halt his incessant advance, but for how long? Had I enough fitness, energy, courage and pride to carry this advantage further? I tried a right cross, it caught him rather high on the head and it seemed to shake him. He seemed rather stung by my attempts, but he came back rather strongly towards the end of the round. I must admit that I utilised some of the more lurid experiences of my past during this part of the fight, and suffice to say that his vision could have been slightly impaired. The thumb of an old pro can sometimes have an upsetting effect. Oh, that joyous clanging of a bell again.

You sit on that silly little stool feeling that your whole body is on fire. Deep in your heart you know that you have to be completely mad and/or stupid to be doing what you are doing. The thought that you have three more minutes of this torture still to come is enough to sap all the energy you have left. Now we return to the question of pride, that master ingredient. Hell, how I used all my reserves of that commodity that day. I have to admit that despite all my experience, I had taken quite a hiding for those first two rounds. What is more, up to that point both my ego and my pride had taken one hell of a knock. But I am glad to report that the last round was mine. I hit Chopper with every punch in the book and just the odd one or two that never got as far as a book. Some of the punches I threw I had virtually forgotten ever existed. Long after the fight, one of the spectators asked me when I had last thrown a 'bolo' punch, to which I replied, 'Hell, you have to be at least forty to even remember that punch.' When the final bell sounded I was the one who was going forward and still throwing punches. They were punches thrown by instinct and pride by a man who had been running on an empty tank for at least half of that last bloody and battering round. Please God, let them be the last punches I will ever throw.

On our arrival in Portsmouth, Chopper was given a weekend leave from which he failed to return. His eventual arrest for desertion was made in the full glare of television cameras. This was an obvious publicity stunt arranged, I believe, by his family. It worked; he was eventually released from the Navy.

Despite being a part of the above contest, which was fought pretty fairly, where no quarter was asked or given, a contest that I clearly lost by a large margin of points, I found Chopper to be a very genuine and likable chap. I would have really liked to hear that he had made it big in the world of professional boxing, and I have often wondered what eventually happened to him.

A few days after my eventful fight with Chopper, the Admiral Commanding the Home Fleet, who had been one of the spectators, asked me what I thought of Chopper's chances of making it in the wide world of professional boxing. I stated that I thought his chances were slim. My point was that if a silly old goat like me could sneak the last round off him, he must have something missing.

I would imagine that the ship was somewhere off the north of Scotland when the above boxing tournament took place, and the weather was just glorious. I have traversed that area on numerous occasions, and I have to admit that it is very rare to sail through it in such a flat calm sea as it was during our boxing tournament.

The ship's Chief Bosun's Mate (always known as 'the buffer'), who was on the ship at that time, I had known since I joined HMS *Duke of York* in 1945. He had been a leading seaman then, whilst I was but a boy, so he was obviously older than I was. His surname was Hall, and like most Halls and Clarks, he had acquired the nickname 'Nobby'. The reason that I thought of him at this point in my story was because he had been the one I had consulted about building a boxing ring and as he was both in charge of the upper deck and also a first-class seaman in every respect, he was the man to organise it for me. Another reason was that there was obviously a lot of rope-work involved, of which he was a past master. Every time I think of Nobby Hall the word 'leadership' comes to my mind.

When I first sought promotion to leading patrolman, our class had a lecture that went under the heading 'Power of Command'. Shortly after attending that lecture, I argued that the title was wrong and it should, in fact, have been entitled 'leadership'. My point of argument was that the word 'leadership' bears little or no relationship to 'command'. A man either can lead people or he can't. The ability of leadership is virtually God-given. A lot of people who have a very high ability of leadership do not have a great physical presence or a loud voice to command other people with. Admiral Lord Nelson was a prime example of this. He was a little man with only one arm and one eye, and was evidently quietly spoken. What he had, and in large quantities, was a type of charisma that promotes the ability of leadership. Leadership is the ability to get other people to do what you want them to do, and to do it with the knowledge that they want to please the person who has instructed them to do that task. Nobby Hall had that type of charisma, or ability of leadership, call it what you wish. The seamen on the ship would have followed him to the ends of the Earth. Then if he had said it was necessary, they would have followed him all the bloody way back.

Nobby Hall smoked like a chimney, drank all the booze he could get his hands on (this included my tot of rum most days), but he never seemed to show any outward sign of having taken drink. He was overweight, though not grossly so. Nobby's greatest indulgence though, was women. He was no bowl of roses to look at, but he had that certain magnetism as far as women were concerned. Wherever we went Nobby invariably had a woman on his arm. Put another way, she would, at the flash of his blue eyes, have Nobby in her bed. As I have already said, the seamen virtually worshipped him, but they were all fully aware of his fondness of women and they would take bets wherever we went as to whether or not Nobby would bed a woman. The consequence of our visit to that rather small out of the way place in northern Sweden that I have already mentioned, was that a large amount of money was riding on the fact that Nobby would have no chance of bedding a woman. How wrong that proved to be. One woman was sent up from the British Embassy in Stockholm. She was to act as our ship's liaison whilst we were in port. She was quite a charmer and several of the officers on board fancied their chances with her. Now guess who bedded her, and I bet she was the only woman in the port who was bedded by one of our ship's company (no prizes for the right answer). How much money was won or lost over the incident? I have no idea. If anybody had kept a book for such bets I would obviously have been the one person who they would not have wanted to hear about it.

During this return passage to the UK we did, in fact, sail right down through a very placid Irish Sea as far as Pembrokeshire in South Wales, where we were to do a missile firing on the missile range there. During our several days' stay, we did our firings during the weekdays, and at the one weekend we were there we moored at a buoy in Goodwick harbour. Pembrokeshire is one of my favourite counties in the whole of the country, but unfortunately Goodwick is merely a village, with about two pubs and three churches. When a village of that size is visited by some three or four hundred sailors frustration soon rears its ugly head, and that certainly happened to our ship's company. My fingers became numb typing charge sheets for the numerous offences committed by our frustrated young sailors. Such charges as 1, 'Urinating in an improper place, namely the letter box of the local policeman's house' and 2, 'Creating a disturbance on shore, namely by driving a bull into the saloon bar of the Lonely Cow public house'. Both charges, if I can still remember rightly, came under sections number 39 and 43 respectively of the Naval Discipline Act (such information was from my *Giant Book of Totally Useless Information,* Volume One). Okay, so I tell some fibs occasionally.

We used to make regular visits to that missile range in Pembrokeshire to sharpen up our firing techniques of the Sea Slug missiles which were our main armament, but after the above happenings, prior to any further such visits, as soon as I received a copy of the programme, I used to rush up to the Captain's cabin and suggest that if there was a weekend in the middle of our missile-firing programme, could we possibly go to some port where the population was above ten citizens. In consequence of my requests to the Captain we put into Liverpool for one weekend, and the result was that I did not have a single charge sheet to type. It certainly bore out my theory that bored sailors can be troublesome people.

Whilst on the subject of troublesome sailors and having also mentioned Nobby Hall, the buffer, it seems an appropriate time to tell you about the prize 'ship's idiot' of all the ones that I ever had to deal with in the Navy. He was an engineering mechanic named Blake, and he really was extra-specially useless, and utterly bonkers. It seemed that everywhere he went on the ship he created some sort of a disaster. A reasonable example was when the Chief of his section in the engine room where he was working sent him up for a breath of fresh air on the upper deck. The chief later admitted to me that the reason he had given him a break was because Blake had made so many cock-ups in the engine room that he was glad to get him out of his sight, so that he (the Chief) could relax for a spell. Unfortunately, as Blake took his first two steps on the upper deck he managed to kick over two very large pots of paint. Nobby Hall (the buffer), who I have already mentioned, was in charge of the upper deck, and he had to be restrained from committing a serious offence of assault. As he proclaimed, 'To have kicked over a pot of paint is one idiotic act by someone who must surely be blind. To have kicked over two within two paces borders on pure lunacy. If I see you on the upper deck again I swear you will be visiting the bloody fishes, and I hope to hell you can't swim.'

The only useful thing I can think of about Blake was that I used him as a kind of a yardstick or guinea pig, such as, if I devised a printed form for a specific purpose. An instance I recall is an occasion when I had to send a party of men on leave from one port and get them back to the ship whilst she was in another port. I would first send for Blake and ask him to fill the form in as if the proposed problem was going to happen to him. I would obviously first have to spend some time convincing him that he was not getting the leave suggested on the form; then, if he got the basic gist of it, I knew that everyone else on the ship would find it problem-free. In other words, if the 'ship's idiot' could get it anywhere near right, all the remainder of the ship's company would find it easy.

We had cause to visit Devonport Dockyard (Plymouth) to load our rocket magazines prior to heading to the West Indies and the USA for quite a long period. We were due to sail from there early on a Monday morning and head westward across the Atlantic. On the Sunday evening prior to sailing, I was relaxing in my cabin when I received a phone call from a police sergeant in Gloucester, who asked if we had a character in the ship's company named Blake, to which I replied in the affirmative. I then quickly added a rider that I hoped that he was being held for a serious offence and that we could anticipate not having him returned to us prior to our early morning departure the following day. The sergeant sounded a little surprised by my attitude towards Blake, and asked if he was the criminal type. I replied that the man was too stupid to be a full-blown criminal. I then went on to ask what Blake had been up to that would make it necessary to phone the ship. The sergeant then gave me the whole sad story.

There had been a fire in a large building in Gloucester, and when the firemen had arrived to extinguish it, Blake had reprimanded them for not being up to the job for which they had been called and that he would show them how to fight fires in the traditional Naval manner. The police were in attendance at the fire, and because of Blake's behaviour they considered that he was the suspect arsonist and arrested him. The sergeant obviously wanted to know if Blake had any previous record of arson. My primary reaction was to sound hesitant so as to give the sergeant some suspicion and then I hoped that he would find it cause enough to hold Blake until the following morning, but I am afraid that my basic honesty took over and I just had to tell him that the man was the 'ship's idiot' and had no record of arson. Then I told him that due almost wholly to Blake's stupid behaviour he had, by that time, committed almost every other offence in the book except arson. I cannot remember now but there is a very strong likelihood that I would have suggested to the sergeant that he should return him to the hands of the firemen and let them hose him into the fire. I do vaguely remember asking if there was just a slight possibility that he could be held for just a few more hours, thereby ensuring that the ship would have sailed prior to him getting back to her. A desperate request on my behalf with which the sergeant was naturally, though unfortunately, unable to comply. It seemed that my only hope was in the fact that he would not find his way back to the ship because of the very limited time there was left for him to complete the journey.

In cases where a man was unlikely to get back to his ship prior to her sailing, it was normal for the person in charge of the man's mess to have his kit packed and ready to land just before the gangway (or brow) was hoisted. When I phoned the Chief Engineering Mechanic and told him that there was a possibility that Blake might not get back to the ship before she sailed, his cheers could have been heard all over the dockyard. I was later told that he danced around his mess for at least ten minutes prior to giving the order to have Blake's kit packed. The news spread around the ship like wildfire. Within minutes of my call to the Chief, both the Engineering Officer and the Commander had phoned me and rather jubilantly asked if the news of Blake possibly missing the ship was true. I confirmed the news, but emphasised that it was still only a possibility, though obviously rather a joyful one. I later heard that both the Commander and the Engineer Officer bought a round of drinks in the wardroom, which was a fair indication of their jubilation, because both were notoriously tight-fisted, both having short arms and very deep pockets.

Our departure day dawned and the ship was prepared for sea. We were all biting our nails and were scared to look at the gangway (brow) as it was prepared for hoisting. Blake's kitbag was the only one we had pre-packed, labelled and left on the jetty. The transport had already been ordered to take it to the Naval barracks after our departure. The slings were secured to the gangway and, at last, it was hoisted into the air. Our umbilical cord was severed, and we left the jetty and made our slow passage into the main channel of the harbour and headed out to sea. Past the Torpoint Ferry, through the restrictions of Cremyll, leaving Drake's Island to our starboard side, then the ship was swung rather hard to starboard and headed on through Plymouth Sound to the breakwater, where we would drop our pilot and splash off out into the deep blue sea. Alas, this was the very point where disaster struck us. Before the pilot could get his foot on the top wrung of the pilot's jumping ladder to leave the ship, there was a shout from the pilot cutter. 'Hold it, there is a passenger to board before the pilot leaves the ship.'

It is almost impossible to exaggerate the look of utter disappointment on the faces of all the spectators as Blake climbed that ladder. He was grinning like a Cheshire cat, and waving a slip of paper that he had received from the Gloucester police, proclaiming that he had been delayed through no fault of his own and testifying that he had been found totally innocent after being held on suspicion of arson.

Blake haunted us for several more months, and the way we got rid of him was an idea dreamed up by the Engineer Officer and the Chief Engineering Mechanic. On the day prior to sailing for a further long stretch abroad, Blake was landed with notes suggesting that he had been recommended to undergo a course for promotion. This was then countermanded by a letter from the Engineer Officer, who claimed in his letter that the wrong man had been accidentally nominated and an investigation was being made into who was responsible for such a blatant error, particularly in view of Blake's record. The letter was naturally timed to arrive at its destination when the ship was well out to sea and there would be no possibility of him being returned to us. So, in true Naval tradition, the first turn of the screws solves most of our problems.

I have often wondered who was unlucky enough to have had Blake drafted to them after we managed to get rid of him in that sneaky and surreptitious manner. When I attend regulator's reunions I prick up my ears when the subject of 'ship's idiots' arises (and it often does) in case the name Blake crops up. I do not know what my reaction would be if it did. My conscience will never be clear on the incident, and I often wonder if the other participants in that dastardly plot ever have pangs of conscience about it. The man really had the ability to sink a ship by his sheer stupidity.

As well as 'ship's idiots', who are mostly harmless, there are other types of people who are usually much more troublesome, they are a virtual thorn in the side of the master-at-arms, and seem to be permanently a hair's breadth from committing an offence. One such person was a character by the name of George Crane. There were several relatively small things that went wrong on the ship and I knew that he was the one responsible for them, but I could never prove it. One of the major snags to nailing him for an offence was the fact that he was a man of very strong and rather dominating personality. He was an able seaman and although he was accommodated in the seaman's mess, where there were at least seven or eight leading seaman, he virtually ruled the roost there. No one in the mess, including the leading seamen, would dare to say a word against him, or to stand up against him. He had that mess sewn up really tight, so no one would utter a single disparaging word against him. I must admit that I found the whole situation very frustrating. I often spoke to the leading seamen after such offences I have mentioned, and I could see by their expressions that they were aware that I knew Crane was behind such offences, but none of them would give me the answer that would have helped me to nail him to the wall, as the saying goes.

This point in my reflections strikes me as a very good time to introduce an antecedence as to my relationship with the leading hands of the messes. I had always stressed my belief that some of the most important people on any RN ship as far as I, or the general running of the ship, was concerned, were the leading hands of messes. Without their co-operation and assistance my job, and the ability for anyone of authority to run the ship, would have been virtually impossible. Any officer or senior rating who did not appreciate this fact would have been worse than useless at his job. In consequence of this firm belief which I had always held, I created a routine whereby, about every six months or so, I would invite all the leading hands of the messes down to my cabin for a chat. It would mean a 'standing-up only' procedure as my cabin was not really very big. I used to lay on a crate of beer to put them at their ease and to loosen the 'verbals' a little. I am pleased to say that I always had the feeling that I had conveyed my impression of their importance in the running of the ship across to them. But my most important message to them was that I was there at all times to listen to their views and to help in any way I could, and that they had access to me at any time. Any sailor worth his salt will say that being the leading hand of a mess, on a seagoing ship, is one of the hardest and most difficult jobs in the Navy. To live cheek by jowl with a group of people whilst maintaining authority over them is surely one of the world's hardest tasks. I had lived many years on broadside messes, so in consequence I certainly realised and appreciated that fact, and for that reason I was always very supportive of them. To me, no one on the ship was more important than they were in running an efficient and happy ship, and I, as the master-at-arms, would suffer nothing less than an efficient and happy ship. My whole life in the Navy had been spent in attaining the ability to strive for that goal. I can only hope that history will proclaim that I helped in acquiring success.

And so, back to Crane; I must admit that several times I did question myself as to whether or not I was carrying out a personal vendetta against him, and I even spoke to my deputy about such feelings, but he was of the same opinion as myself; and in fact he found the situation just as frustrating as I did. Worse was yet to come though, and our frustrations were due to be carried to a much higher plane.

Rosters for promotion were kept at a centralised office in Gosport in Hampshire. A ship would be notified when a person was due for such promotion, and unless the ship had strong reasons for not doing so, the person was promoted by the ship's captain. The office receiving this information had to inform me when they received such notifications, because I was the person who organised the ceremony of promotion by the captain. One day I received the dreaded news that Crane was due to be promoted to leading seaman. I was staggered, I had not realised that he had even passed the exam for leading seaman. Within seconds of receiving the news I was up aloft to see the Commander (who was the executive officer). I told him of my fears if Crane was promoted and that I was bitterly opposed to it. I put my emphasis on the fact that though he was certainly a leader he was very irresponsible, and the type of person who would lead in the wrong direction. The Commander told me to leave it with him and that he would consult both Crane's Divisional Officer and the Captain. When I next saw the Commander he informed me that because the Divisional Officer had given Crane a glowing report and said that he would be a good leader, the Captain had agreed to promote him on the recommendation of the Divisional Officer. My answer to him was that with all due respect Sir, Hitler had been a good leader in the eyes of the entire population of Germany, and that I looked upon this promotion with similar trepidation. I thanked him for putting my views to the Captain and sadly left his office. I cursed myself for not having taken my opinion to the Captain personally when I had first heard of the possibility of the promotion; unfortunately, I could not go over the Commander's head at that late stage. I realised what a stupid fool I had been, and perhaps I said a little prayer and hoped that things would turn out all right. Oh, how I wish that that could have been so!

On promotion, Crane was given the job of quartermaster, which meant that he steered the ship when she was at sea, and in harbour he was in charge of the ship's gangway staff. Within days of him taking over the job and whilst the ship was in London, the officers held a cocktail party on the quarterdeck (the after, or back end of the ship). A lot of booze was flowing around and the party went on much later than was normal for cocktail parties. Crane had the first watch on the gangway (8 p.m. until midnight). Some time around 11 p.m. the Bosun's Mate, who was one of Crane's staff, was found wandering around on the for'ard (forward) part of the ship in a very drunken state. A search was then carried out for

Crane, who should have been on the quarterdeck, but he could not be found. The Bosun's Mate was questioned at length, but he claimed that Crane had sent him for'ard to check on something and whilst he was making the checks that he had been instructed to do by Crane, he had been apprehended by the duty Petty Officer for being drunk.

The ship was, as I have already stated, in the River Thames in London, and in fact she was secured alongside the cruiser HMS *Belfast*, which is a museum ship permanently moored there. Searches were carried out for the rest of the night both on our ship and on HMS *Belfast* for the missing Crane, but there was no trace of him. The following morning the Permanent Naval Shore Patrol in London were brought into the investigation, and all known friends of Crane who resided in or around London were interviewed, but no trace of him was established. I and my staff interviewed every man on the ship who even remotely knew Crane, and we made copious notes, but all was totally in vain. We were due to leave London for Portsmouth only a couple of days after Crane went missing, but by that time I had acquired an awful feeling that the conclusion to this incident was going to be nasty; and so it proved to be.

We received a signal to the effect that a body had been found in the Thames, and on investigation it proved to be that of Crane. He had a large amount of alcohol in his blood and had obviously fallen into the river whilst in a virtual drunken stupor. The Thames has a very strong rate of tide flow and he had been caught in an ebb tide, which had very quickly carried him downriver. He would have had a superhuman struggle in the darkness to have survived had he been cold sober, but in his state of inebriation he did not have a snowball's chance in hell.

Crane committed an act of total irresponsibility whilst he was in a position that required an act of total dedication to the job he had been allotted to perform. The ship was sitting in a strong tidal flow, and his behaviour proved beyond any shadow of doubt that he was totally unsuitable for the promotion that had been awarded him. The Bosun's Mate who was involved in the incident, and who had been found to be drunk by the duty Petty Officer, was awarded some relatively minor punishment.

There was a reasonable investigation into how Crane had acquired the booze that brought about his premature death, but during such times as a party in the middle of London, with booze flowing like a river, there was not the remotest chance that any reasonable conclusion could be reached. I honestly believed that my own presumption was the nearest to the truth, and my belief was that it was a tragedy just waiting to happen.

Crane's parents understandably raised quite a rumpus after the event, and they involved their MP and anyone else who they thought could press the investigation further. Because the incident happened in London, eventually Scotland Yard became involved in their contretemps and two detectives were sent down from London to Portsmouth, where I arranged for them to interview all the people who could have been in any way involved in the incident, and I also produced our own copious notes on the subject. I gave them all the help I could and then left them to absorb and picture the incident from a totally independent point of view. They proved to be very astute people, and soon had a total grasp of the situation. Their conclusion, I am pleased to say, was virtually identical to my own. I was therefore very grateful that they had become involved. The air was at last cleared and the incident put to rest.

A further visit to the Baltic Sea, but on this occasion we took the short cut and went up to it via the Kiel Canal. This was the first and only time that I have been lucky enough to traverse that canal, and I have to say that it really is a most pleasant journey to take. It did seem rather strange to be sailing on a warship through a series of meadows filled with grazing cattle, but oh, what a marked difference between that and the Suez Canal, where one has virtually only sand to look at. Our visit to the port of Kiel was a very pleasant one, and our ship's company became very friendly with the ship's company of the German destroyer *Hessen* which was also paying a visit to the port.

At that period of my time on the ship I often used to go ashore with the Chief Shipwright, and after we had been in Kiel for a day or so we both decided to explore the glories of the port. We had walked a couple of hundred yards or so clear of the dock area when we espied a nice little bar, and we decided to pop into it to wet our whistles. The barman spoke excellent English and was a very friendly character. I ordered a couple of beers, and a schnapps as a chaser. The barman said that he had some Danish schnapps in the bar. He was, in fact Danish, and said he considered that Danish schnapps was the best. We quickly sank the schnapps, and were in the act of washing it down with the beer when one of the German customers who was sitting nearby at the bar corrected the barman and admonished him about his choice of schnapps. He then ordered two further drinks for us, which were in fact one of the several brands of German schnapps that were on sale in the bar. As we drank the second schnapps one of the other customers commented that the last schnapps we had drunk was certainly not the best schnapps available, and he ordered us a further brand. Other customers came over and joined the discussion, their entry fee to the discussion being the cost of two further schnapps for us to sample and pass our opinion on. It was not so very long before the Chief Chippy and I did not know whether we were drinking schnapps or sucking wine gums. We then made our excuses and staggered out of the bar and back to the ship while we still had the ability to steer our feet in the right direction to return to her. We had been ashore less than two hours. So much for the lovely port of Kiel, a really friendly place. But watch out for the schnapps traps.

Back into the Mediterranean and down to our beloved Malta. The place seemed to change very little from my point of view. By the time in question, I had spent more time in and around Malta than I had spent in the town that I was born and brought up in, but more to the point, I knew my way around Malta better than the town I was born in. The Chief Bosun's Mate (who had recently joined in place of Nobby Hall) and I were very good friends, and we often went ashore together to have a couple of drinks in the quiet of the evening. One of our favourite bars was a place we used to call Ma's Bar, which was at the bottom of Straight Street in Valetta; in other words it was at the bottom of the Gutt. I suppose you could rightly call it a 'crappy' little bar. There was a virtually open gents' toilet stuck in the corner of the bar, the flow from which flowed freely into the road outside, adding to the sludge of the Gutt. It would have been the last bar in all the world that I would have wanted to take my wife or mother. The bar was possibly less that twelve foot square, but it normally had the advantage of being a very quiet place to have a drink and a friendly conversation. The Buffer and I had made our greetings to Ma, who we had both known almost since time immemorial, and we sat down to enjoy our quiet drink. Unfortunately I was the last one to enter the bar, and I had been foolish enough to leave the 'bat wing' doors of the bar just a few inches ajar. Rather unfortunately, the seamen's mess were celebrating something special, though for the life of me I cannot remember what it was. As one of them was passing Ma's Bar he must have noticed the Buffer and myself in there. The next we knew was that the bar was full to overflowing, and the crush was such that the Buffer and I decided to make a quick and quiet exit before the singing, generally uncouth merry-making and seaman-type rude and coarse performances got any worse. We had only managed to get some ten or twenty yards clear of the place when we passed both the civil police and the Naval shore patrol storming down the Gutt. *There but for the grace of God*, I thought. I remember saying to the Buffer, 'I feel I am past the stage now of wanting to be involved in a punch-up.' It naturally meant that I had many more charge sheets to type, but luckily enough the Buffer and I had managed to avoid having our names on one of them.

We were off into the Black Sea, which again was a place I had not been before. It was on through the Dardanelles and then into the Sea of Marmara, through the Bosporus and into the Black Sea. What a fantastic journey we had enjoyed! I thought of all the history I had read to date and how so much of it fitted into the channels, seas and territories that we had just traversed. More than that, I thought of the thousands of lives that had been lost fighting for this fertile land and how stupid and senseless such wars had now proved to be.

Now here we were to further pursue the cold war that was rather absurdly being carried out between the Soviet Union and the Western powers. Our reason for going into the Black Sea was to 'fingerprint' the Russian radar. This was just one of the many devious manoeuvres that were carried out during that rather silly period, and I had better explain what this 'fingerprinting' was all about. All radar sets have a slightly different beam pattern, and if you have the right equipment and the radar set is switched on, you can distinguish the type, power, range, position and several other supposedly worthwhile features about the set. The same subterfuges were carried out by the Russians, and as long as we kept outside of each other's territorial waters it was considered fair game and was obviously legal by international law.

On entering the Black Sea, as if from nowhere, we were picked up and shadowed by a Russian destroyer. She was with us the whole of the time we were in that area, mostly staying some two or three miles astern of us. At that time the weather was very good, so, partly to relieve boredom and mostly because of my own liking for a refreshing dip in the sea, most afternoons I would sort out the whereabouts of the Captain and persuade him to stop the ship for a session of 'Hands to bathe'. Then all the sailors not actually on watch could don their bathers and jump over the ship's side. They could alternatively go in the buff if they so desired, as we had no 'lady sailors' in those days. The Captain of the ship at that time was a really first-class man and exceptionally popular with the ship's company, and he was usually just as keen as the rest of us were to get into the sea for a relieving dip, whenever his circumstances would allow him to do so of course. He was also a pretty strong swimmer, and he and I usually had an unofficial race to the perimeter of the area designated for the swim.

Sailing in a sea like the Black Sea at that time meant that our own navigation had to be very accurate, as sometimes we would have to sail very near to the international coastal limits. In consequence, the Navigating Officer hated having to stop the ship for what he considered to be such a trivial reason as 'Hands to bathe', as the time lost would ruin his calculations and give him a great deal of extra work. Possibly because of these interruptions, the Navigating Officer developed something of a hate attitude towards myself. In fact the situation reached the point whereby he would try to deliberately lead me on a false trail when I was trying to find the Captain to request that the ship's company had their 'Hands to bathe', but I developed a way of circumventing his method of false directions. In truth, our cat and mouse games became something of a ship's comedy, quite a standing joke in fact.

One day I went to see the Captain to request our usual swim, and he said that we would have something of a problem as we were in a position whereby we could not fully turn the ship's engines off. He instructed me to announce that only strong swimmers were to enter the water, and that they would have to keep clear of the area around the ship's screws, which would be slowly turning whilst we were in the water. This I duly did, and at the appointed hour the strong and more enthusiastic swimmers lined the deck. The plunge was made, and the Captain and I performed our usual little unofficial race. We had possibly swum a hundred yards from the ship's side when we both looked up to see that the Russian destroyer had 'hove to' some fifty yards or less ahead of us. The Russian destroyer's listening gear had obviously noted that our ship had its engines running, and with the misinformation that the Communist regimes of that time had fed to them, they surely believed that all the men in the water were deserting the ship and heading for their 'Communist Utopia'. As we looked up at the destroyer, which by then was but yards from us, we saw what seemed to be their whole ship's company lowering 'scrambling nets' and obviously expecting many 'Western European visitors' to join them. Both the Captain and myself turned and made rather frantic signals to the men behind us to abandon our 'Hands to bathe'. As they too realised the situation they turned and we all swam for the safety of our own ship, our enjoyable swim having been annoyingly curtailed, but a possible international incident had been avoided.

Several years after the above event, I met that former Navigating Officer in a bar and found that he had mellowed quite considerably with age. We enjoyed a few drinks together, in fact it was several drinks. We eventually got around to talking about our Black Sea escapade. The question he posed was, how did I always seem to know where to find the Captain, despite the fact that he (the Navigating Officer) had given me false information? I told him that all his staff on the bridge used hand signals behind his back to inform me of the whereabouts of the Captain, because they also wanted a swim and knew why I was seeking his whereabouts. I thought the ex-Navigating Officer was going to have a fit. I have never seen a man laugh so much, particularly when the joke was against himself.

Our radar spy work was completed, and we headed back to the Bosporus and had a couple of days in Istanbul, where I was able to have a good roam around the world's largest covered market and buy presents for the family. Unfortunately all this was before the bridge over the Bosporus was built and I have, as yet, not been able to see that bridge. Perhaps one day I will return.

We seemed to have spent several months sailing around the Mediterranean Sea area during the time in question, and I remember a smashing visit to Corsica. I ran the line at a rugby match that we played against a French Navy side one Sunday morning. After the match the Captain came over to me and told me that he was not using the Chauffeur-driven car that had been allotted to him so I could have it for the rest of the day. I got a couple of chums together and off we went up into the Corsican hills. I was truly amazed at the beauty of the island. I had never been there before, though I had read a little about it, and I also knew that it was the birthplace of Napoleon. I was most surprised that such a lovely place had not got a better reputation as a holiday resort. We eventually stopped at a typical little French restaurant and had a snack of bread and cheese. I had never tasted a more mouth-watering cheese in my whole life, so I asked the waiter where I could obtain such cheese, and he directed us further up in the hills. We got to the allotted farm and found that the cheeses were, in fact, goat cheeses. The farmer showed us around the large cave where all the cheeses were stored for many months in order to mature. Knowing that the Captain was, like myself, a cheese addict, I then purchased two of the cheeses, mostly with the intention of repaying the Captain for his gesture of letting me use his car, and we then returned to the ship.

On our arrival back on board, I realised that the warrant officers' mess, which was the one I used as my mess for social occasions, was having a guest night, so I left one of the cheeses there and then went up to the Captain's cabin, only to find that he was also having a guest night. I therefore left the second cheese with the Captain's Steward in his pantry and returned to my own mess, only to find that the whole of the cheese that I had left there only minutes before had all been eaten, mostly by the guests. Later in the evening I had a call from the Captain asking me if I had any of the cheese left as his guests, prior to leaving the ship, had assured him that they had never enjoyed cheese so much in their lives; he then realised that they had eaten the whole cheese before he was able to taste any of it. I explained to him that I was in the same state of cheese starvation as he was, and we both sympathised with each other over the phone.

There was a period of time during our deployment in the Mediterranean when the UK post office had quite a long strike. In fact I think just about everybody and everything was on strike in the UK. We had gone weeks without receiving any mail, and please remember that this was long before the days of mobile phones and easy international phone calls. Then, at last, we received a signal from the UK giving us the joyful information that several bags of mail had been despatched to us from the UK. We were in Italy at the time, and I got our postman ashore and up to the local sorting office as quickly as I possibly could. He eventually found someone who could speak English and explained that he had come to collect mail for HMS *London*. Big searches were made but no mail could be found for us. Investigations as to the whereabouts of our mail went on for several more days, and then at last we got an answer as to what had happened to it. It appeared that someone at the airport in Rome had seen the word London on the mail sacks for us, and as he spoke no English and did not understand what the letters HMS signified, he rushed them onto an aircraft that was bound for London in the UK. The mail arrived in the UK just in time to be caught up in a strike by baggage handlers at London Airport. I think that we eventually got those sacks of mail when we entered Portsmouth a couple of months later.

Ping Pong

Three fine young princes vied for the hand of the beautiful
    Princess Jane.
The King said, 'We'll have a contest to see who will give her his
    name.
My daughter's hand will go to the man who returns within these
    walls,
With the largest collection he can find of ordinary ping-pong balls.'

So the three rode off on their trusty steeds, to return within one
    week,
But within four days the first one was back, the wedding plan to
    keep.
He had almost a ton of ping pong balls that overflowed his cart,
He said, 'The other two won't beat me and they'll die of a broken
    heart.'

The second prince soon followed him back, he was certain that he
    had won,
When his ping-pong balls were all weighed up they were well over
    one ton.
'You can now arrange the wedding,' the second prince said with
    glee,
'The third prince will not beat my score, that you will all soon see.'

It was well over a week when the third prince returned, he'd
    evidently had a fight,
He had a small bloodied sack, which he held in his hand and he
    clung to it very tight.
'The ping-pong ball contest is over, you had one week to return to
    these walls.'
'Oh hell,' said the prince, quite astounded, 'I thought you said
    King Kong's balls.'

Old Bill and the Lift

We had all come up to the city for our Christmas shopping spree,
The decorations looked wonderful, of that we could all agree.
Old Bill looked out in amazement, the first time he'd seen such a
    sight,
He'd never been up to the city before, so we hoped he would be all
    right.

When the shopping spree was over, we went to a hotel for a drink,
But we sat for a while in the foyer to settle our minds and to think.
Then Bill saw a very old lady hobbling painfully into the lift,
The doors soon shut behind her and the lift was gone quite swift.

Bill was really astounded and sat staring at the lift door,
He didn't know what to make of it, he'd not seen such a thing
    before.
The lift door was once again opened and out strode a beautiful girl,
Old Bill looked quite astonished, his mind was now in a whirl.

Then Bill jumped up from the foyer and rushed back towards our
    bus,
I followed him out quite quickly, trying not to make a fuss.
When at last I was able to catch him and ask what was the trouble,
That should make him want to leave us all and exit at the double.

'Gosh,' he said, 'that was magic, what happed in that little room.
An old lady shuffled into it and the door shut with a boom,
Then when the door re-opened she had lost some fifty years,
She then looked so young and lovely, I almost broke out in tears.'

I said, 'I'm sorry if it upset you, Bill, and spoiled your shopping day,
But I'll get the other passengers and we'll soon be on our way.'
'I'm not a bit upset,' said Bill, his smile now fully abloom,
'I want to go home to get my wife and push her into that little
    room.'

The Ham-Fisted Brickie

A ham-fisted brickie named Cannon was busy building a wall,
He wanted to get it finished as the foreman was due to call.
'I'll show him I'm good at my job,' he said, as he spread the mortar
    around,
Perhaps he did not realise that most of it fell on the ground.

The foreman eventually entered the site, cast his eyes upon the wall,
'Good grief!' said he, 'that's awful work, it just won't do at all,
Get down to the office and draw your cards, I'm giving you the
    sack.'
'That's terrible, Boss,' said Cannon, 'but I know of a worse wall
    than that.'

'That's impossible,' the foreman said, 'but I'll give your sacking a
    miss,
If you can show me a building with a wall that's worse than this.'
Cannon took him to another road and pointed to a wall on the
    right,
The foreman almost died of shock to see such an awful sight.

'Okay, Cannon,' the foremen said, 'you've proved a point, my boy,
So now you have your job back, that should give you joy.
But the chap who did a job like this ought to be flushed down the
    loo.'
'Oh don't say that,' said Cannon, ''cause I built this wall too.'

CHAPTER TEN

I was recently watching the TV presentation of a football match from Italy where the supporters of a British team were involved in what, I suppose, could be called a rather serious affray. I thought that the police handling of the situation was causing more of a problem than it was solving. I am fully aware that British football fans now have a very poor record in Europe, from the behavioural point of view that is, and I feel sure that we, the British, should set an example to the rest of Europe and pass the necessary laws prohibiting the citizens of our country who commit offences in other parts of Europe, or for that matter any proven football hooligan, from leaving our shores as football fans, or even from leaving our shores for any reason. In other words, their passports should be withdrawn for a long period.

However, I do have something of a slanted opinion on some of the European police forces, and the following story may help to explain why I have formulated these views. Or, at least, why I have put them into a slightly more condescending perspective from the British football supporters' point of view.

I was always quite pleased, nay proud, of the behaviour of our ship's company, and I had often boasted to masters-at-arms of other ships that I had the best-behaved ship's company in the fleet. There is one little proviso I want to add to that statement, however, and that is that I would not venture ashore on the first night in any port. The reason for this was that when I first took over a ship in the mid-1950s as that ship's master-at-arms, I learned that if there was going to be any trouble it would be on the first night in port when 'Jolly Jack' had money in his pocket. So, I considered it better to remain on the ship on that first night, and to sort out any possible problems rather than to spend hours the next day trying to sort out the mistakes made by people who knew little or nothing about the Naval Discipline Act or Rules of Evidence etc.

The ship had cause to visit Civitavecchia, which is a port quite close to the city of Rome. It is a busy port, with the usual Italian bustle, and one would expect that the populace of the town, especially the police, were well used to the noisy habits of sailors. But, oh that that were true. On the evening in question I was striding the quarterdeck with the Officer of the Watch, with whom I was quite friendly, when a police jeep came to a screaming halt by our afterbrow (that is, the gangway between the jetty and the ship). A seriously overweight police constable panted his way up the very steep brow and uttered possibly the only word of English that he knew, and that word was 'riot'. He then pointed in the direction from which he had just come. I requested the Officer of the Watch to get the 'standby shore patrol' organised and ready to move, whilst I proceeded ashore with this policeman to do all that I could to calm the situation.

I have seen some sad, bad and mad driving in my time, but that evening I experienced some of the most frightening driving I had ever known. How we got through the town and to the bar where the supposed 'riot' was happening, I will never really be sure, because after the first fifty yards I closed my eyes and hung on like grim death. This police officer had surely been told that he was only to have two or less of the vehicle's wheels in contact with the road at any one time, and he stuck rigidly to that method of driving. At last, another screaming halt, this time my nose bashed the windscreen. I was nevertheless glad to bail out of the jeep and to feel both my feet firmly implanted once again on terra firma. But, oh what a frightening sight met my eyes. The bar we had stopped at was surrounded by a dozen or more armed police officers. They were hidden behind vehicles, large plant pots and any other paraphernalia that might have afforded them cover. I thought, *what the hell am I and my usually well behaved ship's company doing in this sort of situation?.*

One of the more senior officers present seemed to have a slightly better grasp of English than the one who had chauffeured me to the scene. He told me that in his opinion the sailors were revving up to take the bar apart. My jaw must have dropped in line with my belly button. I said, 'With all due respect, Sir, my sailors are in there singing, and I can assure you that nothing will be taken apart. What is more I will go in there and request them to leave the bar at once, and I will gamble everything I own that they will all do so.' I am not sure if that senior police officer really had a grasp of what I was actually saying, but by that time I was getting a little uptight and, rather worried about the situation. I said, 'Just after I enter that bar, my sailors will all come out, two at a time, and I want an assurance that there will be no shooting.' To this day I am not sure if I received that verbal assurance, but I felt that, in this situation, I could wait no longer. I turned and put my hands in the air like some ridiculous cowboy in a Hollywood film, and I walked into the bar. The place was occupied by some fifty or sixty of our ship's company. They were all gathered around a piano which one of the men was playing, but I have to admit that the singing was certainly a mile below the standard of a Welsh choir, despite the fact that we had a pretty large smattering of Welshmen on board.

When the men saw me enter the bar with my hands still thrust rigidly skywards, they all looked amazed. 'What the f*****g hell is wrong, Joss?' said someone.

'Right,' I said, 'this bar is surrounded by armed police because they think you are about to cause something like a riot, and by the sound of that bloody awful singing I have a certain amount of sympathy with their views. If anyone thinks that I am here on a skylark, they can look out of one of the windows, and I hope that they don't get any of their vital parts shot off whilst doing so. Now, this is what you are going to do. You will all leave this bar, two at a time, and disperse to the rest of the town, but for God's sake, and in no case, will you congregate in anything like the numbers you are in at present. I hope that you stupid bastards realise the seriousness of the situation and have the sense to leave quietly.' Someone must have looked out of one of the windows, and a whisper quickly spread, it certainly silenced any possible retort.

Like animals leaving the ark, they left the bar in twos, and they did so very quietly. When I was satisfied that the last couple were well clear, I walked out myself. My reappearance was greeted by a cheer from all the police and the quite large crowd of civilians who had by that time gathered. I felt awfully embarrassed. All I had done was to stop some awful rendering of rather bawdy songs. There was never the remotest chance of any serious trouble being caused by our ship's company.

The same policeman who had conveyed me to the incident was given the job of returning me to my ship and I am delighted to report that the vehicle remained on all four of its wheels for almost the whole of the return journey. When we got back to the bottom of the ship's brow, the policeman got out of the driving seat and ran around to my side of the vehicle and as I slowly rose from my seat he gave me a huge and rather embarrassing hug. The Officer of the Watch and all the gangway staff watched this with obvious incredulity, and when I got to the top of the brow the Officer of the Watch said, 'What the hell was all that crap about, Master-at-Arms?' Fortunately the Officer of the Watch and I were friends of long standing, and my reply was, 'I hope you don't mind if I leave the explanations until the morning.' He nodded and bid me good night. I descended to my cabin, hoping that the night would present no further problems, which, I am glad to say, was the case.

The next morning I went to make my usual morning report to the Commander. He was in the company of two other senior officers, and he greeted me with the words, 'I hear that you had an unexpected trip ashore last night, Master-at-Arms.'

I replied, 'Yes Sir, it appears that the Italian police took exception to our ship's company's singing. I have to admit it was pretty awful and I suppose we were rather lucky that they did not shoot any of them.' All three of the officers had a good laugh over what was obviously considered to be my little joke. It then struck me that I could have just done myself a big favour. If a derogatory report from the Italian police was later submitted to the ship, via the British Embassy, stating that they had been considering armed intervention, I would be able to remind the Commander that I had mentioned the possibility of a shooting, and in front of two witnesses. Fortunately, nothing further was heard of the incident.

I have already made it clear that HMS *London* was the favourite ship of my entire Naval career, and the fact that I willingly and totally voluntarily went back to her for a second commission was the undeniable proof of that fact. There were several aspects of the ship that I would like to inform my readers about, though, before I press on to other parts of this story. One of the first points ought to be about the ship's Chinese laundry. A large number of ships in the Royal Navy used to carry a Chinese laundry staff, almost all of whom originated from Hong Kong, keeping in mind that, at that time, Hong Kong was a colony of the UK. I had a very good liaison with the laundry staff throughout my entire time in the Navy, particularly whilst on HMS *London*. The first thing that should be made clear is that the Master-at-Arms was, first and foremost, their protector. If they had any kind of problem, the laundry 'Number One' had access to the Master-at-Arms at any reasonable time. These problems invariably took the form of a failure to pay their bills or dissatisfaction with the standard of the returned laundry. Although there was a specified officer who was nominated as the laundry officer, I was invariably the arbitrator in any such problem and I feel sure that I always did a satisfactory job in that direction. One of the perks of this protection and arbitration however was the fact that the Master-at-Arms always had his laundry done free of charge.

When I first joined the ship in 1965 the laundry staff consisted of four hands, and as I have already indicated they were always known as the number they took in the seniority or hierarchy they held in their jobs in the laundry. In other words the one in charge was known as Number One, and so on down the line. No one in the ship knew any of their names. They were just referred to as

Number One, Two and so on. Shortly after I joined the ship, the laundry had a new recruit in the form of a very young Chinese boy, who obviously became Number Four. For some reason, this new recruit acquired the name Chico. For the life of me I don't know how that happened. In all my time on ships with Chinese laundry hands, I had never heard of one of them having a name, but Chico became something of a ship's mascot. He had the brightest smile that one could ever wish to see and very soon became something of a favourite amongst the ship's company. One of the main points in his favour was that his English was far superior to that of the then Number One, and quite quickly he was the one who was sorting out all the laundry problems. Although he was still but a teenager, he was virtually running the laundry. Number One was soon happy to return to Hong Kong and Chico, because of his excellent command of English, jumped three places from Number Four to Number One virtually overnight.

All the time that Chico was the Laundry Number One, he never had a problem that he had to bring to me. I think that I could safely say that Chico was as competent at his job, or possibly even more so, than any other head of department on the ship. It was always a pleasure to meet him, mainly because of that contagious smile and good humour that just emanated from him.

We were having a short self-maintenance period in Malta for a couple of weeks and several of us took advantage of the situation to get our wives out there for a few days during that period. My wife was very happy to join me, and as we were both quite familiar with Malta it turned out to be a wonderful holiday for both of us. I then had an invite from Chico; he said that there was now a Chinese restaurant opened in Malta, run by a close relative of his. He had invited all the people on the ship who had any dealings with his job, like the Laundry Officer and his lady, the Doctor and his lady, the Commander and his lady and my lady and myself. He had spent the whole day at the restaurant and prepared the whole meal himself, and it was one of the finest meals I have ever eaten. A couple of the ladies present said that they had it in mind to kidnap Chico and take him home to cook for them.

The laundry crews change around quite regularly, and a few weeks after the above event, Chico went back to Hong Kong for what we expected to be a couple of weeks. The few weeks turned into several weeks and no sign of Chico. A couple of signals were sent in an attempt to find out what had happened to him, and then we had the awful news that Chico had committed suicide. It was evidently all due to his love for a woman. I had terrible pangs of sadness whilst writing and telling my wife, who had taken on a maternal, almost motherly, feeling towards young Chico. He was particularly sadly missed by the ship's company, who had all grown very fond of him. He was possibly one of the most popular men on the ship. I wish that I had acquired a photograph of his smile; he really had a great all-encompassing smile. Cheerio Chico, may your God like you and appreciate you as much as the men on HMS *London* did.

After my first commission on HMS *London* I was drafted into the Naval barracks in Portsmouth, which was quite convenient to me because I had already acquired the use of a married quarter in Portsmouth, due to it being the home base of HMS *London*.

I had something of a dead end job in the barracks to begin with, because there were several masters-at-arms on the books there. One of them was quite a long-time senior to me, so he had what was then called 'the chair', in other words he performed the duties, more or less, of a normal master-at-arms on a ship. He was a first-class man however, and we both got on well together, and because I was enjoying normal married life again I was quite happy with the situation. My job consisted of taking charge of what was called the Cell Recess Establishment. We used to take people who were awarded 'cell punishment', which was a period of imprisonment of up to a maximum of fourteen days. I am glad to say that the punishment has long been deleted from the list of Naval punishments. We also processed the sailors who were sent from other ships and establishments to be incarcerated in the Naval detention quarters, which were then in the Portsmouth Naval

Dockyard. I am pleased to say that that establishment has also been closed down.

During my sojourn in the barracks we had a new block of cells built, and because I would be the person in charge of the building when it was turned over to us, I was summoned by the builders to sign for it. I considered that the layout of the building and the general security were totally inadequate for the purpose for which it was to be used and I refused to sign for it. There was quite a rumpus over my refusal to sign, and eventually I was summoned to the Commodore's office. He told me that the signature was only for the acceptance of the building, and I would not be liable for its inadequate security. So, on his assurance, I signed for the new cell block. During the second night of its use, one of the prisoners escaped from it. There had been no escapees from the old barracks cell block in living memory. I tried very hard not to wear that 'I told you so' smile after the event, and I was glad that my staff and I were exonerated from blame because of the building's inadequate security. I was certainly very glad that I had been insistent and that my pig-headedness had taken both myself and my complaint as far as the Commodore.

One other job that I had in the barracks was to act as the Provost Marshal at Naval courts martial. Some of the cases were very interesting, but there were the occasional boobs made by the presidents of the court; they would sometimes forget to stand the poor Provost Marshal (me) at ease, and I could be standing there for an hour or more holding my sword, which weighs about ten pounds or more, at the end of an outstretched forearm. I used to think about trying some type of a hinge contraption for my elbow but I never got around to it.

After a few months at the above jobs, I took over the 'chair' due to my predecessor leaving the service and going to pension. I found the snag of being *the* master-at-arms in a big barracks was the fact that there was a Commissioned Officer of the Regulating Branch who was naturally responsible for the running of all regulating tasks. It was, by that time, alien to me not to be the one in charge, and it was one of the reasons, if not the major reason, why I very soon volunteered to go back to sea, where I would be virtually the master of my own destiny once again.

I contacted the appropriate section of the Naval Drafting Authority, and requested a seagoing ship. I was told that the only one available would be HMS *London*, the snag being that I was very low on the 'back to sea' roster, due mainly to the fact that I had so recently left a seagoing ship. I was told that I would have to wait a while in case anyone else who was higher on the back to sea roster wanted it. After a few weeks I had a call to tell me that my beloved *London* would be mine once again.

The Master-at-Arms on the ship was the one who had relieved me prior to me going into the barracks, and by way of 'turn over' he said, 'You know more about the bloody ship than I do, so it's all yours again.' Some people refer to ships as just a 'big iron box on the water'. To me that lovely lady was something special, and I really was over the moon to get back to her. I know I am something of a sentimentalist but she was my favourite ship, though I am sad to say, the very last one in a long Naval career.

I have often tried to analyse why I so much enjoyed being at sea as a ship's master-at-arms, despite the fact that it was a twenty-five hour a day, eight day a week job. I am sure that the banter of the sailors was a very great attraction to me. Keeping abreast of everything that was happening on the ship was a very important part of my job, and to do that I had to spend a lot of my time walking around the ship. This meant that most of my paperwork was done during the evenings and often well into the night hours. The act of walking around the ship meant that I was in constant contact with the sailors' verbals. I just loved to hear their witticisms and banter; I feel sure that I more than held my own in the replies I gave, though I am sure that I never did it in a bullying or officious manner. I often wish that I had had one of the modern recorders that I could have kept in my pocket to record some of their witticisms. I have no doubt that I could have greatly improved on the laughter that I hope these pages have created.

What a privilege I have had! To have done a job that I loved so much and to have served with so many wonderful people. Life has certainly been very good to me. The only part of my life that could have suffered by this love of my seagoing activities was my marriage. I am pleased to say that I found no weakness in that relationship at any time in my life. From the day I met her until the day she died, I was always totally faithful and very much in love with my wife and I felt sure in my heart that such feelings were reciprocal. I can but emphasise what a privilege I'd had.

In the early 1970s, the warrant officer rank was reintroduced into the Navy. It had been withdrawn in the mid 1950s, and all the then warrant officers had been commissioned as sub lieutenants. Because this threw the Navy out of line with the other two services, who had still retained their warrant officers, and also because the three services were supposedly drawing closer together under the one banner of the Ministry of Defence, it was decided to reintroduce the warrant rank into the Navy, but for the first few years of its reintroduction it was referred to as the 'fleet rank'.

Possibly because of my liking of being at sea as a master-at-arms and the fact that I had always striven hard to do the job to the best of my ability, I was nominated to be promoted to fleet master-at-arms. In one way, I was rather sad about the reintroduction of the warrant rank because it meant that there was not the slightest possibility of my ever going back to sea again, even if I was accepted to sign on for a further five years. Secondly, the fact that a further rank just bubbled up in between the chief petty officer rank and the sub lieutenant rank, it was sure to pose problems for years to come. I know that that concern of mine was justifiably borne out because of the many problems I encountered.

When I was promoted to fleet master-at-arms, I was given the opportunity to sign on for a further fourteen months on top of the extra five years that I was already serving above my normal pension time. This extra fourteen months meant that I would then qualify for a warrant officer's pension. My pension was substantially increased that way, so I certainly had no complaints.

The first job I was offered as a fleet MAA was as transport officer at the NATO HQ in Brussels, which unfortunately I had to turn down because of the problems that it posed to my youngest daughter's schooling. The second was as the deputy regulating staff officer back in Portsmouth Barracks. So for the last two years of my Naval service I very boringly drove a desk (as the terminology has it) in Portsmouth. My wife and I then bought a bungalow in Swansea and for most of my last eighteen months in the Navy I commuted each weekend to South Wales. Throughout most of my Naval career I had been lucky enough to be married to a wonderful woman, who was totally compatible with our gypsy existence. How I was ever so lucky as to meet her, I just cannot imagine. I often just pushed off to sea and left her with the most horrendous problems. Had such problems occurred in the opposite direction I would have possibly committed hara-kiri. I further compounded those problems of hers by writing to her several times whilst I was at sea and asking her to visit the wives of some of the sailors on the ship who had not heard from their spouses for long periods. She then sent me her observations via her letters, and unfortunately the observations were often about having found that some other male was ensconced in the family home (a cuckoo-type situation). The man's Divisional Officer and I would often have quite a problem sorting it out. I have to say that I found the welfare organisation in Portsmouth at that time was not really up to the problems that arose. It was staffed mostly by retired Naval officers and chief petty officer Wrens, who were supposedly trained in family welfare duties, though in my opinion they hardly knew what time of the day it was. I hope, for the sake of all concerned, that there have been a lot of changes since then, and that people with down to earth common sense and an appreciation of normal humanity and basic family welfare know-how have since taken over from the Colonel Blimp types that were there in my day.

For my last few months in the Navy I took over the job of manpower allocation and control officer in the barracks. Again it was a boring desk-driving job, but I was at least more or less my own boss. The one aspect of the job that rather frightened me was that for the first time in my career I had several women in my department. I had managed not to have women under my charge for my whole career until that time. Then there I was, almost at the fag end of my time in the service, and I was burdened with about five Wrens (Women's Royal Navy Service). Fortunately the senior Wren was a petty officer Wren, and she was married to a chief petty officer, whom I soon became friendly with; in fact he became an honorary member of the regulating mess of which I was the president. The Petty Officer Wren (his wife) really proved to be first class at her job and she kept all my female staff well in line. I did not have the slightest hint of trouble from any of them.

The Petty Officer Wren was so good at her job that I recommended that her name should be put forward for accelerated advancement. She was in fact one of only two people working in my department (out of almost a hundred staff) whom I considered worthy of such a recommendation, but it certainly gave me something of a headache. Although she was a member of my staff she was not really part of my division, so I was not her divisional officer. The Chief Officer Wrens and I had quite a row about it and I told her that I was fully prepared to see the Commodore about the problem. The Chief Officer then conceded and backed down. I am pleased to say that it all ended quite amicably, though I doubt that the Petty Officer Wren ever knew anything about the incident.

Every job has something of a drawback, and the drawback of that job was the fact that I used to have the responsibility for ratings who had been left behind by their ships because they had to attend a local civilian court. They were then part of my division until the court case was finished and they could then be sent back to their ships. This meant that I spent quite a lot of my time in the various local courts where I had to represent such ratings, and if asked, I had to give a brief outline of their character, which I extracted from their service documents. In fact, I attended the main magistrate's Court in Portsmouth so often that I eventually became part of the police 'tea swindle' there, and I was on first name terms with almost all the staff.

One other rather minor part of the job was that I had to vet and sign passport application forms, because all sailors had to have passports. The applications should have only been signed by a commissioned officer, but I was cleared by the main passport office in London to sign them. A few days prior to my release from the Navy however, I realised that my own passport would shortly be out of date. Because Naval people had their passports issued and renewed free of charge, I decided to renew mine before leaving the Navy. When my immediate boss, the Regulating Staff Officer, heard about me needing a commissioned officer to sign my application, as I could not have signed my own, he decided to have a skylark about it and forbade any commissioned officer from signing it for me. I am pleased to say that he eventually rescinded his instruction and cancelled the skylark, and in the end he signed it himself. I suppose that was his farewell present to me. He actually was a smashing chap who I am delighted to say was promoted to commander; in fact, he was the first member of our branch to have acquired such a promotion. It was a very well deserved one. I was proud to call him a friend.

On the day I was due to leave the Navy, I was still working at my desk. I suppose that I just could not believe that it was all over. I had been in Naval uniform for thirty-two and a half years, since I was a boy of thirteen in fact. I could hardly imagine myself as a civilian, but there it was, the final day. Out in the wide, wide world. I was to take a government training course to become a plumber. I suppose that I just could not keep away from water in some form.

Old Joe's Winnings

Old Joe had been down to the bookies and at last he had had a
    good win,
He knew that the sum was substantial so he wore his broadest
    grin.
The bookie said, 'Now listen old fellow, you have won three
    hundred pound,
But due to the VAT and the betting tax your winnings are very
    much down.'

The stoppages come to two hundred quid so you are left with
    ninety pounds clear.'
Joe was never too good at figures but he thought that the sum
    sounded queer.
In the pub he spoke to the barmaid, whom he'd known for a very
    long time,
He said, 'Maggie, I need you to help me, as my brain is way past its
    prime.

I have just come back from the bookies, but I'm just not sure what
    they meant.
Now suppose I gave you three hundred quid, less the VAT and the
    tax per cent,
If I was inclined to do that for you, how much would you take
    off?'
She said, 'Everything but my earrings dear, and I'd even risk
    catching a cough.'

Blue Unction

We now have antibiotics and many other wonderful potions,
To cure the poor sick sailors as they sail around the oceans
But prior to that we had one great cure that was used without
  compunction,
This wonderful drug to cure our ills was known to us all as 'blue
  unction'.

It cured fleas, crabs and scabies, *tinea pedis*, ringworm and gout,
Whenever you crawled into the sickbay, the blue unction bottle
  came out.
I once tried to go sick with the toothache, the sickbay staff knew
  what to do,
Out came their bottle of unction, and I left with my gums painted
  blue.

If you were moved to Rose Cottage* having caught a disease whilst
  ashore,
By succumbing to the sexual temptation of bedding a shore-side
  whore,
The doc would smile quite serenely then perform his sadistic
  function,
Of painting all around your crotch with his potion called blue
  unction.

*Rose Cottage was the name given to the mess where all the sailors who
had caught a contagious disease whilst ashore (usually venereal) were
accommodated. It no longer exists.

A Lumpy Problem

Our buffer had developed some problems,
On his forehead had sprouted two lumps.
'There's one thing for sure,' said the doctor,
'They're too bloody high to be mumps.'

He said, 'Tell me what have you been doing?
Have you eaten or drunk something queer?'
'Nothing to raise lumps,' said the buffer,
'Though I did drink some rather strange beer.

The beer was in a green bottle,
And it smelled like a wrestler's crotch.
One gulp of the stuff made me feel really ill,
So I'm sure that I didn't drink much.'

'Oh hell,' said the doc, turning paler,
'That liquid I can now recall.
I can tell you without hesitation
There was no beer in that bottle at all.'

It contained liniment for an old lady.
Her dropped womb was giving her pain.
We were trying to return it to normal,
To help her enjoy life once again.

Well Buffer, we've hit a big crisis,'
Said the doctor, now wearing a frown.
'Those lumps on your head are your testes.
How the hell do we get them back down?'

Mary and the Bull

Mary was quite a bright little girl, though her looks were rather
    plain.
One day she was leading the farmer's cow along a country lane.
The vicar, who was passing, asked where she was taking the cow.
'I'm taking it to the bull,' she said, 'at the farm just over that brow.'

'This is not the job for a little girl,' said the vicar, with face quite
    red,
'This should be done by the farmer's boy, or is he still at home in
    bed?'
'He's a busy chap,' said Mary, 'and his work list is always quite full,
But I'm sure he'd be no good at this job, this has to be done by a
    bull.'

The Birdman

I was trying to arrange a ship's concert,
But the talent was just not to be had.
Musicians, comics and singers,
And all of them sounded quite bad.

One sailor claimed he was gifted,
He said, 'At bird imitations I'm great.'
I said, 'I bet you're as bad as the others,
So you can hop over there and just wait.'

He said, 'If you're going to get nasty
I have no inclination to stay.'
Then he casually spread his arms out,
And he gracefully flew away.

Wishes of the Jolly Old Jossman

I hope that my great grandson, in the fullness of time,
Will strive to enjoy his life, as much as I've enjoyed mine.

Fred's Farewell

I served King, Queen and Country, everywhere under the sun,
But at last I'm in retirement, no more sea time to be done.
I've seen it, done it, been there, I've enjoyed a real good innings,
The world has been my oyster with my pension as the winnings.
So farewell all my mariner friends, may you have calm seas ahead,
But if things get rough, don't call on me, I'll be fast asleep in bed.

This is the end of my story, I hope I have raised a smile,
I hope that you laughed at my poems in a happy raucous style.
The world was made for laughter, so don't be grumpy or sad,
If you're still able to raise a laugh then you should feel really glad.
Now try laughing at your neighbours and shout hip hip hooray,
That is the way I did it. That's why I was put away.